SWEET MYSTERY

THE BROADWAY LEGACIES SERIES

Geoffrey Block, Series Editor
Series Board

Tim Carter
Kara Gardner
Kim Kowalke
Dominic McHugh
Jeffrey Magee

Carol J. Oja
Steve Swayne
Larry Starr, Emeritus
Stephen Banfield, Emeritus

"South Pacific": Paradise Rewritten
Jim Lovensheimer

Pick Yourself Up: Dorothy Fields and the American Musical
Charlotte Greenspan

To Broadway, to Life! The Musical Theater of Bock and Harnick
Philip Lambert

Irving Berlin's American Musical Theater
Jeffrey Magee

Loverly: The Life and Times of "My Fair Lady"
Dominic McHugh

"Show Boat": Performing Race in an American Musical
Todd Decker

Bernstein Meets Broadway: Collaborative Art in a Time of War
Carol J. Oja

We'll Have Manhattan: The Early Work of Rodgers and Hart
Dominic Symonds

Agnes de Mille: Telling Stories in Broadway Dance
Kara Gardner

The Shuberts and Their Passing Shows: The Untold Tale of Ziegfeld's Rivals
Jonas Westover

Big Deal: Bob Fosse and Dance in the American Musical
Kevin Winkler

"Pal Joey": The History of a Heel
Julianne Lindberg

"Oklahoma!" The Making of an American Musical, Revised Edition
Tim Carter

Sweet Mystery: The Musical Works of Rida Johnson Young
Ellen M. Peck

SWEET MYSTERY

The Musical Works of Rida Johnson Young

ELLEN M. PECK

Oxford University Press is a department of the University of Oxford. It furthers
the University's objective of excellence in research, scholarship, and education
by publishing worldwide. Oxford is a registered trade mark of Oxford University
Press in the UK and certain other countries.

Published in the United States of America by Oxford University Press
198 Madison Avenue, New York, NY 10016, United States of America.

© Oxford University Press 2020

All rights reserved. No part of this publication may be reproduced, stored in
a retrieval system, or transmitted, in any form or by any means, without the
prior permission in writing of Oxford University Press, or as expressly permitted
by law, by license, or under terms agreed with the appropriate reproduction
rights organization. Inquiries concerning reproduction outside the scope of the
above should be sent to the Rights Department, Oxford University Press, at the
address above.

You must not circulate this work in any other form
and you must impose this same condition on any acquirer.

Library of Congress Cataloging-in-Publication Data
Names: Peck, Ellen M., 1973– author.
Title: Sweet mystery : the musical works of Rida Johnson Young / Ellen Peck.
Description: New York : Oxford University Press, 2020. |
Series: The Broadway legacies series |
Includes bibliographical references and index.
Identifiers: LCCN 2020014204 (print) | LCCN 2020014205 (ebook) |
ISBN 9780190873585 (hardback) | ISBN 9780190873608 (epub) |
ISBN 9780190873615 (online)
Subjects: LCSH: Young, Rida Johnson—Criticism and interpretation. |
Librettists—United States. | Lyricists—United States. |
Women librettists—United States. | Women lyricists—United States. |
Musicals—United States—20th century—History and criticism.
Classification: LCC ML423.Y68 P43 2020 (print) | LCC ML423.Y68 (ebook) |
DDC 782.1/4092 [B]—dc23
LC record available at https://lccn.loc.gov/2020014204
LC ebook record available at https://lccn.loc.gov/2020014205

Dedicated to my Bushel of Pecks: Mom, Dad, Johnny, and David.

Thank you for your love and support.

CONTENTS

* * *

List of Illustrations	ix
List of Boxes	xi
Foreword	xiii
Acknowledgments	xv
Preface	xvii
1. The Women Who Wrote	1
2. An Old Story in a New Dress: The Emerging Playwright	15
3. Ah! Sweet Mystery of Life: *Naughty Marietta*	33
4. The Old-Fashioned Things Must Go: Musical Comedies	53
5. Just One of the Boys: Young as Co-Writer	77
6. Will You Remember? Operetta in Wartime	99
7. Dream Girl: End of a Career	131
Appendix: List of Works by Rida Johnson Young	145
Notes	147
Selected Bibliography	161
Index	167

ILLUSTRATIONS

* * *

P.1. Portrait of Rida Johnson Young	xxii
1.1. Rida Johnson Young with her plants	3
1.2. Rida Johnson Young at her writing desk	4
2.1. Chauncey Olcott in *Ragged Robin*	24
2.2. Rida Johnson Young and Christy Mathewson in a publicity photo for *The Girl and the Pennant*	27
2.3. Rida Johnson Young at home with one of her dogs	32
3.1. A scene from *Naughty Marietta*	38
4.1. Harry Conor and Forrest Huff in a scene from *Lady Luxury*	64
5.1. A scene from *His Little Widows*	94
6.1. Beth Lydy and John Charles Thomas in a scene from *Her Soldier Boy*	103
6.2. Clifton Crawford and Adele Rowland in a scene from *Her Soldier Boy*	104
6.3. Peggy Wood as young Ottilie in *Maytime*	112
6.4. Peggy Wood as an older Ottilie in *Maytime*	116
6.5. Rida Johnson Young, Peggy Wood, and Charles Purcell planting a tree on Young's estate in a publicity photo for *Maytime*	119
7.1. Rida Johnson Young in her garden	132
7.2. Rida Johnson Young with one of her dogs	143

BOXES

* * *

3.1.	Production Information for *Naughty Marietta*	51
4.1.	Production Information for *Lady Luxury*	65
4.2.	Production Information for *Sometime*	74
5.1.	Production Information for *The Red Petticoat*	87
5.2.	Production Information for *When Love Is Young*	92
5.3.	Production Information for *His Little Widows*	97
6.1.	Production Information for *Her Soldier Boy*	109
6.2.	Production Information for *Maytime*	123
6.3.	Production Information for *Little Simplicity*	127
7.1.	Production Information for *The Dream Girl*	139

FOREWORD

• • •

The subject of Ellen Peck's *Sweet Mystery: The Musical Works of Rida Johnson Young*, the latest addition to Oxford's Broadway Legacies, is the librettist and lyricist Rida Johnson Young (ca. 1875–1926), one of the pioneering figures in American musical theater. During her creative years, Young was in such demand that throughout the 1910s and early 1920s, nearly all the major composers in the operetta genre set her lyrics, a veritable who's who in a musical theater genre that included such luminaries as Victor Herbert, Jerome Kern, Emmerich Kálmán, Sigmund Romberg, and Rudolf Friml. But aside from two popular films starring Jeanette MacDonald and Nelson Eddy, *Naughty Marietta* (1935) and *Maytime* (1937), both of which used Young's lyrics (albeit with new dialogue), her work quietly vanished in the decade following her death, along with most members of the operetta species.

While Young may no longer be a household name and her lyrics, when heard, are usually sounded without attribution, they have demonstrated a surprising durability. Audiences unfamiliar with her name still might recognize Young's song "Ah! Sweet Mystery of Life" from what Peck here describes as Madeline Kahn's "postcoital punchline" in the role of the happy Bride of Frankenstein in Mel Brooks's *Young Frankenstein* (1974). In recent decades, Hollywood and Broadway buffs also noticed that in addition to "Sweet Mystery," a second song originally heard in *Naughty Marietta*, "I'm Falling in Love with Some One," appeared in both the film and stage versions of *Thoroughly Modern Millie*. As with so many lost, forgotten, or misplaced lyricists of Young's era, we may still know some of these songs without realizing that the woman who wrote their lyrics was unquestionably a formidable and central figure in the early years of the twentieth century.

After writing *Brown of Harvard* in 1906, a successful play that included songs set to her own lyrics, Young was selected to write the book and lyrics to what is widely recognized as Victor Herbert's most significant and lasting musical, *Naughty Marietta*, first staged in 1910, a show described by the musical theater historian Gerald Bordman as "The American masterwork of the era." Two years later, Young made history as the lyricist and librettist assigned to Jerome Kern when the untested young future composer of "Ol' Man River" was given his first opportunity to compose the music for an entire score, the obscure but historic *The Red Petticoat*.

In 1916, Young teamed up with composers Sigmund Romberg and Emmerich Kálmán on the hit show *Her Soldier Boy*. One year later, she again collaborated with Romberg on an even greater wartime musical hit, *Maytime* (492 performances), which contained one of Young and Romberg's best-remembered songs, "Will You Remember?" and is credited, again by Bordman, for "keeping the vogue for operetta alive during the height of the war." The latter two works also amply served Young's specialty, the Americanization of Viennese stage stories, for which the librettist heroine of this present volume deserves her fair share of credit. Near the end of the war in 1918, Young teamed with Rudolf Friml, another distinguished operetta composer, on yet another hit show, *Sometime*. A few years later in 1921, she reunited with Herbert on the less successful *The Dream Girl*, which turned out to be the final Herbert musical to be produced when it was performed in 1924, the year of the composer's death.

Young was not alone. In fact, she shared the musical stage with a number of significant female creative companions, perhaps most notably Dorothy Donnelly, who wrote the book and lyrics to three long-running musicals of the 1920s with music by Young's musical collaborator Romberg: *Blossom Time* (1921), *The Student Prince* (1924), and *My Maryland* (1927). But it was Young who got things started, and it's not hyperbolic to conclude that she played a key role in paving the way for successful women creators of the American musical and film. One lyricist and librettist to emerge shortly after Young's death, Dorothy Fields, became the first female to write the lyrics to an Oscar-winning song, "The Way You Look Tonight" from *Swing Time* (1936), and later wrote the book to *Annie Get Your Gun* in 1946 and the lyrics to *Sweet Charity* in 1966. Before too long, librettist Marsha Norman received the Tony Award in 1991 for the best Broadway book, *The Secret Garden*, a feat repeated by Lisa Kron for *Fun Home* in 2015. Between these two milestones, Fields became the subject of the second book published in Oxford University Press's Broadway Legacies series, Charlotte Greenspan's *Pick Yourself Up: Dorothy Fields and the American Musical* (2010). As the author of *Sweet Mystery* rightly points out, in addition to Young, Donnelly, and Fields, "there is no Golden Age without Betty Comden, Carolyn Leigh, and Bella Spewack."

Ellen Peck, associate professor of drama at Jacksonville State University, conveys Young's remarkable story with passion and authority, a story that equals and perhaps even transcends in importance Young's plays and musical collaborations with the most accomplished creative figures and producers of her era. As Peck writes, Young's "works and career offer a window into the American theater world of the early twentieth century," and "more than that, we get to hear Rida Johnson Young's unique voice and discover how she—and by extension, her fellow female theater artists—made a living and made her mark on the American theater."

Geoffrey Block
Series Editor, Broadway Legacies

ACKNOWLEDGMENTS
• • •

I have so many people to thank for supporting this book in the very long time it has taken to research and write it. First and foremost, my mentor at the University of Illinois, Jeffrey Magee, who graciously asked—*asked!*—to be on my dissertation committee and even more graciously agreed to be my director of research. He continues to be a colleague, sounding board, and friend, who is also willing to nudge me along, gently or not so gently, when necessary. Next, I might not have written this book in the first place were it not for another mentor, William Everett, who, on the train to a Song, Stage and Screen conference in the Netherlands, asked what I was working on. When I said I wasn't sure, he said, "You're going to write a biography of Rida Johnson Young. It needs to be written, and you're the one to do it." A few days later, William introduced me to my future editor, Norman Hirschy, who made time at that conference to talk with me and set me on this path. I simply cannot put into words what Norm's enthusiasm for my subject, encouragement, and remarkable patience as I pulled this book together have meant to me. He is a wonderful advocate for musical theater scholarship and a rock of support. I am so grateful for his guidance.

I am also grateful to those scholars who reviewed my proposal and manuscript, especially James Randall, who offered generous feedback and access to a few resources. Series editor Geoffrey Block provided meticulous notes and encouragement. As an admirer of his scholarship, I am absolutely thrilled to earn his approval of this book.

Special thanks must go to the researchers and library staff at the New York Public Library's Billy Rose Theatre Division, particularly Doug Reside and Annemarie von Roessel, whose guidance through the archival materials, wealth of knowledge, and personal warmth made a difficult process so much easier. In addition, about half of the primary material for this book came from the Shubert Archive. I am indebted to archivists Maryann Chach, Mark Swartz, and Sylvia Wang for their enthusiasm and help pulling together the scripts and other materials I needed. I must also thank the incredible network of musical theater scholars I have met over the years through the Song, Stage and Screen conference and the journal *Studies in Musical Theatre*, particularly George Burrows and Dominic Symonds. I feel privileged to be part of the most incredible group of musical theater geeks, who at one moment are sharing groundbreaking research and the next are singing along—loudly and joyfully—to showtunes. When I am in your presence, I feel like I have truly found my people.

On a personal note, I have many friends who have listened to me talk about Rida Johnson Young for years, only occasionally asking whether I was ever going to finish. My dear friends and professors from the University of Illinois—Peter Davis, Mikko Kivisto, Esther Kim Lee, Michelle Mills, Valleri Robinson, Zack Ross, Michelle Salerno, Larry Smith, and most especially Travis Stern and Amy

Stoch—gave me early encouragement and have continued to believe in me and in this book. My many colleagues and friends at Jacksonville State University and throughout Alabama—Linda Adams, Randy and Marleah Blades, Michael Boynton, Fulton Burns, Freddy Clements, Carmine Di Biase, Jennifer Ivey, Jennifer Luck, Neil David Seibel, and Carlton Ward—have offered support and sympathetic ears when I needed them. I would also like to thank my Fulbright Romania family, including Priscilla Ly, David McTier, Rick St. Peter, Leo Zonn, and the rest of the #FulbrightFunFam for your friendship and scholarly inspiration during one of the best years of my life.

And finally, to my dearest friends and family. Diane Ballor and Kari Wilson have proudly cheered me on and were ready with ice cream and peach Bellinis when needed the most. Their unwavering belief in me has lifted me up on the days I thought I'd never finish. My forever friends, the Mercy Girls, were always only a phone call or Facebook post away. Of course, the most thanks go to my loving and endlessly supportive family: my parents John and Joyce, brothers David and Johnny, all of the Pecks and the Joneses, and, more recently, the Steeles and the Jacksons—especially Margaret and Bob—who welcomed me with open arms into their families. And last but not least, my furry writing partner, Cassie, who sat on my keyboard or my lap for hours on end. I'm so happy to finally share this book with all of you.

PREFACE

* * *

The American musical theater has never had a shortage of female writers, yet their representation on Broadway and critical recognition have yet to match those of its men. In recent years, a handful of women have reached success at the highest levels: in 2019, Anaïs Mitchell won the Tony Award for Best Original Score for her music and lyrics[1] for *Hadestown*; celebrated comedy writer Tina Fey broke into musical theater with her book for *Mean Girls* in 2017, for which Nell Benjamin wrote the lyrics; and in 2015, composer Jeanine Tesori and lyricist-librettist Lisa Kron made history as the first all-female writing team to win the Tony for Best Book of a Musical and Best Original Score, for *Fun Home*. Kron and Tesori were also finalists for the Pulitzer Prize, as was Quiara Alegría Hudes for her Tony-nominated libretto for *In the Heights* (2008). Marsha Norman has earned Tony and Drama Desk Award nominations for the books of *The Color Purple* (2006) and *The Bridges of Madison County* (2014). Norman won the Tony for Best Book of a Musical for *The Secret Garden* in 1991, for which she also wrote lyrics, and composer Lucy Simon was nominated for Best Original Score. And there is no Golden Age without Betty Comden, Carolyn Leigh, and Bella Spewack. Women have hammered at that glass ceiling for years, but the occasional breakthroughs are frustratingly few and far between.

Today's theatergoers might be forgiven for assuming that women writing for the musical theater receive little attention because they are only just beginning to disrupt a male-dominated profession. But if a comprehensive history of the musical theater is to be written, it must include its female pioneers, one of whom was the prolific playwright, lyricist, and librettist Rida Johnson Young (ca. 1875–1926). Young, along with Dorothy Fields, Dorothy Donnelly, Anne Caldwell, Fred (née Frédérique) de Gresac, Clare Kummer, and others, established a place for women at the writer's desk well more than a hundred years ago. And even though these women enjoyed lucrative careers in professional theater, garnered critical and popular praise, saw their names on the front pages of theater programs, and were in demand as collaborators, they remain curiously scarce in musical theater scholarship.

I first encountered Rida Johnson Young in a musical theater history class at the University of Illinois. As a voracious musical theater fan, I thought I knew every name in the business. How had I never heard of Rida Johnson Young or her contemporaries Dorothy Donnelly (1880–1928) and Anne Caldwell (1868–1936), also lyricist-librettists? I raced to the library after class and pulled several musical theater histories off the shelves. For all three women, I found the same narrative again and again: if they were mentioned at all, it was after the composers with whom they worked, and the three were almost always grouped together as if they were the only women writing musicals at the time. A few historians had written about them, but the information was strictly biographical: what they wrote and when, and who composed the work. No mention of their individual styles, their voices, or their unique contributions to the form. I realized that if I wanted to learn more about them, I would have to do the research myself. After many, many hours spent in dusty book stacks, the Shubert Archive, and the New York Public Library's Billy Rose Theatre Division—poring through unpublished typescripts, correspondence, and crumbling newspaper clippings—I started to fill in some of the gaps.

I came to admire all three women greatly, but Rida especially intrigued me. She was outspoken and fearless, and her correspondence and interviews reveal a formidable woman unconcerned with public perception. Her brief marriage to actor James Young and subsequent divorce could have posed a barrier to her career, but she dismissed any mention of it without care, and she never remarried. She embodied the tension between the Victorian woman of the nineteenth century and the "New Woman" of the twentieth with disarming frankness. She saw herself as a craftsperson, an attitude that resulted in strong dramatic structure and richly drawn characters. Her female characters in particular seem to be extensions of herself: strong-willed, stubborn, funny, and very bright.

When Young wrote one of her most recognizable lyrics, "Ah! Sweet mystery of life, at last I've found thee!" for the 1910 operetta *Naughty Marietta* (music by Victor Herbert), the up-and-coming playwright was just beginning her career as a musical theater lyricist and librettist. Having written song lyrics for individual performers and plays with music, Young knew how to entice an audience with a sentimental verse. She had included incidental songs in her first few plays—such as the 1906 comedy *Brown of Harvard*—diegetic numbers that did not advance the plots but added "charm" to the scenes. With *Naughty Marietta* Young's skills as a playwright and popular-song lyricist converged. Her characters could express their inner feelings through song when speech became inadequate. And even though Young hesitated to write another musical after *Naughty Marietta*, the pull of this kind of creative freedom—and, she admitted, the extra royalties—proved too much to resist.[2] By the time she died in 1926, she had written nine more musicals among more than thirty theatrical works: *The Red Petticoat* (1912), *When Love Is Young* (1913; only produced in Chicago), *Lady Luxury* (1914), *Her Soldier Boy* (1916), *His Little Widows* (1917), *Maytime* (1917), *Sometime* (1918), *Little Simplicity* (1918), and *The Dream Girl* (1924).

Young's songwriting credits alone should justify her place in American popular-song history. As Philip Furia and Michael Lasser assert, "Long forgotten Rida Johnson Young deserves a better fate, if only because she wrote the book and lyrics for what we usually call 'Victor Herbert's *Naughty Marietta*.'"[3] Music historian David Ewen names her on his list of "the elect of Tin Pan Alley" songwriters—*the only woman on the list*—and includes three of her songs on his "Golden Hundred" list of Tin Pan Alley songs: "Ah! Sweet Mystery of Life," "I'm Falling in Love with Some One," and "Mother Machree." To put this in perspective, his list also includes "Blue Skies" (Irving Berlin), "Embraceable You" (George and Ira Gershwin), "Ol' Man River" (Oscar Hammerstein II/Jerome Kern), "Over There" (George M. Cohan), and "Tea for Two" (Irving Caesar/Vincent Youmans).[4]

Ewen even omits Dorothy Fields, whose career in popular music and musical theater surpassed Young's as the lyricist and/or librettist for such monumental hit shows as *Annie Get Your Gun* and *Sweet Charity*.[5] Yet, like so many American music and musical theater historians, Ewen excludes Young entirely from the rest of the book, save for crediting her as the lyricist of "Mother Machree" in a paragraph on popular Irish songs.[6] In a 1946 *Variety* feature, producer and performer George Jessel attempted to rescue American songbook lyricists from obscurity and listed Young as one of "twelve good men" whose "lyrics are sung and spoken throughout the civilized world and who hardly ever get any credit." Apparently ignoring Young's sex, he included her among such other notables as Oscar Hammerstein II, Otto Harbach, and Ira Gershwin, lamenting that their composers overshadowed them.[7] His curious oversight notwithstanding, Jessel still argued for her name to be remembered, something few others have done. More recently, Young has been included in *New Women Dramatists in America* (Sherry Engle), *Women in American Musical Theatre* (Bud Coleman and Judith Sebesta), and *Boy Loses Girl: Broadway's Librettists* (Thomas Hischak).[8] But there is more of Rida Johnson Young to discover, which is what this book is all about.

Young's professional career lasted from approximately 1900 to 1924, an era that saw an astonishing array of competing theatrical forms, including operetta, musical comedy, vaudeville, burlesque, revue, melodrama, and American realism. A prolific and disciplined writer, Young wrote non-musical plays, musical librettos, and lyrics in many of these genres, as well as novellas and the occasional feature in magazines such as Arthur Hornblow's *The Theatre*.[9] The names of her many collaborators constitute a virtual "who's who" of early-twentieth-century popular entertainment: Victor Herbert, Jerome Kern, Sigmund Romberg, Rudolf Friml, E. H. Sothern, Chauncey Olcott, even baseball player Christy Mathewson. Broadway's most powerful producers presented her plays, including Charles and Daniel Frohman of the Theatrical Syndicate, Oscar Hammerstein (grandfather to the Golden Age lyricist-librettist), George M. Cohan and Sam H. Harris, and Lee and J. J. Shubert. The Shuberts employed her as a staff writer for much of her career; in addition to the plays she wrote and pitched to them, they often gave her other writers' pitches from which to develop scripts. Some of the existing correspondence between them details Young's responses, suggestions, and rejections of ideas that she found questionable or unworkable. The volume of letters that have survived in the Shubert Archive indicates that the brothers regularly sought her input.

Young excelled at fitting style and content to genre, an eminently desirable quality at a time when variety and novelty ruled the entertainment industry. Many composers and writers crossed genres regularly. Young did so fluently. She could provide a romantic anthem for an operetta as easily as a comic star turn for a musical comedy. Additionally, Young was skilled at adapting foreign source material into "Americanized" scripts, a task the Shuberts often assigned her. Two of her most successful adaptations, *Maytime* and *Her Soldier Boy*, came from German plays. Because of anti-German sentiment during the First World War, Young had to excise any overt German elements from these plays (such as characters, settings, and less tangible characteristics such as emotion and cultural aesthetics) and reshape them to please American audiences. In 1916, *Her Soldier Boy* was the first Broadway book musical to dramatize the war as it was happening. Young's ability to navigate different styles resulted in a broad and lucrative career.

Her words are often heard satirically now. Anyone who has seen Mel Brooks's comic film *Young Frankenstein* (1974) will recall "Ah! Sweet Mystery of Life" as Madeline Kahn's postcoital punchline. Many others know Young's lyrics (though not her dialogue) from the immensely popular Hollywood pairing of Jeanette MacDonald and Nelson Eddy, who starred in the film versions of *Naughty Marietta* (film, 1935) and *Maytime* (stage, 1917; film, 1937). Two of Young's songs from *Naughty Marietta* ("Ah! Sweet Mystery" and "I'm Falling in Love with Some One") were used in the 1967 film and 2002 stage musical *Thoroughly Modern Millie*. Audiences may recognize her songs but know so little about the versatile and gifted writer behind them: a woman with business sense and theatrical savvy who held her own in a male-dominated profession. Young distinguished herself as one of only a few women writing for the musical stage at the turn of the century. Notable women wrote plays at this time, but only a handful braved the collaborative—and often stressful—nature of the musical. To the challenge of creating interesting plot and characters, add the pressures of connecting dialogue to song, subsuming plot to musical elements, and making economical song lyrics advance the plot. Writing a musical is not for the faint of heart or the ego. Rida Johnson Young is one of the American musical theater's pioneers, by virtue of her tenacity as much as her prolificacy.

Sadly, Rida Johnson Young did not leave behind personal papers or diaries. Her life and legacy are only to be found in her scripts, songs, interviews, scant pieces of correspondence with various theatrical figures of the era, newspaper articles, and critical reviews. This book is an effort to uncover her voice through close readings of several of her musical works. For each show, I provide a song list, character list, detailed plot synopsis with analysis of the libretto and lyrics, and historical context. If the devil is in the details, then the playwright's ability is in the dramaturgy: the technique, patterns, rhythms, motifs, and structural integrity.

Chapter 1, "The Women Who Wrote," situates Young in the American theater at the turn of the twentieth century and places her within the world of her contemporary writers, composers, and producers. It examines the theatrical landscape for the many female playwrights working at the time: their critical reception, societal expectations, challenges, and self-reflections. Using excerpts from interviews and professional correspondence, I introduce Young's personal voice, approaches to her work, her business sense, and her writing process. The chapter also establishes some of the challenges musical theater lyricists and librettists faced when collaborating with not just a composer but star performers of varying musical abilities, directors, and producers who were looking for box office success. Because musicals were (and still are) more expensive to produce than non-musical plays, there was more pressure on the writing teams to work quickly, make changes at the eleventh hour, and cater to demanding performers. Young's own experiences illuminate the behind-the-scenes processes of the musical theater's wordsmiths. Chapter 2, "An Old Story in a New Dress: The Emerging Playwright," introduces Young's early life and the plays that established her reputation. The chapter looks at her use of dramatic structure, language, diegetic songs, and characters and begins to chart her development as a librettist and lyricist. Chapter 3, "Ah! Sweet Mystery of Life: *Naughty Marietta*," examines the 1910 operetta, Young's arguably most famous show. While many critics and historians consider it to be Herbert's best work, they have less appreciation for—or familiarity with—Young's libretto. My close analysis of the script reveals its strong dramaturgical structure, while the rest of the chapter provides the production history of and critical response to Young's essential first musical. Young has become known for her contributions to operetta, but Chapter 4, "The Old-Fashioned Things Must Go: Musical Comedies," examines two of her musical comedies—*Lady Luxury* and *Sometime*—and uncovers Young's gift for comic writing. Chapter 5, "Just One of the Boys: Young as Co-Writer," explores three collaborations with other librettists and lyricists: *The Red Petticoat*, *When Love Is Young*, and *His Little Widows*. Analyses of these shows examine Young's collaborative process and distinguish her voice from those of her partners. Chapter 6, "Will You Remember? Operetta in Wartime," analyzes the musicals Young wrote during the First World War: *Her Soldier Boy*, *Maytime*, and *Little Simplicity*. The war presented certain challenges to Young and her fellow writers; this chapter demonstrates how Young's approaches to nostalgia and sentiment appealed to war-weary audiences. Finally, Chapter 7, "Dream Girl: End of a Career," documents the end of Young's career until her death in 1926 and her contributions to the American musical theater at the turn of the twentieth century. My study concludes with an assessment of Young's lasting legacy.

I must note that most of Young's scripts exist only in typescript or manuscript form, with few, if any, indications of provenance. The scripts housed in the Shubert Archive and New York Public Library appear to be rehearsal scripts—some have blocking notes and line changes. I have not always been able to ascertain which version of the play I am reading, and in some cases, there are multiple scripts with different notations. Unfortunately for musical theater historians, because musical scripts weren't considered "literature," producers—and even writers—didn't always see fit to preserve them. Theatrical ephemera from the period offer only fleeting glimpses into the past. Even for popular shows, material from this era was frequently lost or destroyed or has decayed in archives and personal collections. Historians face a difficult task in collecting primary material and must often rely on newspaper reviews to get a sense of an original production, which are problematic in themselves. Theater critics only give their own opinions and often focus narrowly on one aspect of a show, whether it be a star performer, the catchy songs (or lack thereof), or the costumes. If the critic has experience with a particular composer or librettist, he or she may comment on how this show compares with the last one. In any case, the review is highly subjective and all too easy to substitute for the real thing when the script is not available.

Figure P.1 Rida Johnson Young. Unknown periodical. Billy Rose Theatre Division, The New York Public Library.

Having access to a musical script from the early part of the last century pays dividends toward (virtually) reconstructing the show and evaluating its textual merits. Even when we cannot pin down whether we are reading a first or final draft, these scripts are time capsules. They reveal the conventions and quirks of the era and, frequently, unexpected substance. Although Young is primarily known today as a lyricist and librettist, this book explores more than just her contributions to the musical theater. Her works and career offer a window into the American theater world of the early twentieth century: its standards and practices; relationships among writers, performers, and producers; and its incredible variety. More than that, we get to hear Rida Johnson Young's unique voice and discover how she—and, by extension, her fellow female theater artists—made a living and made her mark on the American theater. And whenever possible, I use Rida's own words to tell her story. The voice that comes across in her letters and interviews is so much more colorful than any I could try to recreate.

1
THE WOMEN WHO WROTE
• • •

If you look at the new writers, you must note that the woman dramatist is coming into greater prominence than she has ever reached before.

Rida Johnson Young[1]

The turn of the twentieth century brought tremendous social change for American women. Greater opportunities for education and the burgeoning women's rights movements taking place across Europe and the United States opened their eyes to the possibilities of employment outside the home, participation in public office, and voting rights. Women of the upper and middle classes began to imagine a world beyond motherhood and wifely duty. Shifting attitudes toward a woman's place in society led to the emergence of what cultural commentators dubbed the "New Woman." The New Woman was a creature of the new century: ambitious, educated, and eager to fulfill her potential. Women dramatists—musical and non-musical—flooded the professional theater in the early decades of the twentieth century. Like all working women of the time, female playwrights straddled the divide between the nineteenth-century ideal of the "True Woman"—wife, mother, and helpmate—and that twentieth-century harbinger of independence and progress, the "New Woman." Playwright Martha Morton (sometimes called "the dean of women playwrights") founded the Society of Dramatic Authors in 1907, having been denied admission to the American Dramatists Club because of her sex. Susan Glaspell was the dominant creative force behind the Provincetown Players, part of the Little Theatre Movement that launched the career of Eugene O'Neill. In 1921, Zona Gale was the first female recipient of the Pulitzer Prize in Drama for her play *Miss Lulu Bett*. Rachel Crothers addressed questions of women's equality in work and marriage in such critically acclaimed plays as *A Man's World* (1910) and *He and She* (1911). Sophie Treadwell's Expressionist masterpiece *Machinal* (1928) critiqued and unsettled societal restrictions on women. Many women also wrote more "popular" dramas: Anne Nichols's *Abie's Irish Rose* ran for five years (1922–1927) and grossed more than a million dollars in 1920s figures—a phenomenal success for the time. All these women and many more were profiled in newspapers and magazines, including the *New York Times*, *The Theatre*, *Green Book Album*, *Good Housekeeping*, and *American Magazine*.

Unfortunately, professional achievement did not manifest gender parity. Interviews with women playwrights at this time reveal a striking trend toward emphasizing feminine domesticity over their theatrical successes. Women were usually introduced in association with their husbands or referred to primarily as "Mrs. [insert husband's name here]." Theater columnist Ada Patterson's 1918 feature "Wealth Not a Bar to Playwriting" positioned female artists in the domestic sphere as evidence that a woman could have a successful career and maintain her expected place in society. Here is her introduction to playwright and author Ethel Watts Mumford, whose works included the 1919 farce *Sick-a-Bed*:

> Ethel Watts Mumford she is to the reading and play-going world, Mrs. Peter Geddings Grant to the smiling world, that fraction of the American commonwealth with a maximum banking account and a minimum of carking cares. A high brownstone house near Central Park, a country estate . . . membership in the Colony Club, membership in two Oriental clubs that bespeak her world wanderings . . . all these tokens of riches has Ethel Watts Mumford.[2]

And it was not only Mumford's wealth that allowed her to pursue a writing career. "Motherhood supplemented her experiences and enriched her nature," proclaimed Patterson. "Having fully lived she was ready to freely write." (As though motherhood endowed playwriting skills.) Patterson treated Anne Caldwell in much the same way. "The Only Woman Librettist in America" presented Caldwell as "Mrs. James O'Dea," a grieving widow who has carried on writing despite the loss of her husband.[3] If a woman was not married, then some other homemaking hobby or quality was highlighted. In Young's case, columnists made frequent references to her love of gardening. A 1917 feature in the *New York Sun* had this subtitle: "But Rida Johnson Young, Who Is Entirely Unspoiled by Good Fortune, Has Her Mind Turned These Days to the Country and the Kind of Plots that Bear Potatoes, Not Plays."[4] That same year, Helen Ten Broeck's article "Rida Young—Dramatist and Garden Expert," set entirely in Young's plant-filled home on her estate, suggested that the garden provided inspiration for her writing. Young often spoke lovingly of her garden and sometimes even admitted she'd rather be planting seeds than writing plays. But in this case, she may have been playing up her hobby with a twinkle in her eye. She fantasized about winning the county fair, leaving Ten Broeck to muse, "we came away wondering whether she really meant it or if she might not have been working at a little bit of comedy at our expense."[5]

Some columnists looked to a woman's past as evidence of her worth as a writer. In 1906, Virginia Frame situated all of the women she featured in "Women Who Have Written Successful Plays" in their childhoods: "Grace Livingstone Furniss . . . has written since she was a small child, being happiest when there was a pen in her hand." "Charlotte Thomas has written since she could hold a pen in her hand." Martha Morton had "written from the time she was a child, beginning with poems and short stories, and comes of a writing family."[6] The

Figure 1.1 Rida Johnson Young with her plants. The Theatre, April 1917. Billy Rose Theatre Division, The New York Public Library.

image of a small girl clutching a pen and clumsily putting words to paper subtly diminishes these women by suggesting that their plays are nothing more than childish scribbling. Young deliberately resisted any such insinuation. In nearly every interview, she would pointedly uncover the myths surrounding her profession. She remarked how often columnists and admirers expressed wonder at her talents or implied that writing was easy and fun, a diversionary pastime. But Young would have none of it, citing her demanding working schedule: "I go to my desk at a certain hour every day and stay there four hours. Regularity in work is one of the biggest helps to success."[7] When pressed to share where her inspiration came from, she refused to take the bait. "Some lucky writers are able to dash off happy dialogue or work out characterizations whenever the mood happens to be inspiring," she quipped. "I unfortunately am not that sort. If I waited to capture the mood, I am afraid I should never write a word."[8] She described the brutality of the play production process: "It is usually a twenty-four-hour day for both librettist and composer, all the way from the first production at Stamford, or Atlantic City, up to the opening night in New York," she said. "While the actors are calmly sleeping and the manager and stage director are in the nearest café, discussing further tortures for librettist and composer, these two, in a stuffy hotel room, work desperately but valiantly."[9] Young would not glamorize her profession. The work was hard, and she wanted her public to know it.

Figure 1.2 Rida Johnson Young at her writing desk. The Theatre, April 1917. Billy Rose Theatre Division, The New York Public Library.

"THE MOST BEAUTIFUL PLAYWRIGHT IN CAPTIVITY"

Women writers were subject to scrutiny of their physical appearances as well as their achievements. One newspaper clipping identified Young as a "tall, stately brunette, and has the reputation of being the handsomest of the women dramatists of the country."[10] Isidore Witmark declared, "One of the most beautiful women ever to come from Baltimore—and Baltimore is noted for its beautiful women—was Rida Johnson Young."[11] A 1917 article assured readers that her beauty could make "even a disgruntled rival . . . lose his grouch if he could see her and talk with her. She is uncommonly 'easy to look at.' She wears her beautiful clothes so well that one cannot envy her the riotous royalties which enable her to buy them."[12] The *Baltimore Sun* reported: "She takes as much interest in a millinery opening as does a puffy society dowager, and she is as much interested in the fit of a shirtwaist as in a dramatic situation."[13] Even before her theatrical fame, Young's wedding announcement praised her "magnificent mass of hair and soulful eyes."[14] One newspaper rather ridiculously called her "the most beautiful playwright in captivity."[15] As was often the case, Young's talents and achievements took a backseat to her public image. Her clothing, hobbies, jewelry, and homes (she owned several homes during her career, including a luxury estate at Southfield Point in Stamford, Connecticut) confirmed her status as a society dame first, working woman second. However, as with questions about what inspired her, Young would deflect attention away from the superficial and back to the grueling writing process. Young certainly played by conventional rules but adeptly subverted them when necessary. Even when downplaying her talents, she fiercely defended her profession, its standards, and her earnings. She spoke passionately about dramaturgy in the same breath in which she compared playwriting to gardening.

Fortunately, Young and her fellow women playwrights did see their hard work lead to growing admiration from the critics. A feature in the *Brooklyn Times* boasted, "Women Writers Now Occupy Important Place on American Stage," with pictures of Crothers, Edith Ellis (who also directed Young's 1909 smash hit *The Lottery Man*), Olive Porter, and Young with the caption "Rida Johnson Young—Wealthiest of Women Playwrights." The brief—and unsentimental—piece positioned female writers in the male-dominated milieu:

> Women are taking a large part of the lion's share of dramatic honors this season. Theatrical producers are being brought to a realization of the importance of the woman playwright, and recently a few remarkable contracts have been entered into between certain managers and women writers which go to show the tendency. Doubtless the most successful woman dramatist of the present time is Rida Johnson Young, who now has two successful pieces to her credit.[16]

And women playwrights had at least one champion in columnist Cady Whaley, who wrote a piece about Young in 1906 for *The Billboard*, titled "The Woman Playwright of the Current Season":

> Verily, the women who can write plays are about the most strenuous, busy pieces of femininity to be found. I have had the pleasure of interviewing quite a number of them within the last ten days, and for the most part each one is possessed of an interesting personality—slender, delicate creatures, but of that never-give-up, nervous, energetic, do-or-die sort of disposition. They are snappy, quick, determined, showing broad culture, wide scholarship, and a well-balanced philosophy of life. They should succeed, for in the name of all that's just and good they deserve to.[17]

A "WOMAN'S TOUCH"

In his volume on Broadway lyricists, Thomas Hischak suggests that the women writing for the theater at the turn of the twentieth century brought a "woman's touch" to their craft.[18] As tempting as it might be to assume that gender influenced lyric writing, women in the business were competing with men for very few opportunities. They would do well to shape their own work to match the styles of the men who wrote regularly for Broadway. When Young began her career, she would likely have known the works of two prominent men: Harry B. Smith and Henry Blossom, both of whom often wrote with Victor Herbert. Smith was the era's most prolific lyricist-librettist, credited with writing more than three hundred librettos and approximately six thousand songs. He first collaborated with Herbert in 1895 on *The Wizard of the Nile*; their other works together included *The Fortune Teller* (1898), *Miss Dolly Dollars* (1905), and *Sweethearts* (1913). Blossom teamed with Herbert for *Mlle. Modiste* (1905), *The Red Mill* (1906), and *Eileen* (1917), among others. Both were celebrated by critics and the public, both in demand by producers. I have chosen a sample from each to illustrate their styles and what Young may have aspired to. Here is Smith's "Gypsy Love Song" from *The Fortune Teller*:

> Slumber on, my little gypsy sweetheart,
> Dream of the field and the grove;
> Can you hear me, hear me in that dreamland
> Where your fancies rove?
> Slumber on, my little gypsy sweetheart,
> Wild little woodland dove,
> Can you hear the song that tells you
> All my heart's true love?[19]

And from Blossom, "Thine Alone" from *Eileen*:

> In thine arms enfold me, my beloved!
> Let thine eyes look fondly into mine!
> For thy love bears a spell all too wondrous to tell,
> 'Tis a rapture that's all divine!
> So within thy tender arms enfold me,
> For thy loss, the world could not atone!
> Belov'd, I swear that I will e'er be true
> And forever thine alone![20]

Both songs contain content and themes typical for early American operettas: stirring, overly emotive love songs using heightened language, nature imagery, inverted syntax, and an almost operatic fervor. If Hischak's estimation is correct, a lyric written by a woman would be noticeably more "feminine." Then compare this lyric by Young, "Kiss Waltz" from the 1916 operetta *Her Soldier Boy*:

> Alas, I know I soon must be
> Far from my home and far from thee.
> Then let us have all happiness and joy today!
> Let us dance the fleeting hours away!
> Dreaming, this is but a dream,
> A dream of joy.
> Come, dear one, so close in my arms,
> Here would I hold you and fold you forever!
> Hold me, hold me in your arms!

> Oh, dream of joy!
> Oh, dear one, my own, dear one!
> For you alone are my own evermore![21]

The similarities among the three samples are striking, particularly those of Blossom and Young. All three employ the common devices listed above, especially the hyper-romantic idiom of operetta. Young's lyrics sound no more feminine than Smith's or Blossom's. Rather than classifying Young's writing voice as specific to her gender, I am more interested in the ways in which she drew on popular conventions and developed a style that composers, producers, directors, and audiences wanted to hear.

"THE POOR LIBRETTIST"

Misconceptions about musical theater in the early twentieth century abound, particularly that the writers were virtually invisible. While that may have been true in burlesque, vaudeville, and revues, audiences certainly knew who wrote for Broadway. Theatrical reviews at the time typically listed a show's writers before the cast, and in fact, the librettist and/or lyricist usually came before the composer. As a reviewer of Young's musical with Jerome Kern, *The Red Petticoat*, stated, "It is not often that the composer's name appears first upon a programme. Generally you read who wrote, produced, made the costumes and did all the other things necessary for the production of a piece, before you find out who is responsible for the music. Quite often that is as it should be."[22] Critics usually devoted at least a paragraph to critiquing the writing, often recalling past works and comparing them to the new one. Composers and lyricists were regularly featured in newspapers and entertainment and society magazines. Newspapers reported new projects in the works, marriages and divorces, even European vacations. As with any other celebrities, theatrical figures' lives were fodder for gossip and entertainment. For instance, Young received a very sympathetic write-up in the *Dramatic News* when she had several hundred dollars' worth of jewelry stolen from her estate: "Now when a hard-working girl puts all her royalties into jewelry, it is more than a shame to have them stolen. It is a downright outrage."[23] Articles about Young frequently showed her at home, in her garden, or pictured with other celebrities.

Another popular misconception is that writers cared more about music than plot, that plot existed merely to support the songs and audiences did not care about the plot if the music was good. Critic George Jean Nathan accused the American stage of having "the cheapest, trashiest and most incompetent librettos that the civilized theatre has thus far in its career listened to." He blamed producers for making assumptions about their audiences:

> But, argue the producers, the public no longer cares about a libretto one way or the other. Give the public the right kind of syncopations, a lot of pretty legs,

some good-looking costumes, and maybe a joke or two about Congress and Pottstown, Pa., and the public is richly satisfied. Does the public want a logical and witty book? they ask. And they reply to themselves fortissimo with a very convincing no.[24]

But while many shows from the early era of American musical comedy went for entertainment first and coherence second, the truth is that audiences *did* care about plot—at least, according to the writers. They demanded that even the silliest musical comedies tell a good story. Lyricist and librettist Otto Harbach, whose many works included *The Firefly* (1912; music by Rudolf Friml) and *Rose-Marie* (1924; music by Friml and Herbert Stotthart, book and lyrics co-written with Oscar Hammerstein II) articulated this elusive ideal in 1925:

> You are in a world of Make-Believe where anything is accepted as plausible provided it pleases. But it must please—vividly. Mere glitter and tinsel will not suffice. . . . However fanciful the story, however fantastic the treatment, there must be an underlying reality closer to the human heart than realism—or the audience will not *care*.[25]

Arthur Hornblow praised Young and Romberg's *Her Soldier Boy*, exclaiming, "Nevertheless, remember here is a musical comedy—real music and real comedy—with a PLOT!"[26] In fact, many contemporary critics considered plot as essential as music in determining a show's quality. That Hornblow felt the need to shout about this particular plot indicates a perceived failure on the part of some librettists to deliver the goods; nevertheless, musical comedies needed solid plots just as much as music. Young and her contemporaries were dramatists first and foremost. They strove for clarity and dramatic interest, even in the most lighthearted pieces. Young insisted:

> I think the songs ought to be written about the action. They ought to belong to it; not be just any old song that could be taken bodily and shoved into any comedy at all. Lugging in a song about icebergs when the action takes place in Panama and singing about parrots and palms when your scene is in Alaska doesn't appeal to me. I think a musical comedy can and should be made as coherent and logical as a play.[27]

Producers and critics appreciated her point of view. When the Shuberts signed Young to her first contract in 1907, *The Billboard* reported that she would "supply them with a musical libretto with entirely novel features. This does not mean any wide departure in musical comedy save that the plot will be visible and yet lend itself to musical setting and splendid costuming. The Shuberts will give the play their usual elaborate scenic investiture, while believing a plot has become a necessary factor in musical comedy."[28]

But no matter how the librettist tried, he or she often had to relinquish artistic control, sometimes to the detriment of the plot. Young recounted a painful experience writing a musical—one that she discreetly left unnamed—in a 1917 feature for the *New York Tribune* titled "Lo! The Poor Librettist." The process had started well enough. The entire creative team, including the scenic designer, had been delighted with her script and ideas, so much so that "everybody was patting me on the back." The show, concerning two sisters in South America, had been written for a female star (also unnamed), who decided that her "sister" should be cut out of the plot. Young obligingly made her an only child, and an orphan at that. When the comic-relief actor schemed to insert his own jokes, she tried in vain to remove them, only to find the jokes "seasoned and hardy. They couldn't be killed." The ingénue, a friend of the producer's, insisted on more stage time, prompting the leading lady to throw tantrums until her own part was lengthened. After being forced to change the location of the show from South America to Hungary for a particular actor, and suffering through all the stylistic revisions required, Young realized that no amount of money compensated for her headaches: "One night after weeks of this agony I had a private little brainstorm of my own. I arose from my typewriter, packed my grip and silently stole away. I quit—cold."[29] Young did not identify the musical in question, nor have I been able to ascertain which one it might have been. But Young's experience, although somewhat extreme, was hardly singular. She would find out that these woes came with the territory. Producers added or dropped songs from shows regularly, depending on sales of sheet music or cast changes; one star wouldn't sing another one's songs, so interpolated his or her own; and no matter how the writers tried to maintain dramatic coherence, star performers could wield inordinate power. Writers often had to defer to other artistic temperaments in the process of creating a musical, no matter how high their ideals. One interviewer asked her, "How much does the author count for anyway when it comes to putting a musical comedy on the stage?"

> "Precious little," she laughed. "Everybody barks at the humble author if he ventures a suggestion. It's a good deal like being a dressmaker, I suppose. You can make a costume, but you're not supposed to dictate to the purchaser how, when and where she is to wear it. The only thing you are supposed to do is to make any alterations demanded of you. Everybody, from the star down to the least of the chorus girls has no hesitation in stating what he or she means to do."[30]

Young had a good sense of humor about her lowly status on the creative team. However, her scripts and correspondence demonstrate that she made every effort to abide by her writing philosophy throughout her career.

"A MATTER OF BUSINESS"

Rida Johnson Young prided herself on her shrewd business acumen. Much of her surviving correspondence with New York producers Lee and J. J. Shubert concerns her contracts and royalties. Young negotiated meticulously for every cent owed her, rigorously defending the time and energy required to produce good work. She paid close attention to box office receipts, attendance records, and grosses and always knew where her plays were being produced. When a production of her play *Glorious Betsy* opened in Nebraska without her consent, Young promptly contacted her lawyer to ensure that her royalties were duly delivered. If more than a week went by that she did not receive a check for a show running in New York or elsewhere, she would write J. J. Shubert a reminder, sometimes with the exact amount owed her:

> Mr. Schirmer told me some months ago that he had sent you over five thousand dollars on "Maytime" royalties, and he must have sent more since. The Victor people sold 189,000 records of "Sweetheart" during the first quarter. Will you kindly look into the matter and have Mr. Schirmer's statements sent me, together with a check for 25 percent of all amounts received.[31]

(In this instance, the very annoyed Shubert replied, "I think the air in Stamford [Connecticut] is inflating your ideas as to royalties.")[32] Young could also inject a little cheeky humor into her business dealings:

> I notice that the printing for "The Lottery Man" which you said you would have stripped with my name, is still guarding the dark secret of the author's identity. Also, in all the papers yesterday, while every other author's name was mentioned mine was carefully forgotten. I cannot understand why. It is in my contract, as you know, that my name should be on all the printing and advertisements. This is simply a matter of business with me, as you know it is important to have one's name appear as often as possible.[33]

She could cajole:

> Also, if I am your favorite playwright, will you please not forget me and make some inquiry as to why I have not received the check for advanced royalty.[34]

And when necessary, she would put her foot down:

> I cannot understand why it is impossible for me to get the contract for "One of the Boys" and the royalty which is owing me. It has been in your office now for four weeks and I think it is time it was attended to. I have stopped in the office time and time again about it and I am entirely too busy to take up my time that way.[35]

Lee and J. J. Shubert were notoriously hard-nosed businessmen. J. J. in particular was prone to fits of ego that could render him hostile. He and Young clashed on more than one occasion, sometimes almost dissolving their working relationship. In one especially terse letter from November 1919, J. J. chastised her for turning down a proposed project, fuming, "It must give you quite a bit of satisfaction to feel as independent as you do, but do not forget that we had a lot to do towards making you so. However, I will not bother you any more about writing any plays for us."[36] Young cleverly responded with restraint and intelligence. She managed to apologize for any misunderstanding without compromising her professional status:

> You always have theaters and you always stick to plays loyally and I am more than grateful for the success I have had under your management. You must not blame me if I want to get a more satisfactory contract than I have had before. I think that it is only natural when one has served his apprenticeship in any profession.[37]

Rather than give in to Shubert's emotional outburst, she smoothly brought the topic back to terms he could understand: this was a business deal, and she was entitled to a fair share. She ended the letter with one last carefully worded stroke to his ego: "I should be very sorry to feel that you think me ungrateful and I hope you will let me prove that I am not by letting me do something for you later on."[38] It evidently worked, because Young continued to write for the Shuberts for the remainder of her career.

Her correspondence also reveals that Young—and presumably other writers—had some input regarding how shows were cast. Many letters discuss possible stars as well as character actors and even bit parts. If she wasn't writing for a particular star, she might make several requests or recommendations for various roles, as in this 1918 letter:

> Here are some suggestions for the cast of "Miss I Don't Know." The dancing waiter and the dancing girl could be played by Fred and Adele Astaire. Georgia O'Ramey should be engaged for the part of "Lulu"; Roy Atwell for that of the Professor (and then he can also supply some topical songs of his own), and Harry Fonder for the young American artist.[39]

Young had few qualms about turning down a project if she believed it unlikely to succeed for any reason. Her following letter from 1917 to the Shuberts demonstrates some of the dramaturgical principles that guided much of her work:

> I returned the play "Who's Looney Now" to your office yesterday. I think it would be a mistake to try to make a musical play of this. Even a farce needs some foundation in probability, and that insanity germ idea is too far-fetched. Besides it is such an old-fashioned idea to try to get fun out of supposed insanity. Then too it would be hard to get any sentiment into it and I can work best with material that offers some sentimental interest.[40]

As she so frequently stated elsewhere, the play must be believable and appeal to an audience. Young saw little value in simply turning in script after script and collecting a check; if she was going to expend precious time and energy on a show, it must meet her dramatic standards. She was also keenly aware of her abilities and would not agree to a project for which she felt herself unsuited. When asked to adapt the German play *Alt Heidelberg*, which eventually became the Sigmund Romberg/Dorothy Donnelly operetta *The Student Prince*, Young begged off:

> I have very carefully studied "Heidelberg" and I do not think I could make a successful musical play of it. In the first place there is no University life of that kind except in Germany. I do not see any way to make a happy ending. Then there is no opportunity to put in up-to-date American numbers without

spoiling the atmosphere. I would love to do it for you but do not think I could make a success of it.[41]

By the time of this letter, Young had already successfully "Americanized" two German plays by removing them from their original settings and using on-trend American character types. *Her Soldier Boy* and *Maytime*, both adapted from German sources, contain distinctly American characters, language, musical rhythms, and patriotic overtones. This was likely because she wrote them during the First World War, when Germany was an enemy and, therefore, unpopular with American audiences. Young needed to divorce her versions from their source material. By the time Romberg and Donnelly received the property, anti-German sentiment had waned somewhat, allowing them to dive deeply into a nostalgic German past. Young did not have this luxury, nor was she inclined to tackle its unhappy ending (which Romberg and Donnelly vigorously defended). Her words to the Shuberts indicate that she felt this was the best approach to these scripts given the political climate that still hung over the country in the immediate aftermath of the war.

Young, like many in her profession, often downplayed the artistic merits of her work. Given that they were writing "popular" entertainment, lyricists and librettists (and some playwrights) saw themselves as workers rather than artists. Harry B. Smith made no secret of the fact that he wrote to make money, not art. He admitted that "it is possible to write comic opera that shall be at the same time artistic and popular. I don't do it often myself, for I am merely in the business of filling orders, but it can be done."[42] Virginia Frame claimed that Young "calls herself a 'manufacturer of entertainment' rather than a playwright."[43] When prodded, Young would modestly admit to a few "really great successes," but insisted that she simply gave audiences what they wanted: "The secret of success is merely to know what a million or so people would want in a song, or a play."[44] This should in no way imply that the work was easy or did not require dramaturgical skill; quite the contrary. Otto Harbach insisted that the musical librettist must be equal to or better than the playwright, pointing out that "the success or failure of a musical comedy depends less on the cleverness of the author than on his craftsmanship, is less a matter of brilliancy than of building. . . . No one is equipped to write a musical comedy who is not already a proficient playwright."[45]

Rida Johnson Young was more than proficient. Her early plays, written between 1900 and 1910, honed her dramaturgical process, voice, and sense of theatricality. Her time as a staff lyricist at the music publisher M. Witmark & Sons taught her how to fit words to music. By the time she wrote *Naughty Marietta*, she was well prepared to take on the task of fitting songs to libretto. Her artistry (although she may have scoffed at the word) developed throughout her career to make her even more valuable to her theater colleagues and to the early development of American musical theater. Besides her own significant contributions, she offers us a way into an underappreciated era by representing what was typical for her time. Young wrote in a world that required flexibility, speed, the ability to collaborate (sometimes with many writers), and a thick skin. Columnist R. B. Sheridan remarked on Young's emotional equanimity:

> One of Mrs. Young's characteristics is her extreme diffidence about her work—a quality not often encountered in stage folk, and it has gained her great popularity. Most dramatists regard the success of their own play as an epoch-marking event, and the failure of one of their bad plays as a national calamity fully as disastrous as the San Francisco earthquake or the Johnstown flood. Not so Mrs. Young, who, being not unduly elated by success, has not so far to fall should she meet with an occasional failure.[46]

Despite identifying herself as a "manufacturer of entertainment," Young sought out projects that would satisfy *and* sell. Like many writers in the theater, she disliked sacrificing quality for speed but also knew that producers wanted to put up shows as quickly as theaters became available. Young was never sentimental about her plays, but she did want them to succeed dramaturgically as well as financially. Her work ethic and self-imposed daily writing schedule enabled her to produce work as quickly as her producers requested it. And if quantity alone equaled success, she would have had a fine career. But Young took great pride in her work, thoughtfully crafting plays and musicals with clever wit, interesting characters, and theatrical savvy. She began writing plays long before she understood dramaturgical techniques or the theater business and continued tirelessly even after a play flopped or was panned by the critics. Her sex could have put her at a disadvantage, but her output and financial success did not appear to suffer for it. If anything, she played the game as well as any of her male counterparts and had the earnings and name recognition to show for it.

Some of the women writing plays at the turn of the twentieth century did so as a hobby, in addition to their societal roles as wives and mothers. Rida Johnson Young wrote plays, musicals, songs, and novellas as her vocation. The theater was her life and livelihood, from almost the beginning of her life to the end of it.

2

AN OLD STORY IN A NEW DRESS
• • •
THE EMERGING PLAYWRIGHT

The most successful play is simple. It deals with things that are not over anyone's head. As you realize—for you know about my first play—I had little idea of this when I began.

Rida Johnson Young[1]

Rida Louise Johnson was born in Baltimore on February 28, 1869 or 1875, to Emma (Stuart) and William A. Johnson.[2] According to census records, Rida was the fifth of six children. William's lighterage business—the transfer of cargo between boats of varying sizes—provided a comfortable lifestyle for the family, and eventually a career for Rida's brother, George Stewart Johnson.[3] Rida began writing at a very early age and had some poems and stories printed in local newspapers. None of them appears to have survived, but fortunately, the *Baltimore Sun* reprinted one of her poems in her wedding announcement in 1901:

> DAWNING.
> I saw the fragile, blue-eyed Morn
> Rise blushing from her rest;
> She drew her cloudy garments, torn,
> Across her pulsing breast.
> She girdled them with bands of gold,
> Hung dew-drops in her hair;
> A perfume fell from every fold,
> And languished on the air.[4]

Her early promise is evident here, even without the aid of music or script. This poem, written at least prior to her twenty-fifth birthday, offers a glimpse into her later lyric-writing style. The images call to mind those of the celebrated Art Nouveau painter Alphonse Mucha; "Morn" is a figure of nature both alluring and erotic. Rida's penchant for evocative imagery would later pervade her operetta lyrics.

Sweet Mystery. Ellen M. Peck, Oxford University Press (2020). © Oxford University Press.
DOI: 10.1093/oso/9780190873585.001.0001.

After graduating from Eastern High School in Baltimore and attending a single year at Wilson College in Chambersburg, Pennsylvania, as a music major, eighteen-year-old Rida moved to New York City against her family's wishes to pursue a theater career.[5] But this was not the impulsive act of a teenager with stars in her eyes. Rida had been following the New York theatrical notices for months, determined that she had as good a chance for success as anyone else. She went armed with her first play, an ambitious and sprawling account of the life of Omar Khayyam. (She later acknowledged that the play was not good—it contained nearly a hundred characters and, according to Young, would have run about ten hours.) Ever practical, on arrival she went straight to answer an ad to work for a furniture-polish salesman who offered her four dollars a week and a room in his two-room office/apartment in Harlem. She agreed on two conditions: that she could live elsewhere and that he would give her time off to visit theatrical producers. Several months of shopping her play around followed, none of them fruitful. So she decided to try a different tack and sent it to several leading actors, hoping that one of them would want to play it. The American Shakespearean actor E. H. Sothern, a member of the Old Lyceum Theatre stock company under producers Charles and Daniel Frohman, responded. Sothern had no interest in the play but admired the effort enough to contact the aspiring young playwright for a meeting:

> Perhaps no one but Mr. Sothern, whose great heart and open mind made it possible for him to wade through those pages, would have seen a ray of hope in them. But Mr. Sothern did see something—what it was I can only wonder—that made him write a note asking me to come down to the theatre to see him. I was certain he intended to produce my play, and it was quite a shock when he told me, ever so gently, that he thought it needed a little altering.[6]

What it really needed was some perspective. Rida Johnson had no practical theater experience and little understanding of dramaturgy or stagecraft. But Sothern had seen potential and offered her a place as an actress in his company. He sent her to Daniel Frohman, who initially dismissed her due to her lack of experience. In a move that would foreshadow her future dealings with the Shuberts, Rida held her ground and insisted that Frohman hire her. She traded in her furniture polish for a spot in Frohman's company, acting in small roles and learning the theater business. She toured with her future husband, the actor James Young, son of a Maryland senator. It didn't take long to realize that her talents lay not in performing but in writing. She went to work for the music publisher M. Witmark & Sons for twenty-five dollars a week, first assisting Isidore Witmark in the press department before joining the lyric-writing staff. She later recalled, "we worked as a factory works, turning out songs at a rate that was bewildering. When someone singing in vaudeville made a hit, and an order came in for an encore verse, or two or three, or half a dozen, I sat down and wrote them."[7] Young later estimated that between her time at Witmark and her many plays and musicals, she had written about five hundred songs. She often mentioned her time at Witmark in interviews and expressed her gratitude for the experience she gained there. She gushed in a letter to Isidore:

> I always feel somehow that the Witmarks—and you especially—are responsible for my success. You taught me so much while I was with you, and your confidence in my ability made me venture farther than I should otherwise have done. If I ever do anything really worthwhile in the playwriting line, I shall attribute it to the fact that you gave me a start when no one else would.[8]

BROWN OF HARVARD AND OTHER EARLY PLAYS

After two years of near-constant songwriting, Young briefly returned to acting but soon began to try her hand at playwriting. "Then I settled down to write something that would *succeed*," she said. "I knew by that time that a stage is a small place, not intended for one hundred characters, and that the fewer people in that small space, the better."[9] Her first play, written for her future husband in the leading role, was the mildly successful *Lord Byron* (1900). Rida played James's leading lady, and the *Baltimore Sun* admired both the play and her onstage chemistry with James:

> Mr. James Young gave his historical characterization of Lord Byron before a large and delighted audience at Ford's last night. The talented young author of the play, Miss Rida Louise Johnson, who is Mr. Young's leading lady, shared with him the honors of the evening. Miss Johnson has written . . . a play that is crowded with interest from beginning to end. The lines are filled with romantic beauty, such as appealed to the poetic soul of Byron, while the vanity, selfishness, deceit and moral vagaries of the brilliant young genius are well portrayed by Mr. Young. The intensity of a love scene between Mr. Young and Miss Johnson caused uproarious applause.[10]

Marriage would have to wait, however. Rida's father became seriously ill, compelling her to return to her parents' home, where she stayed until his death later that year. She continued to produce poems and short stories and even received a contract to write a novel of New York, called "The Hedonites of Gotham," although the book never materialized.[11] James kept up a busy touring schedule while Rida assisted her family in Baltimore. Rida Johnson and James Young finally married in September 1901 at the Holy Trinity Protestant Episcopal Church in Long Island City, New York, after a five-year engagement.[12] The Youngs then moved to Manhattan to begin their married life and continue to build their theater careers.

Rida Young immediately resumed writing. Intent on a career in theater, she focused her energies on plays and popular songs. In 1903, "A Song of Yesterday" (music by Anton Heindl) was interpolated into the second season of the comic opera *The Sultan of Sulu* (book and lyrics by George Ade, music by Alfred G. Wathall). The next year, a drinking song she wrote with Manuel Klein, "Here's to the Ones at Home," was featured in the Revolutionary War drama *Captain*

Barrington, a Weber and Fields production. Young's hometown newspaper, the *Baltimore Sun*, proudly declared that the song "has caught the public in a remarkable manner. The song has already been incorporated in many college glee books."[13] These interpolations helped her to get her foot in the door in New York, but her mind was fixed on writing plays.

Her next major project, the college comedy *Brown of Harvard*, was an immediate and surprising sensation. "College plays"—comedies set on college campuses with exuberant coeds—were all the rage in the early twentieth century. *Brown of Harvard* exemplified this trend, with its cast of "students with properly developed college spirit," young romance, and a varsity boat race at its climax.[14] Young had spent six weeks on the Harvard campus in Cambridge, Massachusetts, doing research and soaking up the college atmosphere. Before the play's opening, the *Baltimore Sun* reported that it "purports to take the life of Harvard University by the scruff of the neck, so to speak, and set it down behind the footlights complete and veracious in detail."[15] Rida Johnson Young's first Broadway outing was directed by Henry Miller, one of the original members of Frohman's Lyceum Company and a trusted friend of the Youngs. Rida wrote the title role for her new husband, but when James's touring schedule conflicted with the production, Henry Woodruff took over the role. Appearing as his love interest was a young Laura Hope Crews, who would not only enjoy a robust career in stage and film (you may remember her as the dotty Aunt Pittypat in *Gone with the Wind*) but would also co-direct Young's very last Broadway musical, *The Dream Girl*, in 1924. *Brown of Harvard* opened at the Princess Theatre on February 26, 1906, where it stayed for 101 performances. It was an impressive debut for a woman who had only written one other play.

The play received mostly positive reviews, with some critics quibbling over the trivial plot but enraptured by its energetic and nostalgic portrayal of college life—the party life, that is. As one character describes another: "He's got the proper college spirit—no books for him, fresh air, and something doing every minute. He's getting some good out of his education."[16] The plot concerns the popular Harvard athlete Tom Brown and his fiancée, Evelyn. Evelyn's brother, Wilfred Kenyon, has gotten himself into financial trouble. The altruistic Brown quietly pays off Kenyon's drinking and gambling debts but incurs the wrath of Thorne, a poor student struggling among the rich set with a chip on his shoulder. Thorne's sister, Marian, is in love with Kenyon. Another student coerces Kenyon to use Marian as bait to keep Thorne out of the upcoming rowing crew race against an English team. He will give Marian a check from Brown's checkbook and send Thorne a note saying that Marian is about to run away with a student. When Thorne rushes out of the rowing yard to find his sister, Brown—knowing nothing of the scheme—takes his place on the crew and leads Harvard to victory. Thorne returns with the check and accuses Brown of ruining his sister. When Brown realizes that Kenyon is involved, he risks his own happiness with Evelyn to protect him as well as Marian. Brown eventually convinces Kenyon to confess his scheme, and all is forgiven.

Indicative of the popular theater critics' boredom with "serious" theater, one critic lauded the play, "It is an inspiring and hopeful sign when those trifling agonies of school life, so absurdly vital to collegians, rouse kindly sympathies which are not afraid to be seen and heard above the din of Shaw and Ibsen, of the impulsivists and the satirists and moral iconoclasts."[17] The producers boasted about the cast members' university connections: star Henry Woodruff was himself a Harvard man, and many of the props used on the set allegedly came from his own dorm room. This sounds like a fun piece of trivia, except that the promotional ads also claim that Rida Johnson Young graduated from Radcliffe, as does a brief article in the *Augusta Herald*: "Mrs. Young is not dependent upon intuition alone, for she was seven years a student at Radcliffe, where she absorbed the local color in evidence in 'Brown of Harvard.' She was made president of the Radcliffe Dramatic Society, which organization presented her first play."[18] As absolutely no records exist of her having attended, and Young herself never claimed to, this was likely a publicity stunt on the part of the producers.[19] I also doubt that Woodruff had kept enough memorabilia from his college dorm to furnish a set.

One need only read promotional material for *Brown of Harvard* to understand the appeal of the college play with its unabashed celebration of masculine, youthful virility. The publicity department fell over itself to sing *Brown of Harvard*'s praises, using language bordering on erotic:

> A man who has seen "Brown of Harvard" . . . will say the college play exists and is patronized and admired because it pulsates with youth, life, and manhood, because it presents scenes and characters with which he is familiar from present or recent associations; to the old man it revives vivid memories of the most cherished days of his life. One of the other sex, be she school girl, old maid, or matron, will have an equally ready reply. Let women say what they may, nothing interests them quite so much as man, and the college play shows him at probably the most picturesque and interesting period of his development. . . . Even the blasé—the world weary and satisfied—find an elixir of interest in a play throbbing with an enthusiasm that they have lost. . . . Youth is the time when illusions come thick and fast. The man who retains them never grows old.[20]

The critics generally agreed that *Brown of Harvard* celebrated the best aspects of the college man's life: athletics, hijinks, and sweethearts. However, some could not help pointing out that a *woman* wrote this paean to college masculinity. Acton Davies of *The Theatre* was so unimpressed that he could not be bothered to give the name of the play or playwright correctly—"Brown at Harvard" by "Miss Rita Johnston Young"—and belittled her writing style:

> It is a picture of college life entirely rose colored, and tinted from a woman's point of view. College men may find a great deal to smile at in some of the situations, but for all of that, its sentimentality and enthusiasm have made it such a strong card to women theatregoers that the management have been obliged to give three matinee performances a week.[21]

But the critic for *Life* saw great promise in the newcomer:

> [*Brown of Harvard*] shows a really stronger grasp of dramatic possibilities than the work of the better-known literary men. More than that, it shows a more intimate knowledge of the material she is dealing with and of actual human motives of action. . . . She has infused into her play quite enough of the university spirit to make it recognizable as a reasonably faithful picture. Above all, it carries with it the swing and go of youth in its sentiment, its devil-may-care ways and its villainies.[22]

What this critic saw—and what many future critics would admit, even if they did not like her work—was that Rida Johnson Young had emotional intelligence and a keen ear for language, be it slang or highbrow. The weeks she had spent in Cambridge with her ear to the ground had shaped the tone and spirit of *Brown of Harvard*. She had created familiar, likeable characters that audiences cheered on, inhabiting a world that many of them had only recently left.

And she did not just write dialogue. To help create the authentic campus atmosphere, Young joined forces with Melville Ellis to write incidental songs. It would have been easy to interpolate popular songs, but Young instead drew on her experience writing for Witmark. The pair wrote several diegetic songs for the play, but one in particular stood out: the jaunty "When Love Is Young in Springtime" (music by Ellis), sung by Tom and the boys on the Harvard Yard:

> When love is young in springtime,
> And boys are youthful, too,
> And girls are so alluring,
> What can a fellow do?
> A look, a smile, a dimple,
> You're caught, you're captured, stung!
> There's danger in the very air,
> When love is young.[23]

This is one of Young's earliest examples of her ability to fit tone with character and place. The lyric is casual and catchy and effortlessly evokes the timeless scenario of love at first sight. Young cleverly employs a kind of antithesis in the notion that "a look, a smile, a dimple" could spell doom for a young man. And there is a pleasantly satisfying use of internal rhyme in the phrase "dan*ger* in the *very air*." She would be criticized later for overly florid phrasing in her operettas, but this song captures the spirit of the moment onstage—fraternity boys watching the girls walking by—as effectively as "I'm Falling in Love with Some One" from *Naughty Marietta*. For a good portion of her professional career, "When Love Is Young" was often named as one of her biggest song hits. And the play itself gave her a taste of real success: after 101 performances in its first season, *Brown of Harvard* returned for another 48 in its second, then enjoyed a lengthy national tour. Three film versions followed in 1911, 1918, and 1926.[24]

Flush with beginner's luck, Young finally could call herself a playwright. Producer Charles Frohman (Daniel's brother), hoping to replicate the success of *Brown of Harvard*, sent her on a research trip to Oxford University. But what had stirred her imagination at Harvard was not to be found at the august British institution. "English people were strange to me," she admitted, "and the life at Oxford bore little relation to that of Harvard. I never even attempted to write the proposed play."[25] Instead, Young turned to another kind of youthful experience for inspiration. *The Boys of Company "B"* (1907) took a lighthearted look at life in an army camp. This time, Daniel Frohman—who had once tried to turn away the green Rida Johnson—produced it at his Lyceum Theatre. (Making an appearance as a servant was future Hollywood pioneer Mack Sennett.) Critics balked at its similarities to *Brown of Harvard* ("In this play Mrs. Young has essayed to do for the national guard what in the other play she did for the college boys")[26] but agreed that Young had some potential. She would return to the material a few years later with her nephew, William Schroeder, when they turned it into the musical *When Love Is Young*. *The Lancers*, an adaptation of a German comedy, co-written by Young and J. Hartley Manners and containing songs by Cecilia Loftus and George Spink, premiered the same year but flopped at just twelve performances. However, this one was produced by the Shubert brothers; even though it failed, it established Young's relationship with the producers and laid the groundwork for her later German adaptations for them. The Shuberts next produced *Glorious Betsy* (1908), a pseudo-melodrama about the historical Elizabeth Patterson, for popular ingénue Mary Mannering. Once again, the *Baltimore Sun* praised its city's native daughter: "Mrs. Young's rise in the dramatic world has been rapid. . . . In the autumn of 1905 with 'Brown of Harvard,' Mrs. Johnson [Young] attracted the attention of theatre-goers and critics all over the country. Since then her plays, whether one-act sketches or more ambitious works, have been eagerly sought by managers and stars."[27] Critics and audiences loved Mannering in the role of the woman from Baltimore who married Jerome Bonaparte—Napoleon's brother—but were less enthusiastic about the play itself. Critic Charles Darnton called Young "that marshmallow dramatist" whose play gave "the matinee girl sugar-coated history."[28] Another paper stated, "Miss Mannering Charming," but felt sorry for the leading lady who not only had to slog through a bad play, but also had to apologize to the opening night audience for a scenic effect gone wrong:

> Some cheerful idiot had conceived the idea of representing a fog at sea by means of volumes of steam or smoke sent up from behind the scenes. As it began to pour forth the audience grew restive, and only the prompt action of one or two people who called out loudly "it is supposed to be a fog" averted what might have been a dangerous panic. Miss Mannering in her curtain speech expressed the hope that the audience was not badly frightened, but added that "the actors were nearly scared to death." A more thoughtless piece of business could hardly be imagined.[29]

Though scarcely Young's fault, that fog spelled doom for *Glorious Betsy*, which lasted only twenty-four performances. (The *Baltimore Sun*, so often her champion, was less than kind regarding this play. One reporter later wrote, "It is hard to forgive Mrs. Young for writing 'Glorious Betsy.'")[30]

Even though Young's first two productions with the Shuberts failed, the brothers do not appear to have lost faith in her potential. Their investment paid off with their third venture. At 200 performances, *The Lottery Man* (1909) was Young's first true box-office success and netted her the most positive response from critics yet. It opened at the Bijou Theatre, which had recently suffered a long streak of failures. All the critics commented that *The Lottery Man* lifted the "funereal atmosphere" off the theater and fully praised Young for her comic skills. The *New York Dramatic Mirror* declared the comedy of a man who raffles himself off as a husband to settle a debt "as bright a farce as one could wish to see."[31] Acton Davies—this time spelling Young's name correctly—proclaimed that the "witty farce raises the curse which for so many weeks has lain upon the Bijou."[32] Another critic cheered that Young had "hit upon a fresh enough idea, the characters she outlines are genuinely funny, and the dialogue bright and snappy."[33] Alan Dale fawned over the play: "Thank the kindly fates for 'The Lottery Man.' Thank 'em also for Rida Johnson Young, who has stamped herself upon the flabby season with a brand-new idea in a gorgeously funny play."[34] Even the notoriously picky critic and cultural commentator George Jean Nathan felt that Young had hit exactly the right note:

> "The Lottery Man" is a mighty bright farce. The program styles it with comedy, but farce it is straight from the funnybone. What if the playwright's conception of newspaper workings is decidedly academic so long as she exploits it merely to amuse "tired business men"? A writer of farce may add two and two and make it anything he chooses. The result must be laughter—that is the only demand. And "The Lottery Man" fully meets it.[35]

Young had never seen such glowing reviews. Her previous plays had been mildly popular, and audiences seemed to enjoy them, although the critics often credited performers like Woodruff, James Young, and Mannering for boosting ostensibly trite plots and flimsy dialogue. *The Lottery Man* signaled a turning point for both her playwriting ability and her critical reception. One critic even lauded Young as a feminist in her own way (although it was something of a backhanded compliment): "While there are women in other parts of the globe who are hurling stones and carrying banners and refusing to eat in order to prove at least the equality of the sexes there are others here who have taken to writing farces that entitle them to a vote by the American public."[36] After five outings on Broadway, perhaps Young was finally a serious contender. Some critics suggested that *The Lottery Man* succeeded because it was a "new" idea, but Young disagreed: "It does not have to have a new plot. Managers insist that the public demand novelty. . . . I have an idea that what people want most is an old story in a new dress."[37] It almost sounds as if she is advocating for the woman playwright, dress pun intended.

While Young must have enjoyed having a legitimate Broadway hit, the businesswoman in her fought to protect her intellectual property. When someone tried to recreate the plot in real life, she fumed in a telegram to J. J. Shubert:

Understand thru papers Miss Lavone Livingston of Tacoma, Washn [sic] offers herself as a matrimonial prize in a lottery conducted by a Newspaper[.] From Press reports she is using exactly the same idea as my play The Lottery Man is based on and my idea being protected by Copyright, I demand you institute legal proceedings to stop this young woman from carrying out her proposed plan. No doubt the plan was engendered in Miss Livingston [sic] mind by witnessing a performance of the play recently.[38]

There is no evidence that the Shuberts followed through on Young's request. However, the play's director, Edith Ellis Furness, also claimed intellectual property rights to *The Lottery Man*. Furness was an experienced playwright, actress, director, and acting theorist. She maintained that the Shuberts had hired her to revise or rewrite scripts submitted to their offices and that she had made substantial rewrites to *The Lottery Man* when it arrived in 1909. Furness further asserted that she had helped revise the play in rehearsals. In 1912, she brought a suit against the Shuberts and Young for $40,000 in royalties and damages. Rida vehemently denied that Furness had contributed any new material to the script, as told in this excerpt from the trial reported by the *Baltimore Evening Sun*:

> "I claim that Mrs. Furness did no rewriting of the play," testified Mrs. Young, darting a glance at Mrs. Furness. "She only did such work on the play as comes within the scope of duty of the stage producer."
>
> "Well, if I should show you eight entire pages inserted in that play by Mrs. Furness, would you still say she did no rewriting of 'The Lottery Man'?" asked the plaintiff's attorney.
>
> "I should say that Mrs. Furness simply copied what I brought in," replied Mrs. Young.
>
> "Well, bringing out points in the play more emphatically—isn't that playwriting?"
>
> "No, that is stage directing."
>
> "Well, inserting a scene or changing a plot—isn't that playwriting?"
>
> "It would be if I, as author, did it," replied Mrs. Young.[39]

Several producers and directors also testified that a play director might add stage business to the play, thereby increasing the running time, but should not be considered an author of that play. Ultimately, Furness failed to prove her case, and the court sided with the author and producers.[40]

CHAUNCEY OLCOTT AND "MOTHER MACHREE"

Young's early plays contained incidental songs for which she wrote some or all of the lyrics. Many of these songs became popular on their own and further increased her recognition. But it was probably her work with actor-singer Chauncey Olcott, which trained Young in the art of collaboration, that would serve her so well as a lyricist and librettist. An American actor and singer, Olcott (1858–1932) began his career in minstrel shows and eventually became a beloved Irish-style balladeer. He specialized in sentimental comedies with music that drew on his Irish lineage—two of his most famous songs were "My Wild Irish Rose" and "When Irish Eyes Are Smiling." Young's first project with Olcott was the 1910 play *Ragged Robin*, for which Young wrote the script and co-wrote diegetic songs. Olcott's wife, Rita, also contributed material and designed the costumes, although Young insisted, "It was Mrs. Olcott's story, and I put it into form."[41] In it, Olcott played a wealthy young man banished from his home to become a wandering Irish minstrel. When he comes upon a small village, a drink from a magical well casts Robin and a village maiden under a love spell. But she is engaged to another man. A few years later, he returns to the village, having reconciled with his family, and saves the girl from her husband's financial ruin. *Ragged Robin* received very positive reviews, but because Olcott was so popular, none of the critics mentions his collaborators. One critic gushed, "As long as Chauncey Olcott can set foot upon a stage, as long as he can make even a pretense of romping through his merry lines, he will still be popular, and audiences will turn out en masse to greet him."[42]

Young and Olcott's 1911 play with music, *Barry of Ballymore*, introduced the song "Mother Machree" (music by Ernest Ball), which would become an

Figure 2.1 Chauncey Olcott in Ragged Robin. Billy Rose Theatre Division, The New York Public Library.

enormously popular hit for both Olcott and Young. In it, a young man pays homage to the first love of his life:

> Sure, I love the dear silver that shines in your hair,
> And the brow that's all furrowed
> And wrinkled with care.
> I kiss the dear fingers, so toil-worn for me,
> Oh, God bless you and keep you,
> Mother Machree![43]

Later in the song, Young demonstrates a flair for internal rhyme that, though simple, lands pleasingly on the listener's ear and gives the verse a lilting tone: "Was made *bright by* the *light* / Of the *smile* in your *eye.*" Young's use of the Irish vernacular—words like *colleen* ("girl" or "girlfriend") and *Machree* ("dearest"), and "Sure" where an American character might sing "Oh"—gives the song an authenticity that would later lead to its being mistaken as a traditional Irish ballad. Helen Christine Bennett's article, "The Woman Who Wrote 'Mother Machree,'" explained:

> The name of Rida Johnson Young appears on every copy of the song and on every phonograph record. Yet, curiously enough, there is a widespread impression that "Mother Machree" is an old song which has come down to us through the years. During the war, some of the newspapers, in commenting on the songs that were favorites with the soldiers, told how the boys especially loved "the old songs, like 'Mother Machree.'"[44]

The song immediately struck a chord with the public and sold more than two million records and copies of sheet music. It remained a favorite for Chauncey Olcott's fans as well. In one of Olcott's obituaries, the author recounts his first public performance of the song: "He took seven encores before he was allowed to return, trembling with emotional exhaustion, to his dressing room."[45]

But it was not just Olcott's plaintive Irish air that moved audiences; the song's popularity was a testament to Young's talent for understanding her audience and creating evocative images with her lyrics. And while the casual listener may not be conscious of it, solidly structured songs are pleasing to the ear, intellect, and emotion. "Mother Machree" succeeds dramaturgically, as Philip Furia and Michael Lasser point out: "Clearly, Young knew her trade; her lyric uses internal rhyme, alliteration, and antithesis effortlessly."[46]

The song was still so popular ten years after its premiere that Young donated a month's worth of royalties to a fundraiser for her alma mater, Wilson College, and wrote a novella based on it. But Young was as stunned by its popularity as anyone. "The enormous success of the song was a surprise to me," she admitted. "Love songs are the ones on which writers depend for hits, although occasionally a 'Mother' song does make one. Why poor old father can't get a look-in on this heart-interest business, I don't know."[47] Young had tapped into a sentimental vein like no other and would return to it later in the wartime musical *Her Soldier Boy*. Olcott and Young's collaboration would last as well; they would write three more plays together—*Macushla* (1912), *The Isle o' Dreams* (1913), and *Shameen Dhu* (1914)—all of which drew inspiration from Olcott's Irish heritage and characters.

AN OUTING WITH "MATTY"

Young collaborated with many theater makers in her career, but one partnership took her into another world entirely. Baseball as the setting for a play has an unlucky history on Broadway, *Damn Yankees* notwithstanding. Even Young admitted, "There is a tradition among theatrical people that no successful play can be written around baseball. At any rate, no play dealing with baseball has been successful. But the subject is such a popular one the managers keep on trying, hoping that someday a really big success will come."[48] Sadly, Young's collaboration with New York Giants pitcher Christy "Matty" Mathewson, *The Girl and the Pennant* (1913), was not that success. The idea seemed promising: pair a popular ballplayer with a seasoned playwright, send the playwright to spring training to learn everything about baseball, model the leading character after the popular playwright, and use real sports figures for inspiration. Why shouldn't America's favorite pastime play on the American stage?

The Girl and the Pennant took its plot from recent events in the world of baseball.[49] In 1911, Helene Hathaway Robison Britton had become the first woman owner of a major-league baseball team, the St. Louis Cardinals. She shared a contentious relationship with the team's manager, Roger Bresnahan, who on at least one occasion declared that he would not be told how to do his job by a woman.[50] The plot concerns a young woman who inherits a baseball team and faces scrutiny from the team and its leadership. Young and Mathewson populated the fictional Eagles with names that the audience would vaguely recognize, like "Cy Dobb" (Ty Cobb) and "Fred Terkle" (Fred Merkle). Even the manager's name—John Bohannon—would have been familiar to those who had been following baseball news. Some critics compared it unfavorably to *Brown of Harvard*, and there certainly are some similarities. The baseball grounds share the hyper-masculine atmosphere of the Harvard men's dormitory, and women are only permitted when the men invite them. The men are by turns heroic, chivalrous, and brutish, claiming the territory as a "man's place." The women in these plays serve as pawns in the men's schemes. But the two plays also demonstrate Young's growth as a playwright. The dialogue in *Brown of Harvard* comes off as fussy and dated, while Young's characters for *The Girl and the Pennant*—written less than a decade later—sound confident and truer to life. The humor is effortless, even with her broader comic characters, like the prim matron Miss Squibbs. And, unlike the victimized female characters in *Brown of Harvard*, the women of *The Girl and the Pennant* exercise some agency over their respective roles. The titular "girl," Mona Fitzgerald, is forced to defend her position and credentials several times but helps her team win the pennant with some clever coaching. While it is not an overtly feminist play—the women all end up with romantic partners and the implication that they will be protected from here on out by their men—Young and Mathewson stepped into potentially controversial territory. As Travis W. Stern explains, many in the baseball world at the time resented Britton's presence at the head of a major-league team and feared the "feminizing" of baseball.[51] *The Girl and the Pennant* effectively lampoons those fears.

Originally titled *Fair Play*, the baseball drama premiered in Young's hometown of Baltimore on September 29, 1913, a month before its New York opening. Critics in New York cautiously praised the effort. It is not known how much Mathewson actually contributed to the play. Even contemporary critics weren't sure how the

Figure 2.2 Rida Johnson Young and Christy Mathewson in a publicity photo for The Girl and the Pennant. *Unknown magazine. Billy Rose Theatre Division, The New York Public Library.*

two authors divided the work. One reviewer's headline read: "'Matty' Does a Play/ Or at Least Assists Mrs. Rida Johnson Young in Doing One."[52] If he didn't write any dialogue, he most certainly advised Young on baseball culture, game play, and personalities. There is little doubt that Young modeled the leading character of Copley Reeves on Mathewson himself. As Stern describes him, "Copley is shown to be a hard-working, respectable man and a paragon of virtue and fair-play in baseball—qualities that might have been recognizable as Mathewson even if his name did not appear as a co-author of the play."[53] Notably, Mathewson did not attend the play's opening or subsequent performances—a disappointing twenty— and the play was later published without his name on it.

"PARADOX INCARNATE"

Young's early hits (and occasional misses) put her name on the public's radar at a time when women were making serious headway in the professional theater. The *Chicago Daily Tribune* dubbed 1907 the "Women's Year in the Drama," thanks to the presence of so many women playwrights:

> Most of the successes either are written or played by women. Although there is confessedly no woman dramatic author of the first rank in the world, and although there never has been, there are working today so many women dramatic authors that are successful, even if they are not great, that they as a force must be reckoned with.[54]

Sexist commentary aside, women playwrights *were* stepping up to the plate, and Rida Johnson Young was leading the pack. In only a few years, the legendary director, producer, and playwright David Belasco would cite her as "one of our very successful women dramatists" while encouraging others to follow in her footsteps:

> The average woman certainly has a greater power of intuition than the average man. Her dramatic sense is keener, and while it may be true that the man from one point of view may have a wider outlook on life, the woman, within her scope, goes more into the details and has a greater knowledge of life in general. Emotionally she is man's superior, and as a student of human nature she is certainly his equal.[55]

But Young didn't need Belasco to validate her. "Playwriting is a field in which there are no handicaps for a woman and where she does not have to unsex herself to compete with a man," she insisted. "A woman may be a dramatist and still be a woman."[56]

Young found some measure of equity in her business dealings as well. A contract for the 1911–1912 season found in the Shubert Archive provides insight into the kinds of agreements the Shuberts made with their writers:

> We have to produce personally and give 50 performances during the season of 1911–1912. Royalty 5% to 4000.—7 ½% to 10.000.—10% on all over. We have

the right to but one company and cannot produce in New York before Oct. 15th, 1911. We have to print her name on any advertising of whatever kind of the play. We have no publishing or operatic rights. We pay $50 for each performance under 50 we fail to produce. . . . We can place in stock after two years by giving author half the stock royalty with no deductions and she has the right to copy all stock contracts.[57]

If this was a standard contract, an author stood to make a tidy profit if a show did well at the box office. As we have seen, Young made it her business to keep close track of all box-office receipts for shows playing in New York and on the road and did not hesitate to contact her producers if she did not receive her checks in a timely manner.

Young's insistence paid off handsomely, as she quickly amassed a salary that allowed her to purchase a modest home in Greenwich, Connecticut—and, later, larger estates in the wealthy Belle Haven community and Southfield Point in Stamford, Connecticut—and help support her mother and siblings. The Belle Haven house was in an area dubbed the "Great American Playwright Belt," a stretch of waterfront neighborhoods on the Long Island Sound occupied by many known playwrights of the time. A newspaper feature on the area described her home and workspace in the "millionaire suburb":

> The author of "The Lottery Man" has a large, roomy stucco house. It sets well back from the road and is screened by many splendid oak trees. Mrs. Young has two acres in the heart of exclusive Belle Haven. Back of the house is a sunken Italian garden, and well away from the house is a roomy stable and garage, built of the same material as the house. The dramatist does all her work in a room on the second floor, and she could not very well be called "a little ink lady" for the reason that she does all of her composing on a typewriter. All that is to be seen in this workshop are the photographs of several famous actors and actresses, a roll top desk, a typewriter and table, and a case of pigeonholes in which are kept copies of the many plays that Mrs. Young has written.[58]

After the Belle Haven home was robbed, she moved to the even wealthier neighborhood of Southfield Point—also the home of some of America's wealthiest families, including the Vanderbilts.[59] During the theatrical season, she lived in hotels, traveled with a lady's maid, and was known for her taste in clothing and jewelry. The *Baltimore Sun* noted, "She is a familiar figure in the best hotels in New York, London, and Paris, and has been traveling extensively on the royalties from her comedies."[60] This female dramatist had, within only a few years, built up a lucrative, steady career on Broadway. Producers and performers sought her out; critics and audiences knew her name. "Yes, I have been a busy woman for these last four years," she gushed, "but don't you think I have been fortunate, the managers who have taken my plays, the stars who have played them? There never has been a luckier woman. Things have just come my way, one after another."[61] She saved her most glowing praise for the producers who had weathered two flops with her before hitting the virtual jackpot with *The Lottery Man*: "Now I am most fortunate of all, for Mr. Lee Shubert has been as helpful as the others, and the Shubert management is ideally generous."[62]

While her career soared, Rida's marriage to James Young faltered. They divorced in 1909, and James married actress Clara Kimball in 1910.[63] Another actress he'd been rumored to be dating "showed no special emotion when told of Mr. Young's marriage. Neither did Mrs. Rida Johnson Young when informed by telephone of the happy event. 'Fine! Congratulations and happiness to both!' was Mrs. Young's blasé message to her former husband and his wife."[64] It seems that little love was lost between them. James would marry and divorce a third time; Rida never remarried, nor was she ever mentioned in connection with any romantic partners. Curiously, after Rida's death, James claimed to have co-written all of her early plays, stating, "but at that time I was an ambitious actor and, not desiring any literary distinction, I claimed no credit for my work."[65] There is simply no evidence to substantiate this. Rida never spoke of James in any of her many interviews and certainly did not suggest that he had contributed anything to her plays.

But Rida Young *was* quick to praise her collaborators whenever anyone complimented her writing. She would not take credit for someone else's work. She wisely learned early on that her script was only the starting point of a production. When Henry Miller directed *Brown of Harvard*, the inexperienced playwright frequently disagreed with his suggestions for script changes, even to the point that he kicked her out of the theater for interfering with his direction. "When I was forced to rewrite and rewrite, to cut and elaborate, I felt that Mr. Miller was murdering my child," she recalled. "I saw it after it was produced; saw how all my crudities had been softened, all my mistakes corrected . . . and how mistaken I had been. And from that day I tried to work with my director and to believe him."[66]

Young's reminiscences of her early days show her as an eager student of all things theatrical. Her willingness to take any work in the theater and seeming fearlessness in the face of rejection positioned her to make the right contacts in New York. Once her foot was in the door, she was a sponge, taking in all the education she could get. A publicist from Wilson College marveled at Young's ability to write from experiences outside of her own: "Paradoxes are fascinating. A woman without Irish ancestry writes the greatest Irish ballad hit. The graduate of a women's college writes a stage success of Harvard. Truly, woman is paradox incarnate."[67]

Rida Johnson Young was no paradox; she was a smart playwright. She had not spent her entire adult life in theater companies, surrounded by the era's great actors, directors, and producers, without having learned something about how audiences respond to what they see on the stage. For all the feature writers who chalked it up to a feminine sensibility, Young was astute. She knew who was coming to see her plays:

> I think I know more about what people who come to the theatre *don't* want than about what they do. For one thing, I know that a play cannot succeed if it

does not please women. . . . Except in vaudeville houses, I do not think I ever saw a theatre audience in which the men outnumbered the women. I am supposed to write musical comedies which will please the "tired business man." But if they do not please the lady whom the tired business man brings with him, the show will not last long.[68]

But one aspect of Young's personality that comes out in her interviews *is* a bit paradoxical. Although she unquestionably worked very hard, she frequently undercut herself by throwing off assumptions about her devotion to her craft. Take, for instance, this 1910 interview with Shirley Burns for the *Green Book Album*: "I never had any trouble in getting my plays on, and I think I am very lucky, since there are so many really good plays going begging. But I don't call mine plays. They aren't my idea of a play. They are just amusing little things—I don't know what you'd call them."[69] She often downplayed her work, sometimes changing the subject to gardening or other hobbies. She would also claim that she was just "after the money."[70] But her work ethic, prodigious output, and involvement in the production of her plays belie her seemingly nonchalant front. Her plays are not mere sketches—they are lengthy, expertly crafted dramas. It is hard to call plays that run three acts and around a hundred pages—as many of her plays do—"little things." Many of her works are collaborations, either with other playwrights or with composers and co-lyricists, and collaborations require intensely hard work. Plus, she talked about that work ethic in nearly every interview she gave throughout her career, including the one with Burns. It seems to have been very important to her that the public understand that she wrote for four hours every day, that she traveled for research, that she was involved in casting and rehearsals, and that she knew exactly how much money she was making on every production.

Young didn't do anything *but* write plays. She had no husband or children and averaged about one play on Broadway every year until her death, in some seasons as many as three. But because she was writing for the popular commercial theater, she may have discounted her plays as silly in comparison to American Realist playwrights. Young followed the work of the more "serious" playwrights almost as much as her commercial colleagues. "I admire Eugene O'Neill extravagantly. He is a real dramatist. The rest of us are merely play carpenters," she explained in an early interview. "I admire Rachel Crothers's work also for its sincerity and enlightened study of young people, sex and society. My interest in young people, however, is more in their comic and sentimental aspects, and I suppose this is a somewhat unique attitude for these days."[71] Still, her plays required a great deal of work, careful collaboration, and thoughtful plotting. The idea that she saw her work as trifling is wholly disingenuous and, I believe, simply untrue.

Young spent the first several years of her career honing her playwriting skills and becoming a regular name on Broadway marquees. Her early plays were produced by the most powerful producers in New York: Daniel Frohman and

Figure 2.3 Rida Johnson Young at home with one of her dogs. New York American, December 1920. Billy Rose Theatre Division, The New York Public Library.

the Shuberts. Clearly, they could count on Young to collaborate with directors, star performers, and composers; more important, she could write a play—and fast—that would make money. In 1909, the *Baltimore Sun* boasted that its native daughter was "one of the most successful women that ever wrote for the American stage"—when her greatest successes were still in her future.[72]

3
AH! SWEET MYSTERY OF LIFE
NAUGHTY MARIETTA

> Someone with a grudge against me must have wished this musical comedy business on me. Of course I'd rather write plays.
>
> Rida Johnson Young[1]

Musical entertainments dominated the New York stage at the turn of the twentieth century. A glance at any season—1907, for example—presents a dazzling array of options for an evening of musical entertainment. On any given night, a typical theatergoer might choose: Keith and Albee's Union Square Theatre for family-friendly vaudeville; the long-running hit musical comedy *The Red Mill*, featuring the antics of comedy duo Dave Montgomery and Fred Stone; the recently opened Hippodrome for a triple bill of an "operatic extravaganza," a circus, and a melodrama that boasted cowboys, Indians, and a full cavalry, followed by an underwater spectacle; a revival of George M. Cohan's patriotic vehicle of 1904, *Little Johnny Jones*; the debut of up-and-coming impresario Florenz Ziegfeld and his *Follies of 1907*, headlined by the charming Anna Held; or the all-black show *The Shoo-Fly Regiment*, by Bob Cole and J. Rosamond Johnson.

It was only natural that Young, having proven herself as a playwright and lyricist, should try her hand at a musical. She first forayed into the musical business in 1907 when she collaborated with her nephew William Schroeder on a musical comedy, *Sweet Sixteen*.[2] The Shuberts optioned it and first offered the starring role to Blanche Ring, who requested changes to the script. Over the course of its three-year gestation, the title changed to *Just One of the Boys*, and Lulu Glaser took over the leading role. Glaser played Cherry Winston, owner and manager of a lumber camp in the Michigan woods whose mannish upbringing by three woodsmen has nurtured her into a rough tomboy. When a handsome young boarding-school man falls in love with her, she goes to a New York finishing school to become more feminine. Glaser received glowing reviews, but the show did not. *Just One of the Boys* toured in early 1910 but closed before it made it to New York. A Washington, D.C., critic lambasted it:

> There are only two acts of it—which is its chief redeeming feature—and one of them . . . is about as inane a conception as one can imagine. As a test of the patience and indulgence of an audience it is supremely successful, but in no other respect.
>
> The second act may be accepted as an apology for the first, because it has some claim to the complaisance of the public. The plot of the play, or what passes as such, is attenuated almost to the point of evanescence.[3]

Young may have been a successful playwright, but her first musical flopped. She had no doubt figured out that knowing how to write a play did not necessarily mean one could easily cross over to musical theater. As we have already seen, Young considered a coherent plot essential: "Maybe I think more of plots because they are what give me the most trouble. Characters and dialogue are easy. But I would sit up nights, if it were not against my principles, over plots."[4] The Washington critic had roasted *Just One of the Boys* for its thin plot; she would have to do better.

AN AMERICAN OPERETTA

In his biography of the early shows of Richard Rodgers and Lorenz Hart, Dominic Symonds states, "Perhaps more than any other cultural idiom, the Broadway musical strained the fault lines between European and American culture, and between highbrow art and popular entertainment."[5] This is probably nowhere more evident than in the American operettas that waltzed all over Broadway in the early 1900s, particularly in the wake of Franz Lehár's megahit from Vienna, *The Merry Widow* (Vienna, 1905; New York, 1907). After overwhelming popularity in Vienna and London—where the music played in "Merry Widow cafes," the costumes influenced fashion and introduced the "Merry Widow hat" to the world, and even wallpaper with scenes from the show made its way into homes—New Yorkers saw the show more than four hundred times in its initial run. American audiences already loved the comic operas of W. S. Gilbert and Arthur Sullivan, and American composers John Philip Sousa, Reginald De Koven, and Victor Herbert enjoyed popular success. Herbert was undoubtedly the most successful in this idiom, with *The Wizard of the Nile* (1895), *Babes in Toyland* (1903), and *Mlle. Modiste* (1905), among many others, to his credit. He had worked primarily with librettist-lyricists Harry B. Smith and Henry Blossom, two of the leading writers of the day.

The opera impresario Oscar Hammerstein tapped Herbert to write a new operetta to premiere at the New York Theater, formerly his Olympia Theater.[6] He asked Young to write several plot outlines from which Herbert would choose. In late May 1910, Young traveled by train to Herbert's summer home in Lake Placid, New York, scenarios in hand. The meeting at Herbert's idyllic Adirondack cottage must have gone well, because Herbert and Young signed contracts and began work soon afterward on *Naughty Marietta*, a work that has since come to be known as one of Herbert's greatest operettas and the first true American operetta.[7]

The comic operetta about a runaway countess's adventures in eighteenth-century New Orleans starred Italian soprano Emma Trentini in the title role and tenor Orville Harrold (sometimes called "The Little Caruso") as her love interest, Captain Richard "Dick" Warrington. The show was an instant smash and would later prove an enduring one for Herbert and Young, not only in national tours but also in royalties from its beloved songs (including "Ah! Sweet Mystery of Life," "I'm Falling in Love with Some One," "Italian Street Song," and "'Neath the Southern Moon"). Neither writer would live to see its well-received 1935 film version starring Jeanette MacDonald and Nelson Eddy, the 1955 television adaptation with Patrice Munsel and Alfred Drake, or its establishment in the repertoire of light opera companies all over the United States. But they would enjoy its immediate success, and Young would embark on a new phase of her writing career.

Many original reviews lavished praise on Herbert's score and panned Young's libretto, although not her lyrics. As a result, general critical consensus holds that while the lyrics fit the tone of the music and the operetta genre, the book is decidedly flimsy. Herbert biographer Neil Gould opines that "the weakness of the book stood out in strong relief to the brilliance of the score."[8] Raymond Knapp, in his analysis of *Naughty Marietta* and its themes of American values, cites "a certain ineptitude on the part of the librettist" as one reason the plot is sometimes considered confusing. Although he acknowledges that the show possesses "a guiding intelligence," Knapp does not fully credit Young as its architect.[9] And operetta historian Richard Traubner maintains that "the book—no matter how thoroughly revised—remains a silly framework" for the songs.[10]

However, a close reading of the script reveals Young's sophisticated management of three plot lines, lively characters, and subtle explorations of racism, feminism, and upward mobility. In fact, the libretto abides by standard operetta conventions on the surface even as Young's characters playfully subvert them. It is important to bear in mind that while operetta librettists tried to write strong books, the focus usually rested on the music, much as it does in opera. Musical theater librettists faced a veritable mountain of dramaturgical hurdles. Henry Blossom explained the complicated job to the readers of *The Theatre*:

> In the first place a librettist must be able to tell a unified story, and that story must be of sufficient strength to hold the interest of audiences for two hours and a half. Then he must write his story in such a manner that the composer shall have every opportunity of displaying his best melodies. He must know how much time to allow between these musical numbers to enable the chorus

and principals to change costumes; he must be able to carry on that story in the lyrics if he is a lyricist as well as librettist; he must be able to build up scenes and situations for the proper dramatic effect; he must know humor, and sprinkle the libretto with a generous number of these humor points; he must know a thousand and one details before he even begins to place his story on paper.

But Blossom knew that no matter how hard the librettist worked, the job was ultimately thankless. As he put it rather bluntly: "We librettists know beforehand that we are going to be eternally damned.... If the production is a success, the critics maintain it is because of the music. If it is a failure, it is because of the librettist's book."[11]

Librettists had many egos to please and countless variables thrown at them while writing a script. For *Naughty Marietta*, Young had two principal singers who barely spoke English (Trentini and French contralto Maria Duchene), a producer who insisted on vaudeville-style comedy, and a costume designer who dictated that the time period be changed.[12] When a reporter asked Young about the period of the play, she replied, "We don't know ourselves. You see, we selected one date, and then the costumer decided that another would give him more latitude in the designing of his costumes, so it is all a little indefinite, but it is sometime during the eighteenth century."[13] Herbert and Young seem to have had a positive working relationship. Young praised Herbert's process: "The rehearsals for this piece were comparatively painless. Mr. Herbert is the original stand-patter. What he writes for a play is sung in that play. The librettist does not have the usual agony of sitting up nights and writing new lyrics during rehearsal time and for many nights after the play is produced."[14] *Naughty Marietta* was not Young's strongest libretto, but it hinted at the potential she would later develop. Herbert biographer Edward N. Waters also points out that Herbert was less than discerning about his librettists: "Rida Johnson Young may not have produced a literary masterpiece, but it was certainly better than many a book the composer so uncritically accepted."[15] In any case, most critical commentary on *Naughty Marietta* tells its history from Herbert's point of view, sometimes even Trentini's. This chapter takes a closer look at this much-maligned libretto and Rida Johnson Young's contribution to the show and to its ultimate success.

PLOT AND SUBPLOTS

Naughty Marietta depicts the Italian countess Marietta d'Altena, who has fled a family-imposed convent life in France by joining a group of "casquette girls," women sent to New Orleans by the French king, carrying gold and land grants locked in small caskets to find husbands. Marietta has escaped from the casquette girls and is hiding in New Orleans. She repeatedly sings an unfinished melody that she believes only her true love can complete (listed in the score as the "Dream

Melody," which will eventually become "Ah! Sweet Mystery of Life"). Captain Dick Warrington has orders to either return her to France or compel her to marry, but when he finds her in New Orleans, she insists that he find her a disguise. The two bicker and deny any romantic feelings toward each other, but there is no doubt from the beginning that Dick will be the man to finish Marietta's song. Instead of returning her to France, he agrees to put her in a local marionette troupe posing as the long-lost son of its Italian owner, Rudolfo.

The first of two subplots begins even before the title character enters the stage. A pirate named Bras Piqué (a French term meaning "pricked arm" or "tattooed") has been menacing the high seas, and Captain Dick and his men have been engaged by the king of France to capture him. But Bras Piqué resides in New Orleans—he is actually Etienne Grandet, the son of the lieutenant governor. The real governor is being held captive on a remote island by Bras Piqué's men. Etienne plans to take over New Orleans, but his attraction to the fiery Marietta and trouble with his quadroon mistress, Adah, disrupt his schemes. The second subplot involves the comic character Simon O'Hara, a servant with lofty ambitions, and Lizette, a casquette girl who cannot get a husband and latches on to Simon.[16] Simon, wishing to "throw off the yoke of servitude," schemes to replace Bras Piqué and instead ends up as the official "whipping boy" of the lieutenant governor.[17] The plots collide at the end of the play, when Dick uncovers Etienne's secret just as Marietta is about to marry the pirate; then he finishes Marietta's "Dream Melody," thus proving himself her true love.

Naughty Marietta's dramaturgical structure is one of its strengths. Managing multiple plot lines takes careful planning and skill. An effective dramatist must keep the plots distinct from one another, connect the subplots to the main plot thematically, and keep secondary characters in the mix. In *Naughty Marietta*, Young gives two of the plots nearly equal stage time and the third a significant amount. Dividing the script into French scenes—smaller increments than the overall act and scene breakdown—readily reveals the structure of the plot lines.[18] In act 1, the first subplot—the introduction of Etienne, his mistress Adah, and his double life as the lieutenant governor's son and the pirate Bras Piqué—occurs right after the opening number. The main plot begins immediately afterward, with the entrance of Captain Dick and his men and the news that they are seeking both Bras Piqué and wives for the men from the crop of casquette girls. The scene finishes with Simon, who is looking for a way out of his servitude and provides the second subplot. From this point on, Young deftly alternates among the plots; the Marietta/Dick plot takes precedence, followed closely by the Simon/Lizette story, then the Etienne/Adah story, and she follows this pattern through the second act as well. The three plots intersect at times, yet none seems dependent on any of the others. However, Young was an accomplished playwright who knew that the subplots must connect to the main plot, no matter how tenuously, in order for an audience to follow them. Young devised subtle ways to mirror Marietta's journey with that of the secondary characters, thus ensuring that all three stories would hold the audience's interest.

Figure 3.1 A scene from Naughty Marietta. *Photo by White Studio. © Billy Rose Theatre Division, The New York Public Library for the Performing Arts.*

AMERICAN RURITANIA

Location and period in large part distinguish operetta from musical comedy. Whereas musical comedies usually take place in contemporary urban settings, operettas are set in a glorified past, usually in a fictional, bucolic European village removed from modern life, that invokes a pseudo-nostalgia for a time and place that feel utterly familiar despite the fact that they never existed at all. Anthony Hope coined the name "Ruritania" in his 1894 novel *The Prisoner of Zenda*, set in a fictional central European country ruled by an autocratic king. Fraught with political intrigue, adventure, and passion, Hope's Ruritania captured readers' imaginations; other writers adopted the practice of setting their works in fictional Balkan countries, creating the genre known as "Ruritanian romance." Musicologist William Everett describes Ruritania in operetta as "synonymous with lands of dimwitted royals, colorfully dressed peasants, and extravagant foreigners . . . all of whom lived blissfully oblivious to the real world in some sort of suspended nineteenth century."[19] Instead of Europe, Young and Herbert chose arguably the most exotic city in the United States and populated it with both patriotic and treasonous Americans, European immigrants, and a sophisticated glamor that the historical New Orleans probably did not possess, effectively inventing an American Ruritania.[20]

Naughty Marietta's original title was *Little Paris*, an early nickname for New Orleans. Set in 1780, the New Orleans of *Naughty Marietta* is a highly fictionalized one, ruled by French aristocrats at a time when the Spanish actually governed the city. France ceded its struggling North American colony to Spain in 1762, effectively abandoning New Orleans and cutting off its expatriates from their mother country. Moreover, the French made up only one part of what had become a rather diverse colony in the less than one hundred years of its existence. Between its founding in 1718 and the Spanish occupation of 1767 to 1800, New Orleans was home to a German settlement, Creoles (broadly defined as native-born during the French occupation, regardless of color), African and Caribbean slaves, Canadian refugees, and American Indians who predated colonization. Those who had come to New Orleans from France in its early days were primarily prisoners, prostitutes, and other "unwanteds," with a much smaller percentage of nobility and merchants, many of whom died en route. While Young left behind no notes indicating what kind of research she did on New Orleans, if any, her characters and situations strongly mirror some aspects of the city's history. Shannon Lee Dawdy, author of *Building the Devil's Empire: French Colonial New Orleans*, calls the colony

> a devilishly difficult corner of empire to control. Instead of developing into an exemplary French-dominated "opulent metropolis" as intended, New Orleans quickly became the untamed hub of a Mississippi-Caribbean frontier. The town had a savage and disorderly quality due to its smuggling activity, ethnic diversity, social mobility, "spirit of insubordination," and the confusing animosities and intimacies of slavery. New Orleanians in the French period were prone to be pragmatic rule-breakers and undomesticated travelers, independent-minded and imaginative in their strategies for survival.[21]

Marietta is a runaway in disguise, Dick is the leader of an independent company of rangers who roam the territories as they please, and Etienne is a pirate. By Dawdy's estimation, they would have fit right into the historical New Orleans.

As unlikely as Marietta's story may seem, it is actually rooted in historical events. In its efforts to increase Louisiana's population, France found that it could not send prostitutes—also called "correction girls"—to the colony and expect high-born men to marry them. After establishing a convent of Ursuline nuns to secure a Christian presence in New Orleans, the French government began importing young women of good breeding from among whom unmarried men could choose brides. They were given small caskets containing clothing and other necessities, resulting in the nickname "casket girls," or *filles à la cassette*. When they arrived, the nuns housed them under strict protection until they got married. But *Naughty Marietta* confuses some key facts about the practice. For one thing, their use of the name "casquette girls" is a major translation error. "Casket" in French is *cassette*, not *casquette*, which is actually a type of cap. Second, the "casquette girls" in *Naughty Marietta* are carrying gold and land grants from the French king as dowries. However, Herbert Asbury's *The French Quarter: An Informal History of the New Orleans Underworld* provides a typical casket girl's packing list: "two coats, two shirts and undershirts, six headdresses and various other articles of clothing."[22] No mention of gold or land grants. Most likely, the men choosing brides already had land—they needed wives and children to work the land and make it profitable. Despite any historical inaccuracies, Marietta's disguise as a casquette girl and the promise of gold in Lizette's casket both provide high-stakes plot points. And while it seems highly unlikely that one of these girls would have been able to escape the marriage contract ordered by the king, Grace King offers a tantalizing anecdote in her history of New Orleans, written in 1895: "Once, one of the girls sent out refused to marry. . . . And thus, also, this girl has been a fruitful theme for idle feminine musings breeding the still more idle longings to know more of her, her name, her reasons, her after life."[23] Could this young woman possibly have inspired Herbert and Young to create Marietta?

Interestingly enough, art imitated life in casting Emma Trentini as Marietta d'Altena. Hammerstein discovered Trentini in Italy, working in her family's deli by day and singing in a cabaret at night. He brought her to New York and installed her at his Manhattan Opera House, where she played Musetta in *La Bohème* and Olympia in *The Tales of Hoffmann* to great acclaim. She was petite, charming, and vivacious, but her temperament earned her the nickname the "Merry Little Devil of the Manhattan Opera."[24] Her English was only passable, so she learned much of her part in *Naughty Marietta* phonetically. Herbert wrote Marietta's music to fit her voice, which he may have regretted later. The *New York Times* reviewer noted: "Mr. Herbert has written a part for her which would tire any prima donna to sing every night, and those who would hear all the high notes, roulades, and trills which are in the score now, had best hurry . . . because sooner or later it will probably be found expedient to take some of them out."[25] Waters describes the eventual fallout between Herbert and Trentini as "an incredible hodgepodge of a prima donna's eccentricities which finally ended in a clash with Herbert himself."[26] As it happened, Trentini did complain about the number of encores she was compelled to do, by the audience, Herbert, and Hammerstein. When *Naughty Marietta* went on tour after its New York run, Trentini felt free to play the show as she wished, refusing encores and difficult passages and throwing the occasional tantrum. Herbert experienced her stubborn will firsthand when he conducted her in a gala performance of the operetta, during which she embarrassed him by walking off the stage instead of singing an encore of "Italian Street Song." Herbert refused to work with her ever again and pulled out of writing a planned second vehicle for her. As her "difficult" reputation was established before *Naughty Marietta* was written, Young managed to work her nickname into the script:

> BLAKE. Yes, she was a fiery Italian girl and when the little devil learned that every casquette girl was obliged to choose a husband, she said she'd take Dick.
> ETIENNE. No!
> BLAKE. Yes—and when Dick politely refused her, she up and struck him across the face with her gloves.[27]

RISING AMERICANS

Much research has been done on the ways in which musicals reflect, celebrate, and grapple with American values.[28] *Naughty Marietta* plays on themes surrounding the American experience and the nationalistic leanings of its characters. Of chief concern to them are personal and national agency. Marietta wishes to be independent, Etienne believes he can rule New Orleans both legally and illegally, and Dick and Sir Harry Blake lead a band of merry men beholden to no country. Their entrance early in the show ("Tramp! Tramp! Tramp!") establishes the overarching theme:

> Tramp! Tramp! Tramp! along the highway,
> Tramp! Tramp! Tramp! the road is free.
> Blazing trails along the byway,
> Courers des bois are we![29]
> Tramp! Tramp! Tramp! Now clear the roadway,
> Room, room, room, the world is free,
> We're planters and Canucks,
> Virginians and Kaintucks,
> Captain Dick's own infantry.[30]

In this, one of her most famous lyrics, Young was actually quoting herself. She lifted a line from her second Broadway play, *The Boys of Company "B,"* from another group of rough-and-tumble men. Early in the play, a brash young militia man tells his fellow recruits that they will not be riding to their next camp; they will set out on foot: "Think of it, fellows, rain or shine, hot or cold. Tramp, tramp, tramp, the boys are marching, half the length of this glorious state."[31] The song and the dialogue that follows identify different American groups—the "Virginians and Kaintucks" (residents of what was then Kentucky territory) and the hyphenated Americans: transplants from France, Ireland, England, and others. The men share this tense dialogue with the first New Orleanians they meet:

> ETIENNE. Is it the girls or the well filled caskets which the king sends with them that attracts the men?
> BLAKE. Sir. That is not a very gallant remark for a Frenchman.
> ETIENNE. No harm meant. You, I take it, are Irish?
> BLAKE. Take it or leave it, I am.
> SIMON. And I, sir, am a rising American. Submerged at present, but looking for my opportunity.[32]

This exchange mirrors a national conversation at the turn of the twentieth century: to what extent do immigrants leave behind their native cultural identities and "become" American? These men take pride in being from specific locations, but Simon declares himself a "rising American" several times and repeats the phrase "This may be my opportunity" in almost every one of his scenes. For him, the generic "American" identity eclipses all others. In Young and Herbert's New

Orleans, Americans are pioneers, trailblazers, and at liberty to shape their own destinies. Another word about this particular song: when Dick's men stomped in, musically and physically, it also established a song type that would become a staple for all American operettas, the men's marching song. Later examples of this would include "To the Inn We're Marching" from *The Student Prince* (1924; lyrics by Dorothy Donnelly, music by Sigmund Romberg) and "Stouthearted Men" from *The New Moon* (1928; lyrics by Oscar Hammerstein II, music by Sigmund Romberg).

Young also explores the desire for American status through the theme of social mobility. Many of the principal characters are trying to escape their class, be it low or high. Marietta frequently denies her highborn status, and not just to protect herself from capture:

> MARIETTA. Now look you, Captain Dick, consider I have never had one—what you say—a good time in all my life.
> DICK. It is your own fault.
> MARIETTA. My fault? Santa Maria! In Italy I was banished and sent away to a convent to learn to be a lady—
> DICK. Where you should have stayed.
> MARIETTA. You could not expect me to like that.[33]

Marietta is not just trying to escape a life of familial duty and avoid being sent back to an angry father. She yearns for adventure and excitement, something neither the convent in France nor her family could give her. When Marietta joins Rudolfo's marionette troupe and sings the joyful "Italian Street Song," the very title signifies her wish to be a "commoner." The lyrics do not state the title, but the pure abandon and exuberance of the song, sung among itinerant Italian peasants, reveal Marietta's desires. Her motives become much clearer in act 2, when she settles into a carefree life with Rudolfo's troupe. When Rudolfo scolds her for not taking puppetry seriously, she laughs and replies, "All the world's a joke! Oh, how I am happy for the first time in my life!"[34] Marietta has never known autonomy. Her noble status means nothing to her—it has only made her miserable.

At the other end of the spectrum is Simon, who is trying to rise from his lowly station as a servant. In a way, he and Marietta mirror each other in that they are traveling in opposite directions: he wants to climb the social ladder, and she wants to descend it. As Marietta has her recurring dream melody, Simon has the mantra "This may be my opportunity." He sees every possible vocation—actor, pirate, wealthy landowner, even whipping boy—as a way to propel himself to a higher class. He declares his frustrations and ambitions in his first song, "If I Were Anybody Else but Me":

> I must have been changed in my cradle,
> By my nurse or something like,
> For I ain't turned out what I ought to be,
> And nothing seems to be right.

> So sometimes I get to dreaming,
> As a fellow will, you see,
> Of the kind of a sort of a "me" I'd be,
> If I wasn't the me that's me.[35]

Simon believes he is destined for a higher life, as evidenced by the rather preposterous fantasy that he was switched at birth. If only someone would give him an opportunity, he would prove himself worthy of higher things.

Etienne's plot deals more explicitly with issues of class status. He lives in two worlds: his position as the son of the lieutenant governor of New Orleans affords him every luxury, but he has also joined the lowest possible class as the leader of a notorious thieving community. At the same time, his mistress, Adah, is a quadroon (a white woman with one-quarter African blood) and is Etienne's property.[36] New Orleans is preparing for its annual "Quadroon Ball," at which the wealthy men of the city will choose quadroon women to enter into a sort of concubinage.[37] Etienne has taunted Adah that he may or may not love her anymore and asked Marietta to accompany him to the ball:

ADAH. You have asked her to go to the ball?
ETIENNE. I have! And I told her to come early that she might see the sale of those slaves who have displeased their masters by boring them with jealousy!
ADAH. You dare not sell me!
ETIENNE. *(Sarcastically)* Sell you! Not while you are so gentle, so sweet, so confiding, so trustful! Ha ha![38]

This is the darkest of the three plot lines, dealing not just with infidelity but with the much more serious treatment of the life of a quadroon. Even if she were set free, her blood would keep her from ever being allowed to marry. Perhaps she loves Etienne hopelessly, as indicated by her song "'Neath the Southern Moon," but she also clings to him because she knows she can be sold at any time. Etienne may be cruel to her, but while she is with him, at least she knows what tomorrow will bring. Young adds depth to the light and frothy tone of the other two plots with Adah's story. Although *Show Boat* frequently gets credited as the first musical to deal with serious themes, including racial inequality and the legal and emotional challenges of mixed-race status, *Naughty Marietta* preceded *Show Boat* by seventeen years. The racial issue does not take prominence here, but Young calls race-based social mores into question.

As Candice Marie Coleman effectively argues, *Naughty Marietta* depicts a pervasive objectification of women. Marietta, Adah, and Lizette are valued by the men in the show primarily for their family connections, money, and social status. Coleman asserts that *Naughty Marietta* manifests misogynist tendencies that reflect the time period in which the show was written and mirrors the plight of American women attempting to break out of nineteenth-century Victorian expectations of them as wives and mothers.[39] Yet the female characters also defy the type of objectification to which their community subjects them. Although the men value Marietta and Lizette only for their gold, the women do not allow themselves to be taken so easily. Adah, the victim of an unforgiving caste system, breaks out of her oppression by revealing Etienne's double life as Bras Piqué to Dick.

Marietta bucks the stereotype of the "damsel in distress" at every turn. At the beginning of the show, she has managed to escape from both the convent *and* the ship providing her escape. When Dick reminds her that her acceptance of the king's casket obliges her to marry, she reveals that she threw it in the sea. Marietta manages to manipulate Dick throughout the play, first by pleading nicely, then by demanding he help her. If Dick refuses, she will find some other way to get what she needs; after all, she has gotten this far on her own. Marietta's determination and self-reliance are not undermined by her decision to marry Etienne in act 2; he may be her quickest way out of banishment back to France. That she immediately regrets the decision speaks to her innate distrust of Etienne and the need to follow her heart. Marietta has two goals in this show: to find freedom and to find her true love. Recognizing Dick as her love and choosing to give herself to him do not erase her attempts at independence. Even though the play ends with their love duet, there is little reason to assume that she will be submissive or subservient to Dick after they are married.

Although Dick has the authority to capture Marietta and send her back to the French convent, Young never allows him to gain the upper hand when it comes to Marietta. She continually outwits him, and he comes away from every encounter with her frustrated, confused, and, as he later discovers to his dismay, more attracted to her. They butt heads from their first scene together, when Marietta insists that Dick find her a disguise:

> MARIETTA. Accordingly—you must arrange for me something!
> DICK. I—why should I—
> MARIETTA. Who else? You are my friend—it is arranged—is it not?
> DICK. It is not—arranged!
> MARIETTA. Besides—the whole—thing is your fault.
> DICK. MY fault? Why?
> MARIETTA. Because. Anyway, it is. If you had not make me angry, oh but so angry, at Mozambique—perhaps, I don't know—maybe I not run away.
> DICK. Do you know, I should take you at once to the Governor.
> MARIETTA. But you will not?
> DICK. Eh?
> MARIETTA. You are stupid, but not cruel![40]

And Marietta is right. Dick neither turns her in to the governor nor leaves her to fend for herself. He convinces Rudolfo to take her on as his "son" in the marionette troupe. In fact, Marietta never fails to get her way. Much as Rida Johnson Young did herself in her negotiations with the Shuberts, Marietta works every angle to achieve her objectives.

The critics had mixed reactions to the comic-relief couple of Simon and Lizette, as played by Harry Cooper and Kate Elinore. While some enjoyed their antics, others dismissed them as "low" burlesque. Many pointed to the fact that Hammerstein had insisted on using them in the show. While Young had no sway over the broad nature of their performances, she handled them well on the page. Lizette and Simon effectively mirror Marietta and Dick. Simon is as chauvinistic as Dick and Etienne, especially in his treatment of the awkward Lizette:

> SIMON. I wouldn't cry that way if I were you.
> LIZETTE. You can cry any way you like. This is my way. I can't help it if I'm historical.
> SIMON. Historical—Are you so old as that?
> LIZETTE. Old! I'm only, only—
> SIMON. Better hurry, Madam. Every minute makes it worse.
> LIZETTE. I should say it does—Here I am verging on—twenty, and would you believe me, I have never had a proposal.
> SIMON. I would believe you.[41]

Exchanges like this are funny, but Simon never passes up a chance to insult Lizette. Even though he is a servant (and a rather disliked one at that), he still sees himself as higher than her. And while Lizette has the casket, and therefore the upper hand, her position is such that she needs Simon, since no other man will have her and she cannot take the gold and land for herself. She allows him to talk her into opening the casket, which actually serves to bind him to her. Later, he tries to pawn her off on the lieutenant governor in order to get out of the contract he unwittingly entered. But Lizette, for all her nervousness and naivete, shares Marietta's spirit. When no man chooses her, she goes in search of one. Like Marietta, Lizette fights for herself, insisting to everyone she meets that the king of France has promised her a husband and that she will hold him to that promise. In her second-act character number, Lizette reveals her determination to find a man but will not compromise:

> I don't deny, I burn to be
> The pet, the joy, the life,
> Of some brave man who would make me
> His lawful wedded wife.
> But if a wretch should dare to breathe
> A word that wasn't right,
> I'd give a whack!
> Say, "Villain, back!
> I wait for Mister Right!"[42]

THE SONGS

Young's lyrics and placement of songs in *Naughty Marietta* demonstrate that she understood how to use them effectively to support character development and underline the emotion of a scene. And she understood standard operetta conventions and structure, no doubt aided by Herbert. While some of *Naughty Marietta*'s songs arise from plot, many serve to reveal atmosphere and character, including the character of the New Orleans portrayed onstage. The opening number depicts almost every level of this society, from the street sweepers and flower sellers, to the convent girls, to the quadroon belles. We observe the day unfolding in this make-believe New Orleans and watch as the social hierarchy reveals itself. We are brutally reminded of that hierarchy in act 2, when the rich men of the town gamble at the Quadroon Ball ("New Orleans Jeunesse Doreé") while the quadroon belles, Spanish dancers, and French girls entertain them ("Loves of New Orleans"). Both songs foreshadow the terrible quadroon auction to come.

Of the fourteen individual songs in *Naughty Marietta*, nine of them—including the three just discussed—reveal character more than plot. For instance, we find out before we meet Marietta that she has escaped from her wealthy family and the casquette girls and is thought to be hiding in New Orleans. Her first song, "Naughty Marietta," explains *why* she escaped and tells us what to expect from her (with a tip of the hat to Henry Wadsworth Longfellow):

> Come a time to the convent they sent me straight off,
> I'm not fond of dat, not me!
> I say my pray'r, well most ev'rywhere,
> And better than gold I be.
> But the naughty Marietta dat's also me,
> Make dat convent so warm, 'twas torrid!
> 'Cause when she was good, she was very good indeed,
> But when she was bad, she was horrid![43]

This is an early example of a song type that still exists in contemporary musical theater: the "I Am" or "I Want" song, in which major characters introduce themselves and/or sets up their superobjectives. There are countless examples of this song type, but the title song to *Naughty Marietta* serves as a reminder of just how long this convention has been used. In this particular case, art again imitates life, as interviews with Trentini reveal an origin story eerily similar to Marietta's:

> I was ten years old when they sent me to a convent school. Then the silent Emma died, and the impish Emma was born. What a dreadful Emma! It is because I remember her well that I am able to play Naughty Marietta. She played tricks on her schoolmates and on the good sisters, the imp, Emma Trentini, and she crowned her naughtiness by running away. Because she wore the uniform, the costume, of the pupils of the convent, she was discovered and brought back. I am afraid she made her entrance into the convent grounds kicking and scratching her captors. I am quite sure of it. I do not know what would have become of the imp, Trentini, if they had not discovered in her a voice.[44]

Etienne's character song comes at the beginning of act 2. Although he has already been established as a rogue and a playboy, "You Marry a Marionette" reveals how deep his disdain for women goes. Before the song, he has just tried to persuade Marietta to give up her disguise and marry him, but she haughtily rebukes him and storms off. The frustrated Etienne exclaims, "She is a witch! What puppets we are, the strongest of us can be pulled about by a weak little woman like that."[45] This leads into his diatribe on women as puppetmasters and his advice to the men in the audience:

> So if you're a fool and you're hoping to rule
> The woman you're planning to get,
> Then by the old Harry, be sure when you marry,
> You marry a marionette, my lads![46]

Dick's major number, "I'm Falling in Love with Some One,"[47] couches complexity in a seemingly simple love song. First, the song anticipates the type of duet later popularized by Oscar Hammerstein II in which the intended lovers protest their feelings for each other in a "conditional" love song (as in "People Will Say We're in Love" from *Oklahoma!* or *Carousel*'s "If I Loved You"). But instead of overtly pretending he is not in love with Marietta, Captain Dick tells her in code, repeating that he is in love with "some one" while singing straight to her. Note the subtle progression of Dick's emotions from the beginning to the end of the song. In the first verse, he is almost stammering to find the right words to reveal his love without completely exposing himself:

> I've a very strange feeling I ne'er felt before,
> 'Tis a kind of a grind of depression.
> My heart's acting strangely, it feels rather sore,
> At least it gives me that impression.
> My pulses leap madly without any cause,
> Believe me, I'm telling you truly,
> I'm gay without pause, then sad without cause,
> My spirits are truly unruly.
> For I'm falling in love with some one, some one girl;
> I'm falling in love with some one, head awhirl;
> Yes! I'm falling in love with some one, plain to see,
> I'm sure I could love some one madly
> If some one would only love me.[48]

There is a conversational banality in his rather simple expressions of "Believe me," "At least," and "Now, I don't mind confessing." He uses a couple of sophisticated rhymes, but the overall effect is of a shy teenager telling a secret he does not want anyone to know. The refrain is quite simple, with his repetition of "some one," but could be played in such a way that every time he sings it, he leans in more closely, in an attempt to get Marietta to realize that "some one" is her. However, the second verse is much more complex, with several instances of alliteration ("sort of a sport," "foolish but fond," and "heartily hope") and the rather daring attitude of "I'm looking for trouble and know it." This is a bolder Captain Dick, raising the stakes for himself and risking rejection. When he repeats the refrain, although the lyrics do not change, the intent does. He is even more determined to show his true feelings to Marietta but continues to hold back in case she does not reciprocate his affection. Young adroitly captures the sentiments of a man trying to maintain control while his passions threaten to burst forth.

THE "DREAM MELODY"

A unique characteristic of this show is that it uses a musical theme as a plot device, something only a handful of musicals have done since.[49] Marietta's search for the man who will finish her song serves as her primary motivation for running away from her family. The theme is heard a total of eight times, not as underscoring or incidental music but as a diegetic device. However, the song is not diegetic in the same sense as *Brown of Harvard*'s "When Love Is Young." That song had no connection to the plot or characters—it could be removed from the show without any consequence. So desperate is Marietta to complete the song that she—perhaps without realizing—sings it to herself while hiding in the fountain in the town square, where the whole town hears her. She sings the tune to every major male character (except Simon) in the hopes that he will sing it back to her, each time more urgently. "Ah! Sweet Mystery of Life" is so essential to the plot of *Naughty Marietta* that the show cannot end until the song does.

Audiences loved it, but a closer look at the song shows that it was more than just Herbert's lush melody that captivated them. Young expertly matches the sweeping tone of Herbert's music with an epic ode to romantic love. When Dick finally sings it at the end, the simple tune and vague lyrics heard earlier now explode with passion, clarity, and soaring sentiment:

> Ah! Sweet mystery of life, at last I've found thee,
> Ah! I know at last the secret of it all.
> All the longing, seeking, striving, waiting, yearning,
> The burning hopes, the joy and idle tears that fall!
> For 'tis love and love alone the world is seeking;
> And 'tis love and love alone that can repay!
> 'Tis the answer, 'tis the end and all of living,
> For it is love alone that rules for aye![50]

First, the use of the phrase "sweet mystery of life" to describe true love fits Marietta's attitude not only toward love but toward the elusive lyric she has been seeking. Dick reveals both his love and an intimate understanding of Marietta's mind, supplying exactly the words she's been trying to find all along. Here, "love" is more than romance; it is an all-encompassing ideal, as the rest of the song so clearly states. The somewhat archaic language ("at last I've found thee" and the song's final phrase "for aye" to mean "forever") places the show in an idealized past. Young shows a remarkable gift for lyrical economy, conveying the idea of love as "the end and all of living" in only thirty-two bars of music. Using the evocative string of "longing, seeking, striving, waiting, yearning" and fitting three stages of yearning (hopes, joy, and tears) into one line, Young effectively describes a universal search for love and delivers it with a satisfying dramatic punch.

Naughty Marietta received generally favorable reviews, with critics almost universally praising Herbert's score and Trentini's charming performance as Marietta. Young, however, caught some grief for her book. *The Theatre* harshly declared, "The less said about the book of this opera the better. It is simply stupid and will interrupt no one's drowsing. This is the weak spot—that and the fact that the comedy introduced is far, far below the level of the rest of the work. It is vulgar at times, and not funny at its best."[51] Charles Darnton unkindly called the book "rather desperate."[52] Another New York critic called Young's script "an incomprehensible hodgepodge of rot."[53] But a few critics genuinely appreciated Young's work, even if they found the libretto lacking. Amy Leslie of the *Toledo Blade* noted that Young "has a certain happy spirit of her own and is prolific, if not varied, and abundantly vital."[54] The *New York Times* critic made no mention of Young's book—surprising, as she had already had critical successes as a playwright in New York. The show ran for five months, then launched a lengthy tour, with Trentini reprising her role. Despite the show's popularity, Young and Herbert would team up again only once, both at the end of their lives, for the less successful *The Dream Girl* (1924). *Naughty Marietta* would prove to have a staying power neither could have predicted.

NAUGHTY MARIETTA ON FILM

Although *Naughty Marietta* initially had a modest run, the show stayed in the public consciousness, partly due to the popularity of the songs. A film version in 1935 paired Jeanette MacDonald and Nelson Eddy, but the script was highly revised (as Young had died in 1926, she was not involved in the film script) and only retained a few of Herbert's songs. Gus Kahn wrote additional lyrics and revised some of Young's. Screenwriters Frances Goodrich, Albert Hackett, and John Lee Mahin put all of the plot's focus on Marietta and Dick and eliminated the play's two subplots. MacDonald plays a French princess named Marie engaged to the Spanish duke Don Carlos. She trades identities with her maid, Marietta, to get on the ship sailing for America with the casquette girls. When the ship is captured by pirates just outside of New Orleans, Captain Dick (Eddy) rescues the girls and strikes up a friendship with "Marietta." When Marie's father sends Don Carlos to New Orleans to bring her home, Dick reveals his love by finishing her "dream melody" and escapes with her. The spirit and humor of Young's characters survive, and her lyrics are mostly intact, with only a few tweaks, so she is not entirely removed from the final product. (She would not fare as well with the MacDonald/Eddy film version of *Maytime*.) The film also launched the onscreen pairing of MacDonald and Eddy, starting his career and elevating hers. "Ah! Sweet Mystery of Life" became one of MacDonald's signature songs and would be associated with her for the rest of her life—and at her death, as it was blasted over loudspeakers at her funeral in 1965. Audiences and many critics loved the movie (and still do), but the industry insiders at *Variety* found that leaving out so much of Young and Herbert's original material hurt the film:

> Much of the original score, plus a couple of added tunes, is included. . . . It might also be because the boys were afraid of the story and sought to cover up by cramming in the songs. If so they've but padded the film into two reels of surplus length. . . . The comedy being insufficient to sustain this much footage, with no especially exciting action, due to the exaggerated theatrical license necessary to transplant this type of book show to the screen, provides serious handicaps. In other words, although Marietta may have been naughty in 1910, after 25 years and Joe Breen if she's still naughty it's her secret.[55]

A live television adaptation in 1955, starring Patrice Munsel and Alfred Drake, went back to the original stage plot and used more songs from the stage version but was cut down significantly for time.

Ultimately, *Naughty Marietta* operates quite effectively within the operetta idiom. Young's script supports Herbert's music and gives the characters individual voices. As is often the case with works of the early twentieth century, some perspective matters. Neil Gould offers this observation:

> It has become a commonplace in the literature to blacken the reputations of Herbert's co-creators with snide deprecations. Still, the fact remains that their librettos fostered the creation of a body of work that, in its day, held and dominated the American musical stage. Herbert and his librettists created memorable moments in the theater and in theatrical history; of equal importance, they created an audience for high-quality entertainment, significantly raising the level of audience expectations of what music theater could and should be."[56]

Considering that *Naughty Marietta* was Young's first operetta, the strength of her characters and structure outweighs the libretto's weaknesses. Her later scripts will show that she learned much from this experience and developed a more sophisticated style.

Box 3.1 *Naughty Marietta*

Lyrics and libretto: Rida Johnson Young
Music: Victor Herbert
New York Theater; opened November 7, 1910; closed March 4, 1911 (136 performances)
Producer: Oscar Hammerstein

Major Cast

Marietta d'Altena . . . Emma Trentini
Captain Richard Warrington . . . Orville Harrold
Etienne Grandet . . . Edward Martindel
Adah . . . Maria Duchene
Lizette . . . Kate Elinore
Simon O'Hara (later Silas Slick) . . . Harry Cooper

Songs

"Tramp! Tramp! Tramp!" . . . Captain Richard (Dick) Warrington and Male Chorus
"Taisez-Vous" . . . Casquette Girls
"Naughty Marietta" . . . Marietta
"It Never, Never Can Be Love" . . . Marietta and Dick
"If I Were Anybody Else but Me" . . . Simon and Lizette
"'Neath the Southern Moon" . . . Adah
"Italian Street Song" . . . Marietta and Chorus
"(You) Marry a Marionette" . . . Etienne
"New Orleans Jeunesse Dorée / The Loves of New Orleans" . . . Ensemble
"(The Sweet) By and By" . . . Lizette
"Live for Today" . . . Marietta, Dick, Adah, and Etienne
"I'm Falling in Love with Some One" . . . Dick
"It's Pretty Soft for Simon" . . . Simon
"Dream Melody (Ah! Sweet Mystery of Life)" . . . Marietta and Dick

4

THE OLD-FASHIONED THINGS MUST GO

MUSICAL COMEDIES

A musical comedy doesn't pay the author nearly as well as a successful play does, unless you happen to write some very popular songs and get big royalties from them. And even though your musical comedies make a hit they don't help you as a playwright. People get to thinking of you merely as a librettist, and that makes them skeptical of your ability to do plays. I suppose it is because the average musical comedy has to be gone over with a microscope to find any trace of a plot. But I do try to put the real thing into mine, not merely a shadowy hint of one.

Rida Johnson Young[1]

Young is best known today for her operettas, but of her eleven total musical works, six were musical comedies. Young's sparkling, sometimes sardonic, sense of humor made her a deft comic writer. Musical comedies presented some unique challenges. Producers might insist on specialty numbers, novelty performers, comic relief, and song interpolations to keep the audience engaged. The style of music heard on the New York stage was changing as well, as ragtime introduced a new sound in the nightclubs. Before long, jazz would emerge from the fringes to infiltrate popular music and eventually theater music. The musical theater was slow to embrace it, but once it did, there was no going back. But variety was one of Rida Johnson Young's specialties, as demonstrated in *Lady Luxury* (1914; music by William Schroeder) and *Sometime* (1918; music by Rudolf Friml).

LADY LUXURY

Rida Johnson Young married into an appropriate family name, because "youth" was one of her favorite subjects. The majority of her plays and musicals feature fresh faces bursting with vibrancy and hope for the future. When a reporter noticed this and asked her about it, she cried, "Youth! Do I get youth into my plays? Then it is because I am so fond of youth. I love boys, just the buoyancy and vim and youngness of them. Do you know, I believe in youth!"[2] Young's third venture with composer William Schroeder was yet another testament to her fascination with it. (Their second and third shows together—*When Love Is Young* and *His Little Widows*—are discussed elsewhere in this book.) Although *Lady Luxury* played at two of the Shubert brothers' theaters on Broadway (it opened at the Casino Theatre, then moved to the Comedy Theatre), it was not technically a Shubert production. Young and Schroeder started working on it in early 1913, as evidenced by a letter from Young to the Shuberts in May of that year:

> Have you read "My Lady Luxury" yet? If not, won't you make an appointment and let me read it to you soon? I am moving up to the country on Friday but will come in at any time you appoint. If it is not convenient for you to hear it at the office, I wish you would motor out to my place some Sunday soon and let us read the book and play the music for you there. In that way we would have no interruption, and I should be so delighted to have you come.[3]

The Shuberts evidently sat on it for some time, because this letter appears next in the archives: "Won't you give me a decision soon on 'My Lady Luxury'? I want to place it before I go abroad but don't wish to take it to any other management while you are considering it. Please make an appointment to hear the music soon."[4]

The Shuberts passed it on to Fred C. Whitney, a longtime colleague of Lee and J. J. and owner of Detroit's Whitney Opera Company. Whitney was a Detroit native and the son of Clark J. Whitney, a prominent theatrical manager and music salesman. As was common for the time, *Lady Luxury* did a pre-Broadway tour, opening first at the Detroit Opera House, under Clark Whitney's management, on September 23, 1914. Even with the Shuberts' connection to the piece, Whitney must not have secured their theaters for the Broadway run at that point. Young sent a telegram to Lee Shubert on opening night, hoping to influence their decision:

> I am wiring you Ben Teal's opinion of Lady Luxury—He says book good score melodic both above average with an adequate cast and otherwise thoroughly produced—The piece would strongly appeal to lovers of polite musical comedy—For complete preparation about four weeks required. Rida Young 2:18 am.[5]

It is this last sentence that suggests that Whitney had not yet convinced the Shuberts that *Lady Luxury* would be suitable for their theaters. Shubert replied the next day: "I am glad that your piece is a success, and as soon as you are ready to come to New York, I will be only too happy to arrange a theatre for yourself and Mr. Whitney."[6] The decision must have been made sometime soon thereafter, but the Shuberts evidently left all other production concerns to Whitney. Two more telegrams from the road—the show traveled to Montreal and Providence, Rhode Island—reveal Young's anxiety about getting the Shuberts' blessing:

Telegram to Lee Shubert—Providence RI Dec 21 1914:

Play went over splendidly—Was disappointed that no one from Shubert office was here—Wanted your advice and suggestions—Try to come on for one performance

Dec 22:

Please come and look show over or send representative—Notices excellent[7]

We do not know if the Shuberts made it to the show in Providence, but it did open on Broadway at their Casino Theatre only three days later, on Christmas Day. Whether or not they gave any advice or approval, they gave *Lady Luxury* a theater.

While most musical comedies of the period are not known for their strong books, *Lady Luxury*'s libretto outshines its music. The witty dialogue has sophistication and an energetic pace and shows off Young's talent for writing farce. Young's scripts had always been funny, but the humor in *Lady Luxury* has ease, confidence, and a modern sensibility. At least, the dialogue does; the songs are a bit of a mixed bag. But given the changing nature of music in musical comedy as composers gingerly dipped their toes into the ragtime and jazz pools, growing pains were to be expected. Young and Schroeder included operetta-like duets, a ragtime dance number, a collegiate men's chorus number, interpretive dance, and a minstrel number in the *Lady Luxury* score, representing a wide spectrum of American popular entertainment.

One characteristic that generally distinguishes musical comedy from operetta is that the setting, characters, language, and dances are, to use a popular turn-of-the-century expression, "up to date." Americans were as fascinated by the "new" in 1914 as they are in the twenty-first century. They sought out novelty in fashion, slang, technology, and pop culture. If operetta was synonymous with the "Ruritanian" past, musical comedy lived in the city—usually New York—of *right now*. *Lady Luxury* tipped its hat to the latest fads and animal-inspired dances—like the Fox Trot, Turkey Trot, Bunny Hug, and Grizzly Bear—with characters who spoke like contemporary young men and women, not characters in a classical melodrama. The original costumes were designed by Lady Duff Gordon, also known as "Lucile," whose couture house had revolutionized fashion in Europe and the United States. She later marketed some of the dress patterns designed for *Lady Luxury* to the general public. Despite some operetta touches in the music, *Lady Luxury* fits the musical comedy idiom.

And while the show is quite funny, it also has substance. Of all the shows Young wrote, *Lady Luxury* engages the most with the clash of past and future that drove the American imagination at the turn of the century. Eloise, the newly come-of-age heroine of *Lady Luxury*, struggles to find her identity as a young woman whose old-fashioned sensibilities conflict with more extreme modern views. In his insightful article on *Lady Luxury* for the Shubert Archive's magazine *The Passing Show*, John James Hickey calls it "an overlooked gem of popular theatre that cannily reflected the socio-cultural change and turmoil that was afoot in the years leading up to the First World War."[8] Its two main characters, Eloise and her uncle Edward, represent either side of a generation gap, but the divide is not as clear-cut as it would be later in the 1920s. American women coming into adulthood before World War I were only just beginning to witness the changes that would enable them to vote and occupy more significant spaces in the workplace and public life. While the push toward this progress had been developing for decades, the leap into the new century accelerated it.

"My Lady Luxury"

The action takes place at the home of the overly strict Edward Van Cuyler ("Uncle Ned") on the day of his niece's twenty-first birthday.[9] Uncle Ned has decreed that Eloise does not turn twenty-one until five o'clock, at which time she will claim her inheritance, which includes the house. Terrified that his niece will ruin his stately home with modern decorations and music, he has a nightmare in which the portraits of his ancestors come to life and warn him that his world is about to turn upside down. When Eloise enters a few moments later and sends her uncle off for his afternoon walk, the stage explodes with young guests and servants bearing party decorations and a fancy new dress and makeup for the birthday girl.

Eloise's chosen party guests arrive, each one more outlandish than the one before. First comes her older brother, Jimmy, who has spent the previous year sowing his wild oats—or, as Uncle Ned calls it, his "favorite cereal"—and has brought a cadre of college friends to celebrate Eloise's coming-out party. Next comes the English chaperone, Mrs. Draper-Cowles (whom Young described in early notes as a "Large grande dame type")[10] and her shy daughter, Maude, very distant cousins of Eloise. She has invited them hoping that Mrs. Draper-Cowles will educate her in the ways of the social world, as Uncle Ned has kept her under a tight rein. Maude shows absolutely no interest in Eloise but brightens up at the news that the Italian tenor Count Piniaselli, with whom Maude has fallen in love on the boat from England, is also on the guest list. Next to arrive is the Russian dancer Mischkowa, bearing a case containing thousands of dollars' worth of jewels, who alarms Uncle Ned with her description of her specialty: dancing naked. (Later, she will perform the "Futurist Twirl," possibly inspired by Loïe Fuller's 1891 "Serpentine Dance.")[11] Finally, Piniaselli arrives and just happens to have a case exactly like Mischkowa's, only his contains a special throat spray to preserve his voice—of course, the identical cases will soon cause trouble. In the midst of all this, Jimmy's down-to-earth college friend Sam Warren appears, hoping to find the demure Eloise he had met several months earlier. He is disappointed to find that she has turned into "My Lady Luxury," as her friends now call her, but believes he can convince her that they belong together and get her to change her newfound ways. Eloise, however, declares him utterly brutish and refuses to have anything to do with him. Meanwhile, Maude and Piniaselli secretly meet. Piniaselli wants to marry her, but she refuses, saying her mother will never allow it, as he is poor. He tries to convince her to run away with him, but she dares not go against her mother; besides, she cannot stand the thought of living in poverty.

Eloise's fate takes a turn when Sam and Uncle Ned discover that, as the only sensible people in the house, they have a common bond. They hatch a plan to turn Eloise away from her social whirlwind and get her to fall in love with Sam. Uncle Ned writes a note to Eloise explaining that he has gambled away her inheritance and, ashamed of himself, has run away. He actually climbs into a crawl space above the fireplace in the living room, where he will stay until Eloise realizes that without her money, her friends will abandon her. Sam will supply him with food, cigars, drink, and newspapers while he is in hiding, a task that proves more difficult than they imagined. When Eloise discovers her uncle is gone, another problem mars the birthday celebration: Mischkowa's jewels go missing. The act ends with Eloise vowing to live on her uncle's assets for one year before accepting a life of poverty.

Act 2 begins with a series of misunderstandings: Eloise suspects Sam of stealing food, liquor, and her uncle's clothing (which, of course, he has been secretly delivering to Uncle Ned in the crawl space), then becomes convinced that he has kidnapped her uncle. Everyone in the house thinks Sam is a raging alcoholic, having been seen too often with a whiskey bottle in hand. When Mischkowa's jewels suddenly reappear (having been returned unseen by Piniaselli, who picked up her case by mistake), both Eloise and Sam are suspects. Meanwhile, Uncle Ned gets angry when Sam fails to make headway with Eloise and decides to teach them both a lesson by leaving another note saying he has gone to kill himself. Of course, all is revealed in the end, Eloise returns to her old self, and she and Sam fall into each other's arms.

Another Revolution

Even the silliest musical comedy, if well written, explores a theme that elevates the show beyond pure entertainment. Young took one of the hot-button topics of her day—women's liberation from the confines of the Victorian era—and built *Lady Luxury* around it. Nineteenth-century values collide with the twentieth century; new music, fashions, art movements, and social mores force the old ones out the door, but not without a struggle:

> ELOISE. Now, Uncle Ned. Don't get excited. Remember your heart.
> UNCLE. Excited. My house full of rowdies and dancers, my furnishings torn from their places. My house that has stood since the revolution.
> ELOISE. Well, this is another revolution, Uncle.[12]

Eloise, like many young women of her generation, feels imprisoned by her uncle's strict code of decorum and yearns to break free of it in the most dramatic way possible. Even her brother takes her side, telling Ned, "Don't fight against progress. She's burst the shell. You can't put her back again."[13] She is frustrated by the fact that while Uncle Ned forgives her brother for goofing off after college and running off to Europe, he expects Eloise to remain the prim and proper lady he has raised her to be. In retaliation, Eloise pledges to join the "revolution" and become a new woman (or a New Woman):

> I'm going to have a hundred frocks,
> A hundred pairs of shoes.

> And grown-up stays and negligees,
> In pinks and whites and blues.
> I'm going to have ten motor cars,
> A racing stable, too.
> I'm going to do just everything I've been forbidden to.[14]

Eloise's ideas of womanhood do not include thinking rationally and behaving like an adult. At the same time, having never been allowed to truly express herself, how else could she behave? Young gives Eloise a guilty conscience, making her grapple with the world of choices that has opened up to her and the consequences of her actions. Eloise embodies the dilemma facing American women everywhere at the beginning of the twentieth century. The world was shifting quickly: clothes got looser, hairdos got shorter, makeup got heavier, jobs opened up for women, and suddenly they could make choices their mothers and grandmothers could not. But these young women were also being pulled in two directions. She rationalizes, "I've got to have this breaking out. It's just like the measles."[15] But she also feels comfortable in her modest clothes and secretly likes the idea of moving to Sam's ranch and living a quiet life. She quickly finds that she is not quite ready to throw her old life out the window, but neither can she resist the allure of an exciting social life and the chance to discover a new Eloise. Those readers familiar with *No, No, Nanette* (1925; music by Vincent Youmans, book by Otto Harbach and Frank Mendel, lyrics by Harbach and Irving Caesar) will be struck by the similarity of a character who preceded Nanette by ten years.

Songs

The *New York Times* review lamented that *Lady Luxury* "starts off without any great amount of what is technically known in the theatrical world as 'pep.'"[16] Some critics thought that the show took some time to pick up the pace. While this is a fair assessment, I would argue that Young and Schroeder deliberately slowed some of the top-of-show pacing. Instead of an upbeat number crowded with dancing girls, the first act opens with Uncle Ned lying down for a nap and the portraits of his ancestors coming to life, singing mournfully:

> The old fashioned days, the old fashioned ways,
> The old fashioned songs you know,
> Must pass away in a newer day,
> The old fashioned things must go.[17]
> (*Suddenly, a ragtime rhythm disrupts the song*)
> But you'll wake to be shocked by the Turkey Trot bold,
> Or the Texas Tommy Fly,
> Old songs, old days, old times, old ways,
> The good old days have gone, gone by.[18]

If the number feels slow, that is precisely the point. Young must show Uncle Ned as stodgy and set in his ways in order to set up the main conflict. "Pep" at this point would be inappropriate. Young chooses to serve the drama rather than the expected conventions of the genre. The critics might also have been responding to the length of the first few book scenes and the perhaps overly long time Young takes to give exposition. There are approximately seven pages of dialogue before the first "peppy" number, Jimmy's flirtatious "I'll Take You All." After this, the musical numbers pick up speed, more characters enter and exit, and the dialogue tightens and gets funnier. Perhaps the script could have used some editing at the beginning, but it all serves the story.

We have already seen Young's talent for writing operetta; here she demonstrates a wider range of songwriting talent (hinted at in *Naughty Marietta*'s comic songs) that includes urbane musical comedy. Two in particular, both sung by Jimmy, fit squarely into the musical comedy style. The first is "I'll Take You All," in which Jimmy flirts with the women's chorus, a song type popular in contemporary musical comedy.[19] Here Young shows off her rarely used talent for double rhymes:

> Little one, pretty one, witty one, flitty one,
> If I should choose, for which one would I fall?
> Rosy one, cozy one, posy one, dozy one,
> Each one I see is more charming.
> Maybe you, you would do, number two! No, not you!
> I'm in a fix quite alarming![20]

Young employs the technique of repeating a common word in a list and rhyming the words around it to convey a bouncy sophistication. Although "little" does not technically rhyme with the other words in the first line, it contains the double "t" and the endearing tone of the others. Young also chooses adjectives that all end in a bright, long "e" sound that allows Jimmy to flash a charming smile while he sings. For the last three lines, she replaces Jimmy's compliments with a more definitive attempt to pick one girl, internally rhyming "you," "do," and "two." The song introduces Jimmy as the freewheeling playboy who cannot be tied down to one woman. Later, when he tries to woo Maude with the charm number "Don't You Really Think I'd Do?" his reasons have little to do with love:

> JIMMY. I'm just a simple duffer—a fluffer—I know.
> But I've inherited plenty—yes plenty—of dough.
> And I wish you'd look me over—in clover you'd be.
> For I'm sure I could be good to you, if you'd be good to me.

Maude answers him, just as shallow in her wishes as he:

> MAUDE. I'm just a simple maid, sir, afraid, sir, to say.
> I'm mercenary, very, be wary, I pray.
> I might wed you for your money, but honey you see,
> I'm sure I might be good to you, if you'd be good to me.

Young's clever internal rhymes (like "mer*cenary*, *very*, be *wary*" and "look me *over*, in *clover* you'll be") and strings of monosyllabic words keep the rhythm clipping along. She also connects the characters by starting both of their verses with "I'm just a simple," but neither of them is really simple. If Maude were "just a simple maid," the thought of poverty probably would not bother her. And while Jimmy calls himself a "fluffer"—an airhead or a layabout—he is actually quite cunning. He knows that telling Maude of his wealth will give him a chance with her, and he is likely attracted to her because she has money as well. However, true to musical comedy fashion, the song primarily exists as a showpiece for these performers, not because their characters are actually in love. They have no other interaction in the show, and Maude is enamored with Piniaselli, so there is nothing much to back up this song. Audiences today might question why this couple has a song, but 1914 audiences were accustomed to interruptions in plot for a song-and-dance diversion. And the lyrics are some of Young's most charming.

Because Eloise spends almost the entire show refusing Sam's attentions, he wears her down with two operetta-styled love songs. In "Longing Just for You" and "Dream On, My Princess," Sam woos Eloise with romantic words that pull her away from the glittering social world and back for a moment into her comfort zone. The opening verse of "Longing Just for You" could have come from an operetta:

> Oh, eyes so blue, so true, so tenderly beaming,
> Oh, lips that smile so sweet, but smile not for me,
> Oh, voice that haunts me, every waking or dreaming,
> Though I may win thee never,
> I'll long for someone ever near me.[21]

Young's use of inverted syntax, as in "I may win thee never," gives the song a poetic grandiosity rarely found in musical comedy. It would be easy to dismiss this as parody in the context of a musical comedy, but the lines between musical comedy and operetta have always been somewhat fluid. Comic and florid ballads operate easily side by side because they serve different dramatic purposes. Operettas and musical comedies frequently contain a romantic (read: serious) couple and a comic couple—audiences can have different expectations of them. If anything, *Lady Luxury* uses the stylistic mix to represent the two worlds that Eloise is caught between: the old (operetta) and the new (musical comedy).

The second act number "Dream On, My Princess" is the second dream sequence in the show, again employing heightened lyrics:

> You are waiting for
> Love revealing,
> Soft, soft stealing near.
> Stealing near, do not fear,
> Love awaits your waking.[22]

Just as Uncle Ned's dream in the first act revealed his fear that Eloise would destroy his house, Eloise's dream reveals the fact that she spends most of the show denying that she loves Sam and longs for him to take her away from the mess she has created. While the script does not specifically call for a "dream ballet," the setup and stage directions imply as much:

JIMMY. You'd better wake up. You'll lose Sam. You don't know your own mind. You're living in a dream.

(Eloise goes into "Dream On, My Princess" Number.)

The script does not indicate who sings the song, but the vocal score lists Sam as the singer. After the second verse, the stage directions read:

Orchestra plays refrain again. You waltz round stage and on final eight bars, you come in singing again.[23]

While it is not a dream ballet as later realized in the Golden Age musicals, it is not hard to see the similarities between this dream sequence and "Out of My Dreams" from *Oklahoma!* (1943). The main female character is caught between two possible outcomes, and her unconscious mind reveals her true desires. I do not mean to imply that Rodgers and Hammerstein took inspiration from *Lady Luxury* but simply point out that this kind of device was in use long before the Golden Age.

Operettas usually contain at least one love duet between the primary couple, sometimes two. More common in musical comedy is a variation on the conditional love song, in which one or both lovers vehemently protest being in love. One character actually appears to loathe the other (even though we know they will end up together), as in "Could You Use Me?" from *Girl Crazy* (George and Ira Gershwin, 1930) or "Where's My Shoe?" from *She Loves Me* (Jerry Bock and Sheldon Harnick, 1963). In *Lady Luxury*, Eloise despises Sam—or so she says— and manages to keep up the charade until the end of the show. In a very funny and probably intentionally overblown duet called "It's Written in the Book of Destiny," Sam tries one last time to woo Eloise:

SAM. I'm going to take you in my arms,
 And shelter you from all alarms,
 You'll be my wife, my little joy for life.
ELOISE. Never, never, never.
SAM. But I say yes.
ELOISE. And I say no.
SAM. You can't deny you love me.
ELOISE. Oh.
SAM. Don't fight your fate, 'twill get you soon or late,
 I've lots of time, I can wait, wait, wait.
 For I'm for you and you're for me.
ELOISE. No.
SAM. Yes.
ELOISE. No.
SAM. Yes. It's written in the book of destiny.[24]

(After the song, Uncle Ned opens the door to his hiding place and tells the audience, "It's written in the book of destiny that I'm going to starve in this pokey hole.")[25] Because this song comes so late in the show, and the audience has already seen Eloise's subconscious telling her what she really wants, this number is just fun. Sam knows he has broken Eloise down and plays on her confusion. Three encores follow, in which the two playfully antagonize each other, all while making it clear that they truly are in love. While technically a love song, it never becomes heavy-handed or sentimental, just as the show itself never becomes maudlin.

In yet another instance of following typical musical comedy conventions—and possibly at the producer's behest—Young included a minstrel number for the black servant, Harper, called "Pick, Pick, Pickaninny." This is simply a character number, does not advance or contribute to the plot in any way, and is the longest amount of time Harper spends onstage. Harper introduces the song after Eloise has scolded him, saying, "Everybody's pickin' on me."

> I wish I was a yaller chile,
> Or just a chocolate brown,
> Cos I'm der only coal black
> Inky dinky in dis town.
> When I goes walkin' down de street,
> My blushes you can't see,
> But I'm blushin' somethin' scandalous
> When dat white chile yells at me. . . .
> When the stork was bringing 'round the chilluns,
> I just can't see
> Just why ma Mammy picked a little pickaninny
> Cos dey's always picking on me.[26]

This was the era of the "coon song," originating in the minstrel shows of the nineteenth century, made especially popular in vaudeville, and frequently interpolated into musical comedies. Coon songs stereotyped black culture and depicted black characters—and black music—as buffoonish, slovenly, and stupid. Even though Harper is depicted throughout *Lady Luxury* as an intelligent and faithful servant, even part of the Van Cuyler family, he still gets the minstrel treatment that reminds the audience that he knows his place. This kind of number would have been perfectly acceptable to, and even expected by, Young's audiences. And it is only one of many such songs that she wrote: all of Simon's songs in *Naughty Marietta* fit this type (not specifically minstrel but the comic "other" of the unsophisticated immigrant), and I will discuss her version of the very famous minstrel number "Jump Jim Crow" that she wrote for *Maytime* in a later chapter.

Comic Timing

Young's libretto has an unmistakably modern sensibility, with comedy that remains fresh and playable today. One-liners, setups and punchlines, and comic situations abound, almost at the pace of modern television sitcoms. Rarely does she linger on a joke, but lands it and moves on, as in this example:

> MISCHKOWA. I dance undraped.
> UNCLE. Undraped. In my garden? You'll do nothing of the kind.

> MISCHKOWA. Ah, the dance of spring I do. You should see me as Spring, robed in mist. And as Summer, with the grape leaf.
> UNCLE. Spring and Summer. I hope I wake before the fall.[27]

And this one:

> UNCLE. She's ungrateful. I've done everything for that girl. Why only the other day I had my life insured for her.
> SAM. Fine. Now you won't have to be so careful dodging automobiles.[28]

Young could also write an extended farcical scene, as in the opening of act 2. Uncle Ned sticks his head out of the door to his crawl space and complains to the audience that he is starving. When other characters enter the room, he quickly shuts the door. Harper informs Eloise that someone has been stealing food from the kitchen. A few minutes later, Sam enters with a plate of sandwiches for Uncle Ned but throws a scarf over them when he hears Piniaselli and Mrs. Draper-Cowles coming. What follows is a sequence of mishaps in the classic farce tradition, in which Sam tries three times to deliver the sandwiches but hides them on his person when someone new enters and creates three different excuses for his odd behavior. The door to the hiding space opens and shuts continuously while Uncle Ned tries to retrieve the sandwiches without being seen. The dialogue moves as quickly as the action:

> MRS. D. C. Young man, I'm accustomed to seeing gentlemen rise when I enter a room.
> SAM. I know. Awfully sorry. But—I've got rheumatism. My knees—Doctor's orders—says I must keep them covered when it's going on like this.
> MRS. D. C. Why don't you go to bed?
> SAM. That's just where I was off to when it came on so suddenly.
> MRS. D. C. I suspect you drink too much, young man. I tell you for your own good that everyone knows you are continually carrying a bottle around with you.
> SAM. I don't deny the bottle. It's cough medicine. I've got a weak throat.
> MRS. D. C. I shouldn't call you delicate.
> SAM. No, you shouldn't. It makes me nervous.[29]

Young possesses sharp comedic timing and never relies on bad puns for a laugh. The comedy arises directly from character and situation, resulting in genuinely funny moments. Here, after Mrs. Draper-Cowles calls Sam an "inebriate" as she exits, Sam turns back to Ned's hiding place and quips, "Fine. You've got the thirst and I've got the reputation."[30] Young's comic writing throughout *Lady Luxury* could easily stand up to that of Guy Bolton or P. G. Wodehouse and certainly earns her a place beside them in musical comedy literature. *Lady Luxury* demonstrates Young's uncanny ability to write within the conventions of a genre without being limited by them. The humor is smart and character-driven, while the show delivers all the hallmarks of a crowd-pleasing musical comedy.

Figure 4.1 Harry Conor and Forrest Huff in a scene from Lady Luxury. *Photo by White Studio. © Billy Rose Theatre Division, The New York Public Library for the Performing Arts.*

As was so often the case, reviews were mixed. The *New York Times* found the show "quite pleasing," and Schroeder's music "ambitious, if not entirely tuneful."[31] Another New York paper said, "For the tired Christmas feaster and his wife, for the man dreading the weight of New Year resolutions soon to be shouldered, for all in need of a laugh-tonic—'Lady Luxury' is ready."[32] The *Evening Sun* praised its "youth, melody, mirth and graceful dancing in large measure woven around an original plot."[33] But some critics were not impressed. The *New York World* titled its review "'Lady Luxury' a Sad Dame on Casino Stage," although the critic's issue was with the production, not the material: "It would be cruel to attempt to picture the emotions with which Mrs. Rida Johnson Young, the author of 'Lady Luxury,' must have witnessed the tragedy of its initial production."[34] The reviewer for *The Theatre* wasted no words in slamming the show. Here is the entire review—all eight sentences:

> The sooner the managers will realize that Abe Lincoln was right when he said, "You can fool some of the people some of the time, but you can't fool all the people all the time," the better it will be for them. If anyone can find any excuse for "Lady Luxury," recently presented at the Casino, let him come forward and prove his case. Nothing more amateurish in libretto, lyrics or music has ever been seen or heard in New York. Not even a good cut could save this production from an ultimate and deserved death. Ina Claire's name flares in the big electric sign, but that does not make her a star, lacking the necessary qualifications. Harry Conor, the dear old comedian, struggles hopelessly with a silly part. None of the other perpetrators need any special mention. They are as amateurish as the show.[35]

After its brief New York run, *Lady Luxury* took to the road for two seasons. The DeKalb Theatre review indicates that the audience enjoyed it, reporting, "a large audience expressed appreciation of its charms by frequent and enthusiastic applause. . . . There is not a dull line in the book and the music for the most part is tuneful and catchy."[36] When it reached the Lyric Theatre in Philadelphia, one critic declared it "guaranteed to offend no sensibility whatsoever . . . a sweet, simple and pleasing presentation."[37] Interestingly, the DeKalb Theatre critic stated that it "had a long and successful run" on Broadway.[38] This is not an entirely false statement. Hickey points out that 154 shows opened on Broadway in 1914, and half of them ran fewer than thirty performances.[39] In an era when brief runs were normal, and the years-long runs of today's Broadway shows were simply unimaginable, *Lady Luxury* was among the average. Perhaps not a roaring success, but not a flop, either.

Box 4.1 Lady Luxury

Lyrics and libretto: Rida Johnson Young
Music: William Schroeder
Casino Theatre and Comedy Theatre; opened December 25, 1914; closed January 23, 1915 (35 performances)
Producer: Fred C. Whitney

Major Cast

Eloise Van Cuyler . . . Ina Claire
Edward Van Cuyler . . . Harry Conor
Sam Warren . . . Forrest Huff
Jimmy . . . Alan Mudie

Maude Draper-Cowles . . . Alice Moffat
Mrs. Draper-Cowles . . . Emily Fitzroy
Count Piniaselli . . . Arthur Albro
Madame Mischkowa . . . Emilie Lea
Harper . . . Frank Andrews

Songs

"The Old-Fashioned Things" . . . Ned and Ancestors
"Those Awful Tattle Tales" . . . Eloise (lyrics by W. C. Duncan)
"I'll Take You All" . . . Jimmy and Girls
"Hi There, Buddy" . . . Sam and Boys
"Kiss Me Once More" . . . Maude and Piniaselli
"Whistle When You Want Me" . . . Boys and Girls
"Dream On, My Princess" . . . Sam
"Longing Just for You" . . . Sam
"Pick, Pick, Pickaninny" . . . Harper
"Don't You Really Think I'll Do?" . . . Jimmy and Maude
"It's Written in the Book of Destiny" . . . Eloise and Sam
"When I Sing in Grand Opera" . . . Piniaselli
"Longing for You" . . . Eloise
"That Rag-Tag Dance" . . . Jimmy and Ensemble

SOMETIME

Reminding us that musical comedies concerned themselves with comedy over music and insisting that operetta "attracted the more musicianly composers," Gerald Bordman places the musicals of Rudolf Friml and Sigmund Romberg decidedly in the genre of operetta.[40] So how do we categorize their collaborations with Rida Johnson Young? Both *Her Soldier Boy* (Romberg) and *Sometime* (Friml) contained elements of musical comedy and featured prominent comic performers in roles that were clearly tailored to their talents. However, because of its Belgian wartime setting, use of romantic language for the lovers, and melodramatic plot elements, *Her Soldier Boy* leans more toward operetta than musical comedy. Classifying *Sometime* is a bit more problematic. The *New York Times* called it a musical comedy, the score published by Schirmer calls it a musical play, some contemporary newspapers call it a musical romance, but *Sometime* appears most regularly in books on operetta (often in lists of Friml's credits). The difficulty lies not so much in the fact that shows from this period lacked an accurate labeling system but that this particular show defies categorization. Many of the scenes and songs are highly comic, yet the music resounds with the lushness of an operetta score. The original *Times* reviewer clearly preferred *Sometime*'s operetta sound, disparaging the book and lyrics while gushing over a score that "made one forget the book and lyrics and float away into a true world of graceful and sensuous delight."[41] This reviewer wanted *Sometime* to be an operetta—instead, he got a hybrid of operetta and musical comedy.

Born in Prague and educated at the Prague Conservatory, where he studied with Antonín Dvořák, Rudolf Friml (1879–1972) made his Broadway debut as the composer of *The Firefly* (1912). *The Firefly* was conceived as a vehicle for *Naughty Marietta*'s Emma Trentini and originally given to Victor Herbert. Herbert walked away from the project, infuriated with Trentini for her tempestuous behavior on *Marietta*, and vowed never to work with her again. Producer Arthur Hammerstein then hired Friml for the job. The operetta was so successful that it started the budding classical composer on an unexpected career in the theater. *Sometime* was Friml's sixth operetta and his only collaboration with Young. *Sometime* is also notable for two vaudeville performers who would go on to be bigger stars: Ed Wynn and Mae West. Both had been in numerous Broadway shows prior to *Sometime* but were not yet the household names they would later be.

Working with the original script for *Sometime* proved a particular research challenge. I located two very different versions of the script. The one housed at the New York Public Library (NYPL) is bound, with "Property of Arthur Hammerstein" stamped on the front. The one at the Shubert Archive is marked "Property of Century Library," is typed on thin vellum, and has handwritten notes inside, and the title page calls it "'Some Day' OR 'The Road to Love' OR 'Sometime.'" It looks like an early manuscript but also has a handwritten date of "1919" in one corner, even though the show opened on Broadway in 1918. Because the songs correspond to the opening-night song listing on the Internet Broadway Database and in the Schirmer edition of the vocal score, and because of Arthur Hammerstein's name on the cover, I assume the NYPL script is the final version. (It also contains a detailed lighting plot, which, of course, would not be the playwright's responsibility.) Having both scripts is helpful in evaluating *Sometime*, but it also serves as a reminder of how important access to scripts is to historians. Gerald Bordman was one of the great pioneers in establishing musical theater history as a field of research, and scholars rely on his *American Musical Theatre: A Chronicle* as a reference work and a jumping-off point for further research. But mysteriously, his synopsis of *Sometime* contains several mistakes, and as a result, so does William Everett's in his biography of Rudolf Friml, which follows Bordman's plot.[42] It is unclear where Bordman got his version of the plot, as no extant reviews or versions of the script follow it.

Behind the Stage Door

Sometime is a classic "backstage" musical. The action begins just inside the stage door at Henry Vaughn's theater, where his daughter, Enid, stars in what appears to be a musical revue. Loney (Ed Wynn), the doorkeeper and Vaughn's former business partner, greets the chorus girls as they arrive for the matinee, including the unlucky-in-love Mayme (Mae West), with whom Loney is smitten. Enid arrives, peeks through the curtain to check out the audience, and spots her old flame, Richard Carter. The other girls beg her to tell them her story of lost love, so she leads them to her dressing room and begins to recount the history of how she, Vaughn, and Loney went from running a struggling boarding house to opening the theater at which they now perform. Thus begins a series of flashbacks going back about five years. We learn that Carter was a producer who "discovered" Enid and offered her her first leading role. Although the two love each other, Enid's career comes first. While on tour in Buenos Aires, Sylvia, a chorine also in love with Carter, attempts to sabotage the relationship by pointing out how Enid's success is changing her. Carter realizes that he cannot compete with Enid's career and vows to marry her only when she is ready to give it up. Still, he proposes to Enid with a rare ruby ring, and she excitedly accepts. But the engagement is off when Sylvia enters wearing the exact same ring and claims that Carter proposed to *her*. Enid gives the ring back before Carter has a chance to defend himself—Sylvia has actually bought the ring herself in the hopes of making Enid jealous. Meanwhile, Mayme scolds Loney for taking the lowly—and feminine—job of "wardrobe mistress" on the tour. (In a major change from the original script, the song that Young wrote for Loney was cut to make way for one that Ed Wynn wrote, called "Oh! Argentine!")

The second act opens back in Enid's dressing room in the present. Enid and the girls re-enter, and the girls ask if the Buenos Aires tour was the last time she saw Carter. She reveals in another flashback that she ran into him while performing at a benefit in New York a year earlier. Both are too proud to admit that they still have feelings for each other, and Carter leaves to join the Air Force. Sylvia reveals the truth about Carter's reservations about marrying Enid, and Enid tries to catch him, but it is too late; he is already on a steamer on its way to France. Back in the present, Vaughn suggests that they invite Carter over for dinner, but Enid refuses, saying that he must seek her out. Vaughn gently reminds Enid that her pride has too often kept her from happiness and asks her to reconsider. Enid leaves the dressing room and embraces the waiting Carter as the music swells and the curtain falls.

In *Naughty Marietta* and *Maytime*, Young used both musical leitmotifs and visual signifiers to great effect. For *Sometime*, Young turned to a storytelling device that was gaining popularity in early film: the flashback.[43] The action moves between past and present as Enid recalls her difficult road to success and the love she left behind. While Young's transitions between time periods are not always smooth, her experimentation with flashback proves successful in part because of her understanding of stagecraft. She calls for the focus on a set to fade out as another fades up and builds enough time within the scenes for set pieces to be changed in the dark. The action takes place in several disparate locales: a dressing room, a boarding house, a Buenos Aires garden, and a New York rooftop garden theater. This combination of flashback and multiple settings gives *Sometime* a cinematic sensibility and allows this Hollywood ending:

> *Mysterious scene with great white lights. Big voice is heard singing theme song back of drop. CARTER, in aviator's costume, comes out of the shadows into the light. Has pantomime of waiting and listening to song. ENID slowly emerges from shadow. She*

approaches him slowly and they go into each other's arms as entire chorus breaks into theme number, off, and—Curtain.

This highly theatrical scene anticipates the big movie musicals of the late 1920s and 1930s through its use of specialized lighting and lush vocal underscoring. Although sound in film was still a decade away, Young's cinematic flair comes through in *Sometime*.

42nd Street Language

Elements of operetta and musical comedy intertwine throughout *Sometime*, through dialogue, song, and character. We have already seen Young's ability to create distinct voices for her characters that reveal age, social status, and nationality. In *Sometime*, she uses contemporary slang that sets her characters squarely in the early jazz-age theatrical world of 1918. The chorus girls frequently call each other "Dearie," and at the beginning of the show, the stage manager tells the girls that last night's performance "died the death of a second-hand flivver on an upgrade."[44] An early exchange between Mayme and Loney helps set the tone:

> MAYME. See here, Loney, you wouldn't play a dirty trick on me, would you?
> LONEY. Why Mayme Dean, what do you mean?
> MAYME. Nix on the lyrics. When a man gets poetic, I get suspicious.[45]

In contrast, the lovers, Enid and Carter, speak in a heightened, romantic language:

> DICK. You're positively radiant. You seem to grow happier every day.[46]
> ENID. Happy? Oh, Dick, I never knew life could be so good! To be a success, to have people like one. I suppose it's frivolous, but I love it.
> DICK. And you never want anything more?
> ENID. What more could I have?[47]

Enid speaks with a youthful earnestness, while Mayme, the jaded chorus girl, uses a harsh and brassy tone. Mayme and Loney's exchanges seem to come straight out of a 1920s comedy, while Enid and Carter's conversations have a timeless quality, typical of operetta.

In addition to contemporary dialogue, Young makes several pointed references to New York theatrical life, even giving a nod to her producers when Vaughn declares that if noted theatrical producers Klaw and Erlanger cannot give his daughter a fair contract, he will "take [his] attractions over to the Shuberts!"[48] While in Buenos Aires, Mayme laments that no one there "understands 42nd Street language."[49] Young writes in the American vernacular, an important characteristic at the end of the First World War. Young's busiest and most lucrative years were during the war, with eight major shows in four years, most of them addressing American characters and subjects. In the midst of anti-German sentiment in the United States, Young managed to write operetta librettos that sounded as American as the music sounded European.

"The Tune You Can't Forget"

The songs, dialogue, and actions of Loney and Mayme steer *Sometime* into the realm of musical comedy. Mae West played Mayme, the "vampire with no one to vamp." This was a young Mae West, not yet associated with the scandalous roles of her later career in film. However, she had established a reputation as the "Baby Vamp," a character she frequently played in vaudeville, so Young most likely wrote Mayme as the "vamp" in reference to West's alter ego. Mayme's two major songs—"What Do You Have to Do?" and "Any Kind of Man"—present her as a young, frustrated chorus girl who has as much sex appeal as the other girls but cannot get a man no matter what kind of "Theda Bara tricks" she tries. Both of her songs feature some of Young's most clever lyrics to date, as in this section from "What Do You Have to Do?":

> I see those pink and perfumed pets sink in their limousines,
> Without a single thought in life above their mezzanines;
> I wonder why these dames can reign as lobster palace queens
> While I go home and o'er the gas warm up a can of beans.
> What do you have to do to get it?
> What do you have to do?
> I'm ready to see it through,
> But don't know how to etiquette it!
> What do you have to say,
> To let 'em know you're a live one, too?
> My life is one darn waiting,
> It's really aggravating!
> What do you have to do to get it?
> What do you have to do?[50]

Up to this point, we have seen fairly simple lyrics from Young. She rarely employs intricate rhyme schemes, instead going for economy of rhyme by frequently picking one or two vowel sounds and repeating them. Young pulls out all the stops for *Sometime*, beginning with "What Do You Have to Do?" Although "limousines," "mezzanines," "palace queens," and "can of beans" are not technically triple rhymes, Young matches them rhythmically and makes them sound more complex. She also sneaks in some internal rhymes, with "*pink* and perfumed pets *sink* in their limou*sines*" and "*go home* and *o'er* the gas *warm* up a can of beans." Rhyming "get it" with "etiquette it" sounds vaguely like a Gershwin lyric, although *Sometime* predates the Gershwin sound. Interestingly, this is not the only instance that calls to mind the sophisticated slang and intricate rhyme schemes of a Gershwin musical comedy.

Another specialty number for Mayme is notable for Mae West introducing the provocative "shimmy." Young's lyrics for "Any Kind of Man" could have come from any musical comedy and fit in any burlesque show:

> All I want is just a little—
> Said a little loving,
> Just a little spooning and a squeeze.
> I was really made for turtle doving,
> Lead me to it, lead me to it, please!
> Won't you put your loving arms around me,
> Won't you be my wild man for tonight?
> Grab me in your arms and pull that cave man stuff,
> You know what I mean, kid, treat me rough![51]

According to biographer William Everett, Friml did not want to write for West, especially not the kind heard in a "striptease." But Friml relented when he got to know West better and enjoyed writing for her.[52] Sherry Engel suggests that the lyrics were too risqué for Young and may have been at least partially written by West herself.[53] This is certainly possible but has not been recorded anywhere. The lyrics call to mind those of Ira Gershwin for *Girl Crazy* (1930; "Treat Me Rough") and of Arthur Rose and Douglas Furber for *Me and My Girl* (1937; "You Would If You Could"). And "The Tune You Can't Forget" sounds almost like a prototype of the Gershwins' "Fascinatin' Rhythm" from 1924's *Lady, Be Good!*

> Oh! Don't you start that teasing melody,
> I cannot resist.
> No! Don't you let me get the swing of it!
> I beg you, desist!
> Puts me in a trance,
> It makes me hazy, dazy!
> Makes me want to dance!
> It really almost drives me crazy![54]

Not only is the subject matter the same, but it uses similar slang. Young's lyric mixes highbrow ("I beg you, desist!") with lowbrow ("It makes me hazy, dazy!") and reflects the efforts of audiences to assimilate jazz into their musical vocabularies. These songs provide still further examples of Young's ability to write in modes appropriate to genre and character.

Somewhere, Somehow

If Mayme and Loney represent musical comedy, star-crossed lovers Enid and Carter give *Sometime* its operetta-like qualities. Through their songs, we can sense the tension between the traditional operetta style and musical comedy, seen here in the title song:

> Somewhere, somehow, sometime, someday,
> I know, whatever befall,
> Through the dark of waiting years,
> Heart to heart I'll hear you call.
> Tho' near the gates of Paradise,

> Gladly I'd turn away,
> Just to hear you say, "I love you!"
> Sometime, somewhere, someday![55]

As in the love themes in Young's other operettas, the lovers express themselves with heightened poetry and lofty ideals. Young uses straightforward rhymes ("befall" and "call") in service of an expression of love, and the archaic use of inverted syntax, as in "Gladly I'd turn away." The vowels and imagery are expansive, adding to the grandeur of their epic love. The song stands in stark contrast to the comic numbers and the shallow flirtations of the theatrical life portrayed by Sylvia, Mayme, and Loney. This song bears a marked difference from the love songs in *Lady Luxury*: Eloise and Sam are in no danger of losing each other, while the dramatic stakes for Enid and Richard are higher. *Sometime* followed closely on the heels of *Maytime* (1917), also a show about star-crossed lovers. Perhaps working with Friml on this one at the same time influenced Young's approach to the characters.

Despite keeping one foot in traditional operetta, Young continued to progress in her use of songs that work to advance the plot, as she did in *Naughty Marietta* and *Her Soldier Boy*. A song for Enid that was cut from the show, "So Near, So Far Away" (it does not appear in the revised script or song list), is a great example of Young's ability to use the song to tell a compelling story. After the first flashback, in which Enid recounts the first days of her love affair with Carter, Enid, now alone, looks in her dressing room mirror and sings the opening verse:

> I wonder if my face looks just the same
> As when he loved me in the long ago.
> I wonder if his heart still feels the thrill
> He told me of—ah, will I ever know?
> I wonder if my voice awakes a thought
> Of happy hours still living in my heart,
> I wonder if he feels as I do, so near,
> That Fate still holds us many miles apart![56]

When Enid launches into the refrain, it sounds like any popular song that can stand alone without its verse. But the verse is the most interesting part of the song because it has a narrative. The audience sees Enid at her most vulnerable, when she has been putting on a brave face to the other characters. She still carries a torch for Carter even as she dismisses the chorus girls from suggesting that idea in the previous scene. Without this verse, we can certainly infer her feelings, but Young wants us to witness Enid's struggle to come to grips with her conflicting emotions. Young does it again at the end of act 1, with the reprise of Sylvia's song "Keep on Smiling." When Sylvia sings it, it is an uptempo "look for the silver lining" number. When Sylvia encourages Enid to sing it after Carter has apparently rejected her, it becomes forced and frenetic as Enid tries to show everyone that she can smile through her tears:

SYLVIA. Waste no time in sighing, worrying or crying,
    Smile, smile, smile,
    There's lots of things worthwhile!

> ENID. I will! I will! I'll banish all this vain regret
> I'll sing and dance, live my life and forget![57]

And Enid continues the song, dancing and smiling, until the chorus takes over and she breaks down. Young reprises the song to denote a change in character rather than to ensure that the audience will leave the theater humming. This careful attention to dramaturgy, along with a sense of what would please an audience, made Young a master at her craft.

Among the structural changes to the final script, Ed Wynn's part is expanded while some songs are cut, presumably to make room for him. Also, the original has Loney preaching in every scene about being a vegetarian and all the jokes revolving around it; the revised version drops almost all mention of his vegetarianism. Instead, Loney is perpetually trying out his comedy act—which is never funny. Wynn claimed to have always written his own material, and I suspect this was true for *Sometime*, as Loney's jokes do not match Young's style. Here is the opening scene from the original script, written by Young:

> LONEY. Just keeping myself in condition. I try to counteract a sitting down job with sitting up exercises.
> STAGE HAND. Don't mind me, Annette Kellerman, go on diving for a good figger, all the girls is doing it. There's your dinner. Meatless day today. *(Slaps a sandwich down on the table)*
> LONEY. Every day's meatless day for me. I'm a vegetarian. What's this?
> STAGE HAND. A egg, fried.
> LONEY. Take it away. Don't you know that eggs are a form of animal life?
> STAGE HAND. Some is, but that looks dead all right.
> LONEY. Take it away. Give it a decent burial.[58]

Here is an excerpt from Loney's first scene in the revised script:

> LONEY. Wait a minute. I ought to tell you first how the act opens. You see, I walk on from one side—and my partner comes in on the other side—and I'm supposed to be an inventor, a very eccentric inventor. I walk along the street looking for ideas. Just now I'm looking for tobacco. And as I said before, my partner and I walk on from opposite sides. Then we meet in the center and act surprised.
> VAUGHN. I see. "Enter from right, denoting surprise."
> LONEY. That's right. Ready? *(They walk to opposite sides of the stage.)* Now don't forget to act surprised.
> VAUGHN. *(Shouts)* Why, Loney! How are you?
> LONEY. *(Jumps back startled)* You frightened me. I just wanted you to surprise me.[59]

Loney and Vaughn go back and forth for another page and a half, Loney explaining his act—and interrupting the jokes to explain them—until Vaughn stops him, saying, "Enough of this. It's awful." Given that Wynn was a very physical comedian, I suspect that the long explanations of his jokes were accompanied by blocking and gestures that were part of Wynn's performance style. But the jokes fall flat on the page. Young's quick-witted and tightly paced writing style stand in sharp contrast to Wynn's meandering one. As a result, Loney's scenes come across as disjointed and confusing. They may have made more sense in performance; in any case, Young's voice is absent from large portions of the script.

The critics seemed to agree that *Sometime* succeeded because of Friml's music. John H. Raftery of the *New York Telegraph* called it "a welcome betterment of the current grade of Broadway musical comedy."[60] The *New York Times* said, "Not much can be said for the book and lyrics of 'Sometime,'. . . and nothing here shall be said against them—unless it be dispraise to record that they are of the musical comedy of commerce. . . . There were moments, indeed, when the orchestra was so persuasive that it made one forget the book and lyrics and float away into a true world of graceful and sensuous delight."[61] Despite its mixed reviews, *Sometime* was another surprise hit for Young, with a very healthy run of 283 performances. It even ran into the summer, which was unusual in a time when New York theaters closed for the summers because of the city's oppressive heat. (Air conditioning would not be used in theaters until the mid-1920s.) Whether it was due to Friml's music or the onstage antics of Mae West and Ed Wynn, Young had another major hit.

Box 4.2 Sometime

Lyrics and libretto: Rida Johnson Young
Music: Rudolf Friml
Additional lyrics: Ed Wynn
Shubert Theatre and Casino Theatre; opened October 4, 1918; closed June 7, 1919 (283 performances)
Producer: Arthur Hammerstein

Major Cast

Enid Vaughn . . . Francine Larrimore
Richard Carter . . . John Merkyl
Mayme Dean . . . Mae West
Loney Bright . . . Ed Wynn
Henry Vaughn . . . Harrison Brockbank
Sylvia DeForrest . . . Frances Cameron

Songs

"What Do You Have to Do?" . . . Mayme
"Picking Peaches" . . . Henry and Girls
"Sometime" . . . Enid and Girls
"Keep On Smiling" . . . Enid, Sylvia, and Chorus
"Sometime" (reprise) . . . Enid and Richard Carter
"The Tune You Can't Forget" . . . Sylvia and Chorus
"Oh! Argentine" (lyrics by E. Wynn) . . . Loney
"Beautiful Night" . . . Sylvia, George, and Chorus
"Baby Doll" . . . Enid and Boys
"Any Kind of Man" . . . Mayme

JUST ONE OF THE BOYS
• • •
YOUNG AS CO-WRITER

I wish the reviews had not given me so much credit. I want Mr. Duncan, my collaborator, to have his share. He is such a fine young chap and does such good work. But the press, I suppose, because my name is better known, gave me the lion's share of praise.

Rida Johnson Young[1]

In addition to her collaborations with Chauncey Olcott, which were plays with music rather than book musicals, Rida Johnson Young paired with two other lyricist-librettists early in her career: William Cary Duncan[2] and Paul West. Although Young only co-wrote lyrics and librettos for a few musicals, they are as vital in discovering her writing voice as those she wrote herself. Examinations of *The Red Petticoat* (lyrics and libretto co-written with Paul West, music by Jerome Kern) and *When Love Is Young* and *His Little Widows* (both co-written with William Cary Duncan, music by William Schroeder) further reveal the nature of musical theater writing in this time period and demonstrate how Young blended her style with her collaborators.

THE RED PETTICOAT

The Red Petticoat is a musicalization of Young's play *Next!* which the Shuberts produced in 1911. It seems that Young always intended *Next!* as a vehicle for the comic actress Helen Lowell, who had starred in Young's *The Lottery Man* in 1909. Lowell got her professional start playing bit parts in Gilbert and Sullivan operettas, which led to larger roles in some popular touring productions. By the time she appeared in *The Lottery Man*, she was in great demand. Letters to the Shuberts when Young was writing *Next!* refer to it as "the Lowell play," and Young was particularly proud of it: "Have started on the Lowell play and it promises to be the funniest one I have done yet."[3] She reiterated her opinion when it was

Sweet Mystery. Ellen M. Peck, Oxford University Press (2020). © Oxford University Press.
DOI: 10.1093/oso/9780190873585.001.0001.

finished: "I think it is about the best comedy I have written and I know you will like it."[4] At this point, Young was still in the early stages of her career with the Shuberts, but she was by no means hesitant to fight for fair compensation. She expressed her dissatisfaction to the producers, in no uncertain terms, upon receipt of an early contract for the show:

> I have read your contract very carefully and I cannot sign it. The contract I sent you I do not consider in any way measurable and it is the form of contract I intend to use from now on. I should regret very much having to place the play elsewhere, but must do so unless you will sign my contract. Will you kindly let me know tomorrow morning by phone as I must make a decision as to what I am going to do with the play in the next twenty-four hours.[5]

Correspondence shows that the contract went through at least two revisions before Young signed off on it. Young continued her work on the script, always keeping Lowell's comedic skills in mind: "Have just finished the revision of 'Next.' I think you will find the play much improved. I have cut out most of the sentiment and melodrama and have added comedy. Miss Lowell is an eccentric comedian and there is no use trying to make her anything else."[6] Because the script housed in the Houghton Library at Harvard University contains many scenes that border on the melodramatic, I assumed it was her original. However, an unusual stage direction changed my mind. At the top of act 2, the scene description specifies that a particular rain barrel be visible outside the window as a major plot point revolves around it: "The whole effect of the climax will be lost unless the barrel is much in evidence. This was not done at original performance."[7] Presumably, this version came after the play's out-of-town tryout in New Haven in May of that year.

Next! opened in New York at Daly's Theatre on September 28, 1911, but it did not last even a month. At only eighteen performances, Next! was an unmitigated flop. But Young refused to give up on it and proposed a musical version.[8] David Belasco had captivated audiences a few years prior with his Gold Rush melodrama *The Girl of the Golden West*, with three consecutive New York productions from 1905 to 1908. Very likely, despite the failure of Next! the Shuberts thought Young's script had the potential to capitalize on Belasco's success—plus, they probably saw an opportunity for a quick and inexpensive production as they already had the sets and costumes.[9] And since the audiences loved Lowell, if not the vehicle, Young had no qualms about rewriting the show just for her. As Young was still new to musicals at this point in her career, the Shuberts determined that she needed a writing partner and assigned another of their staff writers, Paul West. Originally from Boston, West (1871–1918) was a newspaper editor, comic-strip writer, and author of society verse.[10] By the time he collaborated with Young on *The Red Petticoat*, he had contributed lyrics and scripts to many musical comedies, extravaganzas, and even Ziegfeld's *Follies* (1907 edition). This would be his last Broadway outing, and his life would have a strange and tragic end. West went to Paris as a Red Cross volunteer during the war. Not long after his unit had been involved in combat, his uniform cap was discovered on a bridge, along with a note that said only, "When this is found, I shall be dead." Police later recovered his body from the Seine. His family believed that the terror of the war he had seen recently led to an incurable depression.[11]

The Shuberts signed Jerome Kern to compose the music. *The Red Petticoat* had the distinction of being Kern's first complete score for a Broadway musical. The young composer had already supplied songs for vaudeville and revues, contributing a song here and a song there, sometimes splitting score duties with another composer. Kern contributed music—and sometimes lyrics—to nearly thirty shows before *The Red Petticoat*, including *Fluffy Ruffles* (1908), the *Ziegfeld Follies of 1911*, and *The Kiss Waltz* (1911). Biographer Gerald Bordman reports that Kern "jumped at the chance" to write his own score to what was initially titled *The Girl and the Miner*.[12] But the Shuberts were in a hurry—they allowed only three weeks of rehearsal before a scheduled Philadelphia tryout on October 21, which was delayed to October 24. Quick stops in New Jersey and Albany, New York, followed before the Broadway opening on November 12, 1912. The title changed to *All After Sophie*, then *Look Who's Here* (its title from the beginning of rehearsals), then finally *The Red Petticoat*. Young's correspondence with the Shuberts chronicles the title changes. In a letter from May 1912, Young asks, "What do you think of the title A BUNCH OF PETTICOATS for 'Next'? We could introduce that line several times in the play and I think it would make rather an attractive title."[13] A letter from September gives its longest-standing title before the final one: "Please don't give up the idea of calling the play LOOK WHO'S HERE. Everyone to whom I mention the title is enthusiastic about it."[14] Bordman suggests that the Shuberts insisted on a new title after the Albany tryout because a reviewer had called it "An Operetta Worthy of More Romantic Title."[15] *The Red Petticoat* arrived on Broadway earlier than planned, which may have hurt its chances of success, as the creative team felt they still had work to do.

My major challenge with these collaborations lies in distinguishing Young's voice from those of her co-writers. Even with Young's original plays to use as comparison, I do not have notes or correspondence between the writers that indicate how they agreed on changes made in the adaptation process. Nor do the typescripts or printed programs provide much clarity. For *The Red Petticoat*, the typescript housed in the Shubert Archive gives the authorship as follows: "Book by Rida Johnson Young and Paul West; Lyrics by Paul West."[16] But the opening-night program reads, "Book and Lyrics by Rida Johnson Young and Paul West."[17] Further, a program from the national tour reads, "'The Red Petticoat' An Operetta of the West By Rida Johnson Young and Paul West; Lyrics—By Paul West."[18] A note from Lee Shubert to Young in the early stages of negotiations for the show suggests that West was, at least at the outset, the sole lyricist: "In accordance with our recent conversation, concerning NEXT being made into a musical comedy, I have arranged for the composer and lyric writer to start work."[19] Young replied a week later: "I am sending you the contract for 'Next' with changes in clauses regarding my re-writing the play. Otherwise it is all right."[20] Of course, without the contract, we cannot determine the nature of those "clauses," but the wording suggests that Young was only handling the libretto. The typescript also provides a clue to its time of printing: the authors settled on the final title during its out-of-town tryout. The script held at the Shubert Archive appears to be the performance version.

The Lady Barber

Lowell starred in *Next!* and *The Red Petticoat* as the spunky Sophie Brush (her name is a play on the "soapy brush" a barber would use to lather a client's face), female barber to a band of ruffian miners. Sophie bulldozes her way into a gold-mining camp, upending the masculine atmosphere, and quickly steals everyone's heart. For a romantic musical comedy, Sophie was an unconventional leading lady: assertive, stubborn, awkward, and matronly. Young describes her in the stage directions as a "thin, angular spinster."[21] Publicity pictures of Lowell as Sophie depict a matron in an oversized plaid wool coat and plain, sturdy shoes, with a slightly too small straw hat; the *New York Tribune* remarked that she "used all her ingenuity to present herself as an artistic fright."[22] Up to this point, Young's leading females were conventionally beautiful and sophisticated. In many ways, though, Sophie shares quite a bit in common with Marietta d'Altena and even Young herself. They all boldly enter men's spaces, demand a place for themselves, and will not accept no for an answer. Young seemed to gravitate toward this type of woman; her leading women in *Glorious Betsy, The Girl and the Pennant, Lady Luxury, Maytime, Sometime,* and *The Dream Girl* all share similar traits.

At the "Up-to-Date Improvement Company" in Lost River Camp, Nevada, Otto Schmaltz oversees a "wild and woolly" band of gold miners who have yet to actually find any gold. The show opens with a riotous number that the stage directions describe as "time-honored Wild West ferociousness."[23] Otto has decided that their long hair and scraggly beards are holding them back from becoming gentlemen, so he has hired a barber named "S. Brush" to come and tidy them up. When the vivacious and pushy Sophie Brush enters, he realizes too late that he has hired a woman. Sophie has learned her trade by correspondence course—along with other jobs, as we will find out through a running gag—and has brought a team of young women with her, plus her pet talking parrot, "Mary Garden" (Young's homage to the Scottish opera singer who had recently taken New York by storm). But this is not a live or stuffed parrot—it is an actress in parrot costume. Bordman recounts that this was at least the second parrot character on Broadway that season: "Performers in parrot costumes threatened to become the rage of the theatrical season."[24] Mary Garden knows English well—too well for Otto's taste. When he tries to swear, Sophie shushes him so that the parrot won't pick up his bad language. Sophie and her assistants claim their territory and start moving in, Otto's protests falling on deaf ears.

Meanwhile, "Sage Brush" Kate, a dancer from Regan's Palace Opera House and Dance Hall across the street, confronts Jack, a miner with whom she has had an on-again, off-again flirtation. Jack has fallen for a new girl in town, Phyllis Oldham. Kate threatens to kill Jack for his infidelity, but after he leaves, Phyllis enters and confides in Kate, thinking they should be friends. (Phyllis knows nothing of Kate's relationship with Jack.) Kate takes advantage of Phyllis's naivete and warns her about Jack: he is nothing but a dirty gambler who will break her heart. When Jack returns a few moments later, Phyllis tries to brush him off, but he woos her in song.

After demanding that Otto take her out for supper, Sophie makes herself at home and shoos him out the door. Phyllis explains that a town on the other side of the mountain has found gold, but the prospectors in Lost River Camp are still coming up empty. Suddenly, Jack enters in a panic. He has just shot local thug Bad Jake in self-defense, and the other miners are after him. Sophie pushes him into the cellar and tells the men that she hasn't seen him. After the men leave, Sophie promises to hide Jack until they can clear his name. Otto returns and tries again to get Sophie to leave, but she and the girls settle in for the night. Just before she goes to bed, Sophie takes off her dowdy traveling clothes to reveal a red petticoat underneath.

Act 2 takes place one week later, and the Up-to-Date Improvement Company has been transformed from a simple shack for miners into a cozy, colorful beauty parlor. The miners sport new haircuts and clean-shaven faces, and even Otto is delighted with Sophie's work. The men fawn over her and clamor to be her next customer. Sophie has been hiding Jack in the kitchen all this time, and the girls delight in taking care of him. When Phyllis begs him to escape before the men find him, he reveals that he has been digging an escape route from the cellar to the nearest cliff. But Kate has been spying on the camp all week and reveals to a miner named Brick that his sister—Phyllis—has been sneaking over to visit the fugitive Jack. The miners interrupt this revelation with big news: they have struck gold! They bring in bags of gold for Sophie to keep safe in the kitchen. When she leaves the kitchen door unlocked, Kate and Bad Jake—who has recovered from his gunshot wound—sneak back in and steal it. Then Jake makes a fatal mistake—he jokingly says "Jake did it!" and the parrot repeats him. They stuff the gold in a nearby rain barrel and escape. When the others discover the gold is missing, Brick accuses Jack. Sophie realizes that the parrot has been in the room the whole time and must have seen something. She coaxes the bird to cry, "Jake did it!" But Jack escapes, leaving the crowd to think he stole the gold, no matter what the parrot says.

Act 3 opens two weeks later, and the gold is still missing. While Otto, now smitten with Sophie, tries to work up the courage to propose to her, the rest of the men continue the search for Jack. Finally, Kate and Bad Jake come to retrieve the gold from the rain barrel, but Jack appears and catches them in the act. Jack reveals that he struck gold while digging his escape route and has staked the claim. He will share the claim with Otto Schmaltz's mining camp. Everyone celebrates as Jack and Phyllis embrace, and Otto finally asks Sophie to marry him.

A Bachelor Girl

Sophie Brush is another typical Rida Johnson Young creation: a whip-smart, tenacious woman who will do whatever it takes to get by. The picture that Young sets up for her first entrance—hat askew, tacky plaid traveling coat, surrounded by all of her luggage and the parrot—signals her indifference to society's expectations. She and her belongings take up the entire doorway, and her first line is simply "Is this the Up-to-Date Land and Improvement Company?" When Otto answers yes, she responds, "Send somebody to get my things out of that old rattle trap. I'm the new barber."[25] Sophie does not tiptoe in or excuse her interruption; she does not demure or simper; she takes charge. No amount of demanding or pleading from Otto will detract her from her purpose. Like her author, Sophie has chosen a profession traditionally filled by men: she is a barber, not a "manicure."[26] She brings a team of manicures with her but insists that since she has a barber's training, that makes her one:

> OTTO. That's me, lady, but you can't be my barber.
> SOPHIE. Why not, I took a correspondence course in everything from manicuring to facial massage and I reckon I'm able to tackle anything around here.
> OTTO. But I wasn't expecting a woman.
> SOPHIE. Well, you need one judging by the looks of things, and I wasn't far wrong in thinking you'd need more than one. That's why I brought my assistants.

When Otto asks if they are her daughters, she tartly replies, "Certainly not. I am a bachelor girl."[27] Again, Sophie chooses a masculine title for herself. Her pride even extends to her parrot. When one of the miners calls it a "canary"—slang at the time for a female singer—Sophie considers it an insult (even though she names the parrot after a famous female singer). She will later reveal other correspondence courses she has taken: shooting, nursing, piano moving, and interior decorating. When Young wrote this, she was a recent divorcee, living in the second home purchased with her royalties, and an established playwright with one of the most powerful producing houses in the country. Her early plays featured women in "traditional" women's roles trapped in antiquated social strictures, like Marion Thorne in *Brown of Harvard*, who is "ruined" when she is caught in a man's dorm room. But with *Naughty Marietta* and Sophie, Young began to write independent women who choose unorthodox paths to happiness, who take charge of their own destinies. Yes, these women will end up with husbands, but they will also dictate the terms of their marriages.

And what about that titular red petticoat? The petticoat itself is only seen once, at the end of act 1, when Sophie is undressing to go to bed. Sophie no doubt surprised the audiences, who were not expecting this uncouth "lady barber" in mannish outerwear to have such a feminine undergarment. Critics remarked on the hilarity of that moment, the *New York Times* calling it "excruciatingly funny." Red petticoats were also seen as alluring, something a woman should have in her wardrobe to please her husband. In the same year as the show's premiere, major newspapers circulated an ad penned by J. R. Hamilton, a former advertising manager for Wanamaker's. He encouraged women to spend money on beautiful clothes: "When a woman begins saying, 'I have been a good wife to him,' she had better look less to her morals and more to her clothes. When your husband begins staying out nights, don't go and get an old lawyer; go and get a new hat. And make it ALARMINGLY pretty." He concluded the ad with, "And remember this always—A bright red petticoat is far more easily forgiven than a dull gray face."[28] A red petticoat had been in the recent news as well, when an Irish girl averted a train's collision with a cart stuck on the tracks by taking off her red petticoat and flagging the conductor down with it.[29]

Book and Lyrics

While it is not entirely clear whether Young *and* West wrote the lyrics for *The Red Petticoat*, there are clues in the style of the lyrics. West wrote light verse, as practiced and popularized by poets like Franklin Pierce Adams (or "FPA," as he was affectionately known), Dorothy Parker, and G. K. Chesterton and by other lyricists, including Ira Gershwin. Adams published light verse in his satirical column "The Conning Tower," which was syndicated in all the major New York newspapers. Light verse was a form of poetry based on witticisms, puns, double entendres, and satire. But lyrics and poetry use different meters, and here is where West's voice is evident in the lyrics for *The Red Petticoat*. In the first musical number, "Sing, Sing, You Tetrazzini," Kate regales the miners with a tale of the time the world-renowned opera diva Luisa Tetrazzini visited a nearby mining camp:

> The boys were all excitement for they'd heard with great delight
> An op'ra star was coming on to sing with them that night.
> They met the coach and took her out, and brought her up with pride
> To Johnson's pioneer saloon and followed her inside.
> They howled and shot their pistols off, and in that awful din,
> The bunch rose up and hollered for the lady to begin.[30]

When read aloud, the verse has a completely straight and even rhythm, with fourteen beats per line. There are no internal rhymes, repeated vowel sounds, or alliterative phrases—only the final syllable of each line rhymes. By comparison, Young's lyrics from *Naughty Marietta* show a very different approach:

> I've a very strange feeling I ne'er felt before,
> 'Tis a kind of a grind of depression.
> My heart's acting strangely, it feels rather sore,
> At least it gives me that impression.
> My pulses leap madly without any cause,
> Believe me, I'm telling you truly.

The meter here changes on every other line for the first four lines, then changes again for the fifth and sixth. Young rhymes internally on "*kind of* a *grind of* depression" and, while not a true double rhyme, cleverly pairs "depression" with "impression." It reads like a lyric, not a poem. Here is a verse from another *Red Petticoat* song, "The Correspondence School":

> I was shy on education,
> And I found to my vexation,

> They regarded me as something of a fool.
> So I thought I'd glean some knowledge
> From a modern postal college,
> Or in other words, a correspondence school.
> First I took a course in cooking,
> And when Mother wasn't looking,
> I prepared a lovely dinner, but 'twas strange,
> When I thought it was completed
> That the people couldn't eat it,
> For I hadn't lit the fire in the range![31]

This verse almost sounds like an extended limerick, another type of light verse. The rhythm is straight, precise, and predictable, with an 8-8-11 count per AAB set. And, like the verse from "Sing, Sing, You Tetrazzini," it is telling an amusing anecdote, another hallmark of light verse. While not every song in *The Red Petticoat* reads like verse, enough do to suggest that Paul West was indeed responsible for the lyrics.

On the other hand, the dialogue strongly suggests Rida Johnson Young's writing voice. When writing a comedy, Young wrote in a style similar to that of modern sitcoms. She does a sort of extended setup and punchline pattern, as in this bit of dialogue from act 1:

> SOPHIE. When I get your beard all cleaned off and the hair cut out of your eyes, you'll feel better.
> BARNES. What, cut my hair? Well, when any woman gets a pair of scissors into my hair, Hell'll be froze over.
> SOPHIE. Then there'll be good skating down below in a few days.[32]

And this excerpt from act 2:

> SOPHIE. You know I ain't responsible for what a parrot says. You know they're dangerous birds to have around.
> OTTO. Yes, I had one once. And the way he would swear when the minister come by the house.
> SOPHIE. No! Where did he learn it?
> OTTO. I'll be damned if I know.[33]

In each example, one character introduces an idea, the other builds on it, then the first finishes it with a laugh line. Young also enjoys using one-liners, as in this line from Otto, when he realizes that Sophie's parrot will repeat his bad language:

> OTTO. I'm going out where I can say in English what I'm thinking of in German.[34]

Presumably in an effort to boost the comedy of *The Red Petticoat*, Young and West made some significant changes to the script. The "western" dialect is significantly toned down, probably to make it easier for New York audiences to understand. And the melodramatic aspects of the plot were lightened, including making Sophie's parrot a sort of deus ex machina who reveals Bad Jake as the thief. Although Young insisted it was a comedy, *Next!* reads as a melodrama, with stereotypical "western" characters and high stakes. Instead of the broad comic ethnic characters of *The Red Petticoat*—the bumbling German Otto (a low-comic "Dutch" role) and the sneaky Mexican Bad Jake—*Next!* has a more "American" cast. The proprietor of the Up-to-Date company is named "Up-to-Date" Prendergast, a teetotaler trying to establish a dry town. Bad Jake is not a simpering Mexican "greaser" but a sinister villain of no specific ethnicity who comes across as genuinely dangerous. And Sophie—who is supposed to be the most outlandish character—is surprisingly down-to-earth and even sympathetic. After forcing her way into Prendergast's business, she admits to Phyllis that she knows she's not wanted:

> SOPHIE. I been puttin' up a good front but I noticed his—coolness, to put it mild—I reckon I gotter "move on."
> PHYLLIS. Oh no.
> SOPHIE. Oh, I'm used to it, child. Seems like I never can find no place where I fit. Ever since I was a kid and use ter peddle shoe-strings in the park, seems to me there's been somebody at my elbow tellin' me to move on.
> PARROT. Move on.
> SOPHIE. See—Isabella's got so used to it, she can say it as natural as a policeman. I did reckon out here the scarcity of females would have made even me welcome.
> *(She swallows hard and is evidently almost on the point of tears)*
> PHYLLIS. Oh, don't. You poor dear, don't feel like that. I'll tell Up-to-Date what I think of him. Oh, don't feel so badly.
> SOPHIE. *(Pulling herself up vigorously)* Go 'long. 'Tain't nothin'. You'll have me actin' like a female in a minute. I ain't a-complainin'. I always believe in makin' the best of everything, but I reckon I'm jes' low spirited and sort of tired of movin' along.[35]

In *The Red Petticoat*, Sophie gets a few chances to be feminine and even a love interest for Otto. In *Next!* she remains mannish and is treated as one of the guys. Instead of undressing down to a frilly petticoat for bedtime, Sophie wears sturdy long underwear. The town of Lost River elects Sophie as its mayor in the third act, a job that would have gone to a man in a similar town. Prendergast shows no romantic interest in her, save for one mere hint at the end, when she is one of the last people in town to stay after reports of gold being struck several miles away. As a dramatic character, this Sophie is actually much more interesting than her musical self. In *The Red Petticoat*, Lowell would only get to play her for laughs.

But changing the title of the show feminized it, necessitating a shift in the main character. The simple choice to give Sophie a petticoat to wear under her spinster clothes instead of long underwear—and branding the entire play with it—forced the possibility for romance, an essential ingredient in musical comedy. The moment the audience saw the petticoat, they expected Sophie to end up with Otto (whose last name, Schmaltz, incidentally, was also code for silly sentiment). After all, when a man and a woman start the show bickering profusely, they must be made for each other—just like Marietta and Dick. Young could create strong, independent female characters, but the musical theater demanded traditional sentiment. The Sophie Brush of *Next!* could become the town mayor; *The Red Petticoat*'s Sophie had to fall in love and marry.

The Shuberts billed *The Red Petticoat* as "An Operetta of the West," and a few reviews even compared it to Belasco's *The Girl of the Golden West*. Critics particularly loved Helen Lowell's performance. "Miss Lowell's impersonation of the female barber is a gem of caricature to be treasured in joyful memory," gushed the *Boston Globe* on its tour stop. "There is fine art in this characterization, and extravagant as it is at times, it always has the semblance of real humanity. We not only laugh at barber Sophie Brush, but we sympathize with her."[36] The *New York Sun* remarked, "Nobody who sees Helen Lowell in 'The Red Petticoat' at Daly's Theatre could fail to recognize a genuine artist in her profession." [37] The *New York Times* gave this guardedly positive review: "Rather surprising on the whole is the result obtained by this mongrel combination of a once primitive melodrama with soothing-syrupy tunes, and though the effect is never distinguished, it is, on the whole, rather pleasant and amusing. . . . 'The Red Petticoat' is better as musical comedy than it was as melodrama. And no one will begrudge time spent in seeing Helen Lowell."[38]

Despite favorable reviews, tickets were not selling well. Producers were starting to move their shows farther uptown, and the Daly was in a less popular area. Young pleaded with the Shuberts to move *The Red Petticoat*: "Don't you think we could do more business with 'The Red Petticoat' if it were brought uptown? I wish you would give it a try. I understand 'The Sun Dodgers' will not remain long at the Broadway. Of course, I can't tell you what to do with your attractions, but I do wish you would give us this chance. I am sure the play would make good up there."[39] The Shuberts evidently agreed, because *The Red Petticoat* moved to the Broadway Theatre on December 16, 1912. But the move failed to boost ticket sales. The brothers closed *The Red Petticoat* and sent it on tour after only sixty-one performances.

Several years later, the show came up again, although not for a revival. J. J. Shubert asked Young to convert either *Next!* or *The Red Petticoat* into vaudeville sketches. Young demurred, although she stated that she "would not object to someone else doing them, provided I can get fifty dollars apiece each week for the use of them."[40]

WHEN LOVE IS YOUNG AND HIS LITTLE WIDOWS

Young wrote four musicals with her nephew (and eventual executor of her estate), composer William Schroeder. The first was the previously mentioned unsuccessful vehicle for Lulu Glaser, *Just One of the Boys*, in 1910. In 1913, they joined forces again—this time with William Cary Duncan co-writing the lyrics and libretto—for *When Love Is Young*, a musical version of Young's 1907 play, *The Boys* of Company "B." After his early work with Young and Schroeder, Duncan would go on to write more notable shows, including *The Royal Vagabond* (1919), *Mary Jane McKane* (1923), and *Yes, Yes, Yvette* (1927), a sort of sequel to *No, No, Nanette* starring newcomer Jeanette MacDonald. Schroeder was a charter member of the American Society of Composers, Authors and Publishers (ASCAP) in 1914, having befriended one of its founders, Victor Herbert. He was a bandmaster in the United States Navy during World War I and composed and conducted a revue

---

Box 5.1 *The Red Petticoat*

Lyrics and libretto: Rida Johnson Young and Paul West
Music: Jerome Kern
Daly's Theatre, Broadway Theatre; opened November 13, 1912; closed January 4, 1913 (61 performances)
Producers: Lee and J. J. Shubert

Major Cast

Sophie Brush . . . Helen Lowell
"Sage Brush" Kate . . . Frances Kennedy
Jack Warner . . . Joseph Phillips
Brick Oldham . . . Donald MacDonald
Phyllis Oldham . . . Louise Mink
Otto Schmaltz . . . James B. Carson
Bad Jake . . . E. L. Fernandez
Dora Warner . . . Grace Field
Slim . . . Allen Kearns

Songs

"Sing, Sing, You Tetrazzini" . . . "Sage Brush" Kate
"I Wonder" . . . Phyllis and Jack
"The Correspondence School" . . . Sophie and Chorus
"Dance, Dance, Dance" . . . Brick, Slim, and Manicure Girls
"Little Golden Maid" . . . Dora and Brick
"Oh, You Beautiful Spring" . . . Dora and Chorus (lyrics by M. E. Rourke)
"Where Did the Bird Hear That?" . . . Sophie, Otto, and Parrot
"(My) Peaches and Cream" . . . Phyllis, Jack, and Chorus
"The Ragtime Restaurant" . . . Brick and Chorus
"A Prisoner of Love" . . . Sophie, Phyllis, and Dora
"Walk, Walk, Walk" . . . Brick and Chorus
"The Joy of That Kiss" . . . Phyllis and Jack
"Oo-Oo-Oo" . . . Otto and Girls
"Since the Days of Grandmamma" . . . Sophie and Girls
"The Waltz Time Girl" . . . Phyllis and Brick

called *Biff Bang!* in 1918 that was performed by naval crewmen. He focused on orchestral music after the war and was elected president of the National Association for American Composers and Conductors in 1954.[41] *When Love Is Young* had a well-received run in Chicago but did not make it to New York. They would do slightly better with the 1914 musical comedy *Lady Luxury* (discussed in chapter 4). Their fourth and final outing would be their most successful: the musical comedy *His Little Widows*, for which Duncan once again co-wrote the words.

When Love Is Young

The title page on the unpublished typescript gives authorship as "Book and Lyrics by Rida Johnson Young and William Cary Duncan." But Young retained most of the play script, with only minor changes, which indicates that she took the lead on its adaptation. The most significant difference is that Young cut the third act and condensed its action to fit the end of the second. Although she had written incidental songs for *The Boys of Company "B,"* she, Duncan, and Schroeder wrote all new ones for the musical. But some of them serve the same purpose they did in the original: they are diegetic and do not function to reveal character or advance plot.

At the musical's opening, a group of young men work out in the home gymnasium of Colonel MacLane, head of the militia unit the New York Grays, Company "B." They are waiting to receive a camp assignment for the following week. A chorus of girls enter with flowers to surprise MacLane's daughter, Eileen, on her twentieth birthday. When she enters, she immediately looks around for Tony Allen, whom she has loved since childhood. But she is engaged to Arthur Stabler, a fussy snob whose wealthy father once helped the MacLanes out in a rough time. Mrs. MacLane is determined that Eileen will marry for money and is trying to make her forget about Tony. When Tony enters to announce the Grays' camp location, Eileen surprises them with the news that it will be adjacent to her home. Tony wants to propose to Eileen, but Mrs. MacLane reminds him that two years ago she asked him to stay away from Eileen so that she could marry for money. Tony thinks that he can convince his uncle to leave him a large inheritance. Mrs. MacLane agrees to let them marry under those circumstances but doesn't believe that his tight-fisted uncle will give him any money—therefore, she will do everything she can to keep Tony and Eileen apart. Eileen overhears part of their conversation and declares that she will marry the man she wants. Tony then confides in Colonel MacLane that if he can get his uncle to join the regiment, he may get him to give Tony the money he needs. Just as everyone is sitting down to tea, Tony gets called away on regiment business. After he leaves, he calls Eileen on the telephone and proposes to her.

The second act takes place in the militia's camp. Most of the men are enjoying their time—all but Tony's uncle, who is exhausted from the training. Tony thinks that he can wear his uncle down to the point where he will give him anything to let him out of his service. Madge, Eileen's beautiful and flirty cousin, arrives in the camp and immediately dazzles Tony. Meanwhile, Arthur and Eileen arrive at the camp. Arthur explains that he will be going to South Africa in a month on business and wants Eileen to accompany him. She tries to tell him how ridiculous that sounds, but he won't listen. They come upon Tony and Madge, who are sharing a kiss. Tony claims it was innocent, but Eileen angrily leaves. A few moments later, Madge meets Chick, a recruit who is sweet and has a lisp. Since she has a lisp as well, they hit it off, and Chick falls in love with Madge. Tony and Eileen enter fighting, Tony trying to explain that his kiss with Madge meant nothing. She is almost ready to forgive him, but not quite. The other boys enter, tossing Chick in a blanket, then drop him, spraining his wrist. Chick wants to write Madge a love letter, but he cannot use his right hand, so he asks Tony to do it. When Madge enters with the note—which she knows is from Chick but in Tony's handwriting—Eileen spies it and assumes that Tony is cheating on her with Madge. She agrees to marry Arthur. He, however, is no more interested in marrying Eileen than she is in him. He has heard from a girl in New York who he thinks will make a better wife. Eileen tearfully decries marriage and says that she will marry no one. But when Tony explains that he wrote the love note as a favor to Chick, Eileen relents and falls into Tony's arms.

Besides the act change and addition of songs, there is really only one major change from the original play: Eileen is more assertive and independent. She is a bit of a pawn in the play version; Tony, Mrs. MacLane, and Arthur all argue over who gets to have her. But Young made a small but important addition to Eileen's dialogue in the musical. During the scene between Mrs. MacLane and Tony in which they set each other up as adversaries, Tony asks, "Say, don't you think it's rather nervy, our settling this thing without consulting Eileen?"[42] But in the musical, Eileen enters to speak up for herself:

> Why should I marry at all? I'm happy and satisfied as I am.... Did your mother build your life for you or did you pick your own flower of happiness? Think, Mother, try to realize what the world looks like through a young girl's eyes. Why, it's a land of glorious adventure. There's a rosy haze over everything, Mother, when you're young. There's no room in your heart for any cold, calculating thought, why you'd even welcome hardship and sorrow and disappointment, if it were by the side of someone you loved.[43]

Eileen is outspoken throughout the play about her viewpoints and will not let anyone push her into a decision about marriage. Young revisited this character six years after the original and wrote *Naughty Marietta* in that time. She was distancing herself from her earlier female characters who had little agency. The endings of the original and the musical adaptation illustrate this subtle shift. In *The Boys of Company "B,"* when Eileen realizes at the last moment that Tony wrote the love note as a favor to Chick, they have the following exchange:

> TONY. Say, Eileen, when I got out of my car just now and stalked to the window like Hamlet's ghost—it was all a bluff. I wasn't really going. I was only letting out the line a bit. I knew I still had the hook on you!
> EILEEN. Oh, Tony!

(He takes her in his arms as the curtain descends)[44]

Tony holds the power in this scenario, almost taunting Eileen and using the old "fishing" metaphor for catching a girl. Eileen essentially falls into his arms and confirms his bravado. While they still end up together at the end of *When Love Is Young*, the stage directions are vague:

> TONY. I said goodbye. But before I go I want to explain that I wrote that letter for Chick.
> EILEEN. For Chick?
> TONY. Yes. Chick had a sprained wrist.
> EILEEN. Cross your heart?
> TONY. You cross *my* heart.
> *(Chorus march in singing. Eileen has a soldier for a sweetheart.)*[45]

Tony does not brag about how easily he can win Eileen back, and Eileen cautiously challenges him before believing him. And does she fall into his arms? The stage directions leave ample room for any acting choice. This is a minor change but an important one. Yes, they go back to being a couple, but Eileen does not *have* to cede any agency to him.

One musical moment stands out in *When Love Is Young*: the act 1 finale, in which the boys look forward to making home at their new military camp. It is not a particularly novel song, but it has one intriguing moment. They sing:

> Up in the morning at break of day
> At the sound of the reveille
> *(Bugles and drums sound "reveille" as the boys sing)*
> We can't get 'em up,
> We can't get 'em up,
> We can't get 'em up
> In the morning![46]

Irving Berlin would do almost the exact same thing just five years later in his ode to military life, "Oh, How I Hate to Get Up in the Morning" (1918). His song also quotes the reveille used to wake soldiers, but with the words "You've got to get up / You've got to get up / You've got to get up this morning!"

Since this is Duncan's first musical with Young, it is useful to look at his lyric writing next to hers. Without a published score of *When Love Is Young*, we do not know with certainty who wrote which songs, except for the few for which the sheet music was published. One is this song attributed to Duncan, "The Girl That Dreams of Me":

> I'll be dreaming then of someone,
> Someone fond and dear,
> Visions of her through the night
> Will hover ever near and nearer.
> In my slumbers I shall smile,
> As in my dreams I seem to see

> One girl alone, my life, my own
> The girl that dreams of me.[47]

Young wrote "The Tango Glide," a diegetic number for Eileen's birthday-party dance. Her lyrics have a similar tone:

> In my dreams, it seems to haunt me more and more,
> As I dance with you upon some heavenly shore,
> Can't you hear that pleasing, teasing melody?
> Calling, calling soft and low to you and me?[48]

The two sets of lyrics fit so well together that either Young or Duncan could have written both of them. There are no obvious stylistic differences between the two. For their first collaboration, Young and Duncan effectively blended their styles to create a cohesive lyrical sound. While I could not find clear attributions for many of the songs, *When Love Is Young* demonstrates Young's ability to write with a partner and, more important, to let content dictate form.

When Love Is Young had what was supposed to have been a pre-Broadway tryout at the Cort Theatre in Chicago. Despite the success of the original play, Chicago critics simply were not impressed with *When Love Is Young*. One called it "an unsophisticated little musical piece," and another sneered at its "namby-pamby young men who are playing at the military life and blushy-gushy girls who admire their theoretical bravery" and concluded that it had a "kind of marshmallow taste."[49] *When Love Is Young* did not make it out of Chicago.

His Little Widows

The 1916–1917 theatrical season was particularly good to Rida Johnson Young. That season included three Young properties: *Captain Kidd, Jr.*, *Her Soldier Boy*, and *His Little Widows*. Her name seemed to be everywhere. Feature writer Mary B. Mullett reprimanded any readers who were confused on this point:

> One statement in regard to "His Little Widows," produced at the Astor Theatre last week, is not quite accurate. A good many persons seem to think that it was the thirteenth or maybe the thirtieth New York production Rida Johnson Young has had this season. The real fact is that this is her third. But even at that she holds the 1916–17 record. With . . . all of them successes, it looks to less fortunate authors as if she were trying to monopolize things.[50]

In fact, since *Brown of Harvard*'s premiere in 1906, there had been only one break—from the end of January 1915 to November 1916—without a Rida Johnson Young play running in New York. Most of the remaining theatrical seasons had not just one but two or three of her shows running at any time. No wonder the public assumed this one was her "thirteenth or maybe the thirtieth." In any case, *His Little Widows* was certainly one of her funniest. It was also one of only a very few shows in her career *not* produced by the Shuberts. G. M. Anderson and L. Lawrence Weber produced it at the Astor Theatre. Anderson and Weber also

> *Box 5.2 When Love Is Young*
>
> Lyrics and libretto: Rida Johnson Young and William Cary Duncan
> Music: William Schroeder
> Cort Theatre, Chicago; opened October 28, 1913; closed unknown date
>
> **Major Cast**
>
> Tony Allen . . . John Hyams
> Eileen MacLane . . . Leila McIntyre
> Holbrook Allen . . . Harry Hanlon
> Arthur Stabler . . . Edgar Norton
> Colonel MacLane . . . George Shields
> Jim MacLane . . . Sam Hyams
> "Chick" Sewell . . . Billy Lynn
> "Babe" Carruthers . . . Jack Winthrop
> George Bright . . . John Madden
> Mike McNab . . . Frank Brownlee
> Mrs. MacLane . . . Helen Hanlon
> Florence Henderson . . . Emsy Alton
> Madge Blake . . . Sylvia De Frankie
>
> **Songs**
>
> "Musical Athletics" . . . Jim, Babe, Chick, and Ensemble
> "I Want to Have a Soldier for a Sweetheart" . . . Florence and Ensemble
> "Birthday Song" . . . Eileen
> "The Girl That Dreams of Me" . . . Tony, Eileen, and Ensemble (lyrics by W. C. Duncan)
> "I Never Like to Talk about Myself" . . . Arthur, Tony, and Boys
> "The Evolution of the Dance" (Introducing the Argentine Tango) . . . Eileen and Tony (lyrics by R. J. Young)
> "I Know I'd Be a Hero If I Only Had a Chance" . . . Allen, Tony, and Colonel
> Act I Finale . . . Eileen and Ensemble
> "Please Send Someone to Love Me" . . . Eileen (lyrics by W. C. Duncan)
> "I Don't Know Why I Kissed You" . . . Tony and Madge
> "The Only Good Answer Is Just That It's So" . . . Jim, George, and the Boys
> "I Don't Care What the Weatherman Says" . . . Eileen and Tony
> "The Yankee Volunteers" . . . Jim, George, Colonel, and Ensemble
> Finale, "The March Past" . . . Ensemble

participated in the burgeoning film industry, Anderson becoming better known later as the western performer "Broncho Billy" Anderson.

Lest anyone think *The Book of Mormon* (2011) was the first musical to parody Mormon life, *His Little Widows* may have opened that door. This musical farce about polygamy won many critics over because of its strong plot and fast pace.

Three upstart entrepreneurs—Pete, Biff, and Jack—have sold shares in a copper mine and are celebrating their success with a lavish party. But everything comes to a halt when Pete gets a telegram saying that the mine has gone bust. Not only have they sunk their families' and friends' savings into the mine, but they won't even be able to pay the party bill at the end of the night. Biff's sister Blanche enters, having just finished a run in a Broadway show that is leaving on tour the next day. Even though she invested in the copper mine, she is more worried about how the boys are going to get out of this mess. Suddenly, several Mormon elders enter, looking for Pete. Elder Abijah Smith tells Pete that his wealthy uncle in Salt Lake City has died and left him three million dollars. The three men are overjoyed, but there is one catch: Pete must move to Salt Lake City and marry his uncle's multiple widows. Much to Biff's and Jack's dismay, Pete absolutely refuses, money or no money. Biff and Jack try everything to convince him, but Pete will not budge. As Jack and Biff try to think of a way to get Pete to Salt Lake City, Blanche approaches Pete to ask why he is so shy around girls, then sings that she is secretly in love with someone. (Even though it is clearly Pete, and he seems attracted to her, this plot line disappears after this scene.) Blanche's producer, Jolson, enters to tell her that the chorus men have all quit the show and he needs replacements for their tour—to Salt Lake City. When Biff and Jack reappear, moaning that they can't scrounge up enough money to take Pete to Utah, Blanche tries to convince Jolson to put Biff, Jack, and Pete into the show. But their audition fails miserably, and Jolson refuses and leaves. The party breaks up, and the boys still have no way to pay the waitstaff, when a doorman brings them their coats. But he has given out the wrong coats—Biff has gotten Jolson's coat, and his wallet is full of cash and the train tickets to Utah. They escape with the money as the act ends.

Act 2 takes place at the late Samuel Lloyd's house, where the Mormon elders wait for Pete to claim his uncle's inheritance. Abijah reveals that the Mormon church officials have condemned polygamy and will not allow Pete to marry Samuel's widows, so they must keep the ceremony a secret. Jolson's show company arrives, with Biff, Jack, and a very unhappy Pete. Abijah reveals that he will receive fifty thousand dollars when the ceremony takes place, but they have a strict deadline of eight o'clock that night, at which time the entire inheritance goes to the church. Abijah calls in the widows—*all eleven of them*. Lucinda, the pushy head wife, makes a beeline for Pete, who tries in vain to run away. Two of the widows, Annabelle and Marilla, confront Abijah and refuse to marry Pete. Jack enters and immediately falls in love with Marilla; then Biff enters and falls in love with Annabelle. Meanwhile, the rest of the widows are chasing Pete around the house. Jack and Biff are excited to get the money, until they find out that Annabelle and Marilla are not just local girls—they are two of Pete's future wives. Blanche and Jolson enter, furious about the scheme. Jolson offers to bring the police after the marriage ceremony is over and annul it, leaving Pete with the three million dollars but free of his obligation. The wedding ceremony takes place, but Jolson fails to show. He has been arrested.

Later that night, Pete is overwhelmed by the attention of his new wives. Abijah has found out that the men conspired to annul the marriage and plans to take the whole lot of them to Mexico to keep them from succeeding. When Pete demands the money owed him, Abijah reveals that it is not cash but savings bonds, which he doesn't have in his possession. Finally, when word leaks out that the marriage has taken place and the authorities are on their way, Abijah relents and says that the savings bonds are for the same copper mine that went bust at the beginning of the show. But it hasn't gone bust; it has flourished. The men are rich and can annul the marriage.

Every major critic remarked that the plot was the show's strongest aspect, such as this one:

> The familiar criticism of musical comedies and light operas that are devoid of plot in no way applies to Rida Johnson Young and William Carey Duncan's new piece which came to the Astor Theatre on Monday night and immediately took rank with the best musical pieces of the year. The story of "His Little Widows," consistent and amusing to a marked degree, begins with the rise of the curtain and continues almost uninterruptedly until its fall, and is so good throughout that the music, melodious and musicianly as it is, becomes almost an incident in the development of the plot, instead of being, as in musical shows, the main feature, with the plot and dialogue merely thrown in to furnish pegs upon which to hang songs and dance numbers.[51]

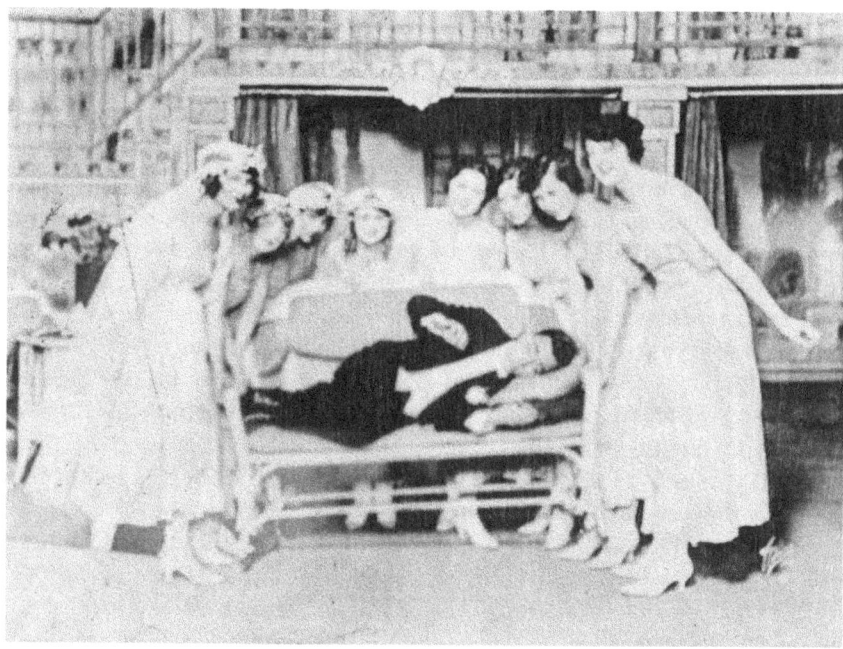

Figure 5.1 A scene from His Little Widows. Photo by White Studio. © Billy Rose Theatre Division, The New York Public Library for the Performing Arts.

On paper, I would agree with the critics. Admittedly, the extant script copies, housed at the Tams-Witmark Library at the University of Wisconsin–Madison, are somewhat difficult to follow. There are two copies, labeled "Prompt Book No. 1" and "Prompt Book No. 2." The first one is a reasonably clean version, with minimal notes but an excess of typographical errors. The second one is very messy, covered in handwritten notes, with entire sections crossed out and line changes. There is another book, labeled "Stage Manager's Guide," that only contains pieces of the score and printed sheet music. Strangely, it also gives the name of the show as "His Six Little Widows." Given that there are eleven widows, I am not sure where the title comes from. In any case, the songs do not seem to contribute much to the action of the play. They feel generic in a way that I have not seen from Young, except in her plays with music.

But the biggest issue I had in reading the script is that it simply does not sound like her voice. The lines are short and the pacing almost too quick to match her style. Young's characters, from the beginning of her career to the end of it, are, well, *loquacious*. They rarely speak in short sentences, even in one-liners. Some of the humor sounds like Young:

> JACK. Besides, it's every man's duty to make as many women happy as possible.
> PETE. Sure. That's why they only let us marry one.[52]

But much of the dialogue looks like this:

> JACK. Now, look here boys, this is the worst blow we've had in our business career.
> BIFF. Business career!
> JACK. But we've reorganized before after a smash and we'll do it again!
> BIFF. Reorganized, on what?
> JACK. On our brains! On our energy! On our nerve!
> PETE. Are you sure we've got all that?
> BIFF. We've got the nerve all right. But brains, I don't know.[53]

The lines come too quickly; they are, in the language of the time, too "snappy." Young could write very clever dialogue and funny jokes, but this style does not seem to have her stamp on it. I suspect that Duncan wrote most of the dialogue. But I believe they are both responsible for one puzzling aspect of the dialogue that one annoyed critic pointed out: the Mormons sound like Quakers, as in this exchange between Biff and Annabelle:

> BIFF. Did you speak?
> ANNABELLE. Nay, verily brother, I spoke not.
> BIFF. Sure you didn't say something?
> ANNABELLE. Nay!
> BIFF. Haven't I met you someplace before?
> ANNABELLE. I know not, brother, hast thou?[54]

The critic from the *Globe* sniffed, "Now as a matter of fact, the Mormons in real life are much funnier than the commonplace inventions of Mrs. Young and Mr.

Duncan. When will Broadway ever learn that human nature, just as it is, invariably is more amusing than the hackneyed jests of cheap imaginations?"[55] Perhaps Young and Duncan were trying too hard to make the Mormons sound old-fashioned or stand out from the non-Mormon characters.

Some of the published sheet music contained in the stage manager's book names either Young or Duncan as lyricist. Some of it was published under the title *Some Little Girl*, which was the name of the show in a later tour. Fortunately, this again allows us to compare the two lyricists side by side. Here is an excerpt from "My Love Is a Secret," with Young's lyrics:

> My love I'm keeping a secret,
> Hid in my heart safe from view.
> No one shall share that rapture so rare,
> And no one shall know that it nestles there;
> My love I'm keeping a secret,
> Thrilling me ever anew,
> Ah, sweet is the charm of a love unknown,
> I never can tell it to you![56]

This has some of the same tone as Young's other love ballads, only without the heightened poetic language of operetta. This next one—again with Young's lyrics—"That Creepy Weepy Feeling," has some of the hallmarks of musical comedy:

> Say, did you feel as I did when I met you?
> Of course I knew at once my heart was won.
> So surely fate would never separate
> Two hearts that have begun to beat as one.
> Don't go away for I can't live without you,
> I'll never leave you, Dearie, that I vow.
> Do not forget that moment when we met,
> I seem to feel that creepy feeling yet.[57]

Young uses contemporary slang like "Say, did you" and "Dearie" that matches both the tone of the libretto and musical comedy convention. Here is a Duncan lyric, from Biff's song, "Oh, You Girls!":

> Gee! I wonder how in thunder
> You can buffalo a man with brains,
> I'm just a joke (Keep you laughing all the time),
> You keep me broke (Bing, there goes another dime),
> With sable sets (Have to put my watch in soak),
> And cigarettes (Why the deuce should women smoke)
> If you fall for a girl, you are stung for your pains,
> She ties you up to her wagon, and then takes the reins.
> They take your cash and blow it,
> Kid and you know it,
> But oh, you girls![58]

Box 5.3 His Little Widows

Lyrics and libretto: Rida Johnson Young and William Cary Duncan
Music: William Schroeder
Additional music and lyrics: Malvin M. Franklin, Thomas J. Gray
Astor Theatre; opened April 30, 1917; closed June 30, 1917 (72 performances)
Producers: G. M. Anderson and L. Lawrence Weber

Major Cast

Jack Grayson . . . Robert Emmett Keane
Biff Hale . . . Harry Tighe
Pete Lloyd . . . Carter DeHaven
Abijah Smith . . . Frank Lalor
Blanche Hale . . . Frances Cameron
Harry Jolson . . . Charles Prince
Sandy Barr . . . John Robb
Lucinda Lloyd . . . Julia Ralph
Annabelle Lloyd . . . Flora Parker
Marilla Lloyd . . . Hattie Burks
Lily . . . Grace Haley
Dahlia . . . Bernice Haley
Tulip . . . Lucile Haley
Rose . . . Mabel Haley
Pansy . . . Alma Pickard
Mignonette . . . Violette Strathmore
Hyacinthe . . . Lucile Zintheo
Narcissus . . . Irma von Nagy

Songs

"When You Waltz with Me" . . . Ensemble
"Oh, You Girls!" . . . Biff
"Saints of the Latter Day" . . . Abijah and Elders
"My Love Is a Secret" . . . Pete and Blanche (lyrics by R. J. Young)
"Johnny Come Follow Me" . . . Blanche and Ensemble
"This Is the Best We Ever Struck" . . . Abijah, Elders, and Ensemble
"I'm Wondering" . . . Annabelle
"I Need Someone's Love" . . . Marilla
"(What Are You Going to Do) When the Animals Are Gone" . . . Dahlia, Tulip, and Rose (music by Malvin M. Franklin, lyrics by T. J. Gray)
"A Wife for Each Day in the Week" . . . Annabelle, Pete, and Jack
"That Creepy Weepy Feeling" . . . Biff, Jack, Marilla, and Annabelle (lyrics by R. J. Young)
"I Want Them All (to Leave Me Alone)" . . . Pete and Widows
"In Cabaret-Land" . . . Blanche and Ensemble
"Salt Lake City" . . . Abijah
"Love Me Best of All" . . . Pete and Widows

Duncan seems to have a better feel for musical comedy style, and his lyrics reflect the dialogue as well. He uses more slang and has a lighter touch with his imagery. Next to this, Young's lyrics for "That Creepy Weepy Feeling" sound slightly fussy, where Duncan displays an ease with the language of these "up-to-date" characters. Their styles blend enough to create a cohesive piece of theater, but Duncan edges out Young for understanding musical comedy conventions.

Overall, the critics liked the show, but some expressed a wish that it had been a straight play instead of a musical comedy. *The Theatre* admitted, "The truth is that 'His Little Widows' is so-so. It would be better if people weren't always interrupting the plot to 'sing.' When they dance, it's not so bad. But the story of the thing is its best ingredient. The lines are frequently bright and the music tinkles, though without distinction."[59] The *New York Evening Mail* praised Young for her restraint in the subject matter: "You can see that a certain delicacy of treatment is necessary with so intimate a subject, and Mrs. Young has succeeded in saving it from anything worse than a common allusion or two. It is not quite so pure as the driven snow, but it is nearly as clean as rainwater, which is pretty good for a polygamous comedy on Broadway."[60] And Lewis Sherwin of the *Globe* certainly had his opinion on how Young and Duncan split the writing duties:

> It is impossible to say which part of the book and lyrics of "His Little Widows" was contributed by Mr. Duncan and which by Mrs. Young. One is tempted to make a guess, but I suppose that would not be fair. At any rate the present condition suggests that somebody started with a capital comic opera idea and that somebody else tried with all the skill of long experience to spoil it but could not succeed.[61]

Clearly, Mr. Sherwin was not a fan of Mrs. Young. But at seventy-two performances, *His Little Widows* was the most successful of the collaborations of Young, Duncan, and Schroeder. It toured in 1918 under the new title *Some Little Girl*, but critics in the tour stops panned it. One claimed that shows like it represented "one of the many reasons why dramatic critics turn gray before their time."[62]

6

WILL YOU REMEMBER?

OPERETTA IN WARTIME

> People who go to the theatre want to laugh. There was a time when they came to weep, but few people come to weep now.
>
> Rida Johnson Young[1]

Beginning with *Brown of Harvard* in 1906, Rida Johnson Young had at least one show on Broadway in every season until 1921. The war years were her busiest, with eight new shows between 1914 and 1918, six of which were musicals. As she had so often before, she told a reporter how hard she worked: "I've had eighteen productions in about ten years. As I tear up half of what I write, you can figure out that I must have worked pretty steadily."[2]

Her first wartime success came in late 1916, a straight comedy called *Captain Kidd, Jr.* This one was produced by George M. Cohan and Sam H. Harris, a producing team from 1904 to about 1920. In it, a small-town bookseller discovers a treasure map that gets an entire Cape Cod town excited to find the buried treasure. But when the bookseller and his partners find the treasure chest, the only "treasure" it contains is some advice for living well: good health, fresh air, and honest work. Happily, the partners come into actual money as a result of their hunt when a cannery owner buys the land the treasure box was on from them and one member of the group gets a book deal. Some reviewers found the plot insipid, but one took them all to task for taking the farce too seriously: "Why anyone should proceed to criticize a comedy labeled a 'farcical adventure in three acts' by the same standards as would apply to a drama is incomprehensible. . . . We owe a deep debt of gratitude to any playwright who can make us laugh as Rida Johnson Young does."[3] Audiences paid little attention to the lukewarm reviews and kept *Captain Kidd, Jr.* open for a very respectable 128 performances.

The Shubert brothers adored operetta; we might call them "superfans" today. Biographer Foster Hirsch explains that J. J. Shubert "became a self-appointed custodian of a superannuated Broadway form, the sugar-spun operetta that took place somewhere over the rainbow."[4] The producers recognized its popularity in the United States and happily capitalized on it. And even though anti-German sentiment during World War I hurt most German imports, Lee and J. J. understood that the best operettas—and sources for American ones—came from Austria and Germany.[5] They offered Young two German-language scripts to develop for American theatergoers; those would eventually become *Her Soldier Boy* and *Maytime*. Hungarian composer Sigmund Romberg would supply the music, and the operettas would provide escapist nostalgia for war-weary American audiences. Young's final wartime musical, *Little Simplicity*, would give audiences some comic relief as the war came to an end.

HER SOLDIER BOY

Sigmund Romberg (1887–1951) was born in Hungary and studied music in Vienna before immigrating to the United States. He started his New York career playing piano in restaurants and supplying songs for Shubert revues, including *The Whirl of the World* and *The Passing Show* in 1914. Romberg proved himself valuable as an interpreter and adapter of Viennese operetta with *The Blue Paradise* in 1915, which led to three more adaptations. His scores for *Her Soldier Boy* and *Maytime* laid the foundation for his later American operetta standards *The Student Prince* (1924) and *The New Moon* (1928).

Young's first collaboration with Romberg may be more noteworthy for its context than its content. *Her Soldier Boy* was the first musical to deal with World War I, made even more significant by the fact that it was produced as the war was happening.[6] The timing created a unique challenge: how could an operetta address the fears and bloodshed of war without offending or alienating the audience? The answer: unabashed sentimentality. *Her Soldier Boy* presents an idealized version of life in Europe during wartime, occasionally addressing the looming danger but focusing primarily on its idyllic setting and romantic characters. *Her Soldier Boy* is based on a German play by Victor Léon called *Gold Gave I for Iron* (*Gold gab ich für Eisen*). Léon, also a native Hungarian, co-wrote the original German libretto for Franz Lehár's *The Merry Widow*. Using a literal translation of the original, Young crafted a new version, this time set in Belgium instead of its original Germany. Young opined, "Nobody would object to that. Everybody loves Belgium in these days. Even the Germans must pity it."[7] Among the changes necessary was a new title. In early correspondence, Young suggested *The War Bride*, *Arms and the Girl*, and *Her Gold for Her Boy*. By the summer of 1916, it was called *The Soldier Boy*. *Her* replaced *The* in the title sometime between its out-of-town tryout and its Broadway opening on December 6, 1916.

The Shuberts cast comic actor and writer Clifton Crawford as Teddy McLane, the American war correspondent and comic relief. Crawford was an Australian native who had come to the United States as an amateur golf champion and was discovered on a golf course by a Boston band director.[8] He went on to moderate fame for his original songs and lively performances of poems. The Shuberts agreed to interpolate some of his songs into *Her Soldier Boy*, and he received favorable reviews when the show opened. But Crawford apparently had some issues with the show. During its Boston tryout, he sent several frustrated telegrams to the Shuberts: "I want to notify you in all seriousness that the play is hopeless. Personally my part is all I could desire but I cannot bear the drama which is the cause of the failure. Therefore ask you to start something new for me."[9] Lee Shubert tried to reassure him:

> In reply will say that the public do not want any regular musical comedies anymore, and I am positive that the "Soldier Boy" will be a sensation in New York. It's the best part you have ever had and what the public seems to want nowadays is something different. . . . I still have a great deal of confidence in this play and don't want you to lose yours.[10]

Lee then alerted J. J. to Crawford's telegram and asked him to reply as well. When J. J. wrote Crawford to explain that he was busy with a hugely successful show at the Winter Garden Theatre, Crawford snapped, "I hope it's such a big success that you can leave it and pay attention to us."[11] There is no existing correspondence to indicate that Young knew of these exchanges or of Crawford's unhappiness, but the Shuberts evidently sided with the production over its star. They managed to placate him into staying with the production but continued to have artistic differences. Two letters from J. J. after the show's opening chide Crawford for trying to change his part. In one, J. J. advises Crawford not to interpolate a new song because "we are doing very well as it is" and reassures him that he will be happy to listen to the new song in the office and put it in if he likes it. Only a few weeks later, J. J. decided he was finished stroking Crawford's ego: "Apropos to submarines and other necessities of life, are you aware that we are running to 11:10 nightly? The show has increased ten minutes within the past three or four weeks. Will you please see what you can cut out, because, putting all jokes aside, our show is running too long."[12]

What did Lee Shubert mean by claiming that the public wanted something "different"? Was he referring to the war, or was there something beyond the typical musical comedy style in *Her Soldier Boy* that Lee felt the audiences would embrace?

Somewhere in Belgium

Her Soldier Boy begins with a prologue at an army camp, "behind the lines, somewhere in Belgium."[13] The soldiers and some local girls, unaware of the enemy's proximity, sing and dance, led by a young soldier named Alfred Appledorp. As the party disperses, two more soldiers, Frantz Delaunay and Alain Teniers, enter and discuss their hopes for a quick end to the fighting so that they may visit Frantz's family in the Belgian village of Ghistelle. Frantz is eager to return after fifteen years in the military, during which time his father has died, his mother has gone blind, and his younger sister, Marlene, has blossomed into a young woman. Alain has heard about Ghistelle so often he feels as though it is his home as well and has fallen in love with Marlene from her picture. Frantz, certain that he will never see his home again, gives Alain a ring his mother gave him and implores him to go to Ghistelle in his place and see that his mother and sister are cared for. Alain tries to dissuade him from his morbid thoughts but promises Frantz he will go. A sergeant enters to tell them that the enemy is approaching, and the two men prepare for battle and sing about the home they long to visit.

Act 1 takes place in Ghistelle, outside the castle in which Marlene and Mme. Delaunay live. Marlene sings happily with a group of children, one of whom reminds her of Frantz as a little boy. She has no idea what her brother looks like now but believes that he must be the most handsome soldier in his regiment. An American would-be war correspondent named Teddy McLane enters, followed by his disgruntled companion, Monty Mainwaring, who, having believed he would be assisting Teddy with war correspondence, has found himself relegated to bellhop. The town elders, Baron Van Artveldt and Vitus Appledorp (father of Alfred), come bearing good news for the Delaunays: Frantz's regiment is on its way into town. Marlene, overjoyed, goes to share the news with her mother. In the meantime, Marlene's American friend, Amy Lee, arrives with several schoolmates en route to Paris, but the war strands them in Belgium. Teddy is immediately smitten with Amy and concocts a plan to impress her, which involves Monty posing as a spy and Teddy heroically "capturing" him. Monty is arrested, protesting his innocence, and Amy becomes suspicious. The regiment finally comes into town, but instead of Frantz coming home, Alain enters, charged with informing the family that Frantz has been killed in battle. When Teddy and Marlene mistake him for Frantz, Alain, not wanting to hurt Mme. Delaunay, decides to go along with the charade.

Act 2 takes place inside the castle. Marlene's engagement announcement to either the baron's son or Appledorp's son (neither man knows the other wants her for his son) is to take place that evening. However, Alfred plans to marry a local girl named Desiree and asks for Teddy's help. Meanwhile, Amy has discovered Teddy's scheme and rescues Monty from prison, then proceeds to wait on the distressed man hand and foot. Furious and jealous, Teddy nevertheless hatches another plan: to trick Vitus into agreeing to any engagement Teddy arranges for Alfred. Vitus, believing that Teddy means to engage Alfred to Marlene, agrees, but he finds out too late that he has authorized the betrothal of Alfred and Desiree. As these various schemes are taking place, Marlene begins to find herself strangely attracted to Alain, even though she thinks he is her brother. Alain is mortified at having to pretend to be Frantz, especially because he is madly in love with Marlene. In two "love" duets (in quotes because Marlene believes she is singing with her brother), "Golden Sunshine" and "The Kiss Waltz," they grow closer, and Marlene finally realizes that Alain is not Frantz. When he explains who he really is, Marlene insists that they keep up the masquerade for her mother's sake, and they resign themselves to parting. Happily, a sergeant comes into town to report that Frantz has actually been recuperating from his near-fatal wounds and is now on his way to Ghistelle. Marlene and Alain now openly express their love, and

Figure 6.1 Beth Lydy and John Charles Thomas in a scene from Her Soldier Boy. *Photo by White Studio. © Billy Rose Theatre Division, The New York Public Library for the Performing Arts.*

Amy forgives Teddy and accepts his proposal of marriage. As the curtain falls, Frantz enters and embraces his family.

Home and "Mother"

Not surprisingly for a show set during the war, recurring themes of home permeate *Her Soldier Boy*. Many of the characters spend the show trying to either get home or find the place where they belong. Perhaps to lend the show universality, this theme extends to both the Belgian and the American characters. All Frantz's thoughts are of his childhood home—which he has not seen in fifteen

Figure 6.2 Clifton Crawford and Adele Rowland in a scene from Her Soldier Boy. *Photo by White Studio. © Billy Rose Theatre Division, The New York Public Library for the Performing Arts.*

years—darkened by a premonition that he will not return home alive. Alain does not speak of his own home but appropriates Frantz's, first in his thoughts, then literally as he impersonates the long-lost son. Although he does so unwillingly, Alain feels immediately as though he belongs in Ghistelle. The two main American characters, Teddy and Amy, are drawn to each other partly because of their shared heritage. Amy sings one of three songs in the show that contain the word "home" in the title, a wistful tribute to America called "I Want to Go Home." For the American audiences at the time, the depiction of Belgian soldiers fearing for their families' safety put a very human face on the war as the possibility of

American troops joining the war became a grim reality. However, the show's sentimentality glosses over the war's darkest aspects. Frantz rhapsodizes about "the little castle, the maple tree, the ramblers, the dear mother, the little sister."[14] The characters that populate Ghistelle speak very little about the war and do not seem particularly affected by it. It is difficult to tell whether Young did this on purpose, in order to spare the audience from coming face to face with the realities of war, or whether she had a somewhat naive view of a war whose horrific impact was not fully realized until it was over.

As a piece of drama, *Her Soldier Boy* shows some marked weaknesses. The balance between the various plots is uneven, even slightly confusing. The two romantic couples—Alain and Marlene, Teddy and Amy—have almost equal stage time, making it difficult to ascertain which couple is the primary and which is the secondary. They are only distinguished by their functions, one couple being the romantic, sentimental pair and the other providing comedy. But in the case of *Her Soldier Boy*, the comic (and presumably secondary) male love interest has several solo songs due to Crawford's interpolations. The two storylines are completely unrelated, except for those occasional references to home. Also, the characters in *Her Soldier Boy* are less fully realized than those from *Naughty Marietta* or Young's next outing, *Maytime*, even two-dimensional.

The real strength of *Her Soldier Boy* lies in its songs. Young's lyrics are unusually whimsical and, unlike her songs for *Naughty Marietta*, often use contemporary speech.[15] At times, Young uses heightened language to distinguish the European characters from the American ones. The songs enhance both the sentimental and the frivolous episodes and keep the more serious moments from becoming maudlin. Only the European characters use inverted syntax, adding another dimension to the quaint depiction of Ghistelle, such as in this section of "I'd Be Happy Anywhere with You," sung by Alfred and Desiree:

> DESIREE. I'll leave you never!
> ALFRED. We shall ever be together!
> DESIREE. Be it fair or stormy weather.
> ALFRED. I have nothing of worth to give, dear,
>   Poor and lowly we'll have to live, dear.[16]

Marlene and Alain frequently sing this way, too, as in "Golden Sunshine":

> ALAIN. How I wish that you would not soon married be.
> MARLENE. I don't care. I'll not wed if you forbid me!
> ALAIN. But, my dear, would you not be sorry?
> MARLENE. Try me then, and you shall see.
> ALAIN. Do you know, I find you quite charming, my dear?
> MARLENE. Such things 'tis odd from a brother to hear.[17]

The American characters use a more familiar, "down home" tone, and Sigmund Romberg's music matches the stylistic differences. While the European lovers sing in an operatic idiom, the Americans' songs are closer to musical comedy.[18]

Amy and the girls, having traveled through Europe and feeling homesick, deliver a musical postcard:

> Home again, no more to roam again,
> You see America first, take a tip from me.
> If you're wise, and you can stand surprise,
> Just go North, East, South or West,
> They will all stand the test.
> You can have tropic heat, or you can freeze your feet,
> We offer mountain, stream or bay,
> The kind of heaven that you want you'll find
> Right in the USA.[19]

The contrast is almost jarring, but we should again consider the context: anti-German sentiment was reaching an all-time high, so much so that Young and Romberg were compelled to change the play's setting. The possibility of going to war loomed over the United States. For the Shuberts, operetta might mean box-office success but could backfire if not handled sensitively. An interjection of patriotism could temper the audience's discomfort with a European setting and musical idiom. We may instead see the stylistic contrasts—even if they do not always work on the page—as Young and Romberg's attempt at a happy medium between romantic sentimentality and light comedy.

Young found another effective use of a common musical convention, rooted in the operatic leitmotif: the reprise. Musical comedies of the era would reprise songs—usually at the ends of acts—in the hopes that the audience would leave remembering the tune and buy the sheet music for it. Young had already experimented with a recurring musical theme as a plot point in *Naughty Marietta*. For *Her Soldier Boy*, she elevated the practice by reprising a full song but changing the words for a new context. "Song of Home"—first sung by Frantz in one scene, then by Alain in another—contains Young's most moving and effective lyrics. In its first iteration, Frantz, suspecting he will die in the next battle, implores Alain to visit his family and break the news of his passing:

> Greet for me the house aglow with flowers,
> Greet the spreading maple tree,
> The haunts that were so dear in childhood's hours,
> Greet them every one for me.
> The arbor where so often I sat dreaming,
> The dreams of youth that are so sweet and long,
> Oh, mother, I can see her fond eyes beaming . . .[20]

When Alain reaches Ghistelle with the news that Frantz is dead, he sings the reprise with new words:

> See, here is the house aglow with flowers,
> Here, the spreading maple tree,
> The place that was so dear in childhood's hours

> Frantz, I greet them all for thee.
> And here the place where often he sat dreaming,
> The dreams of youth that are so sweet and long.
> Alas, no more he'll see the fond eyes gleaming...[21]

Frantz's song has become Alain's. The song's poignancy grows as Alain reveals his final moments with Frantz. Young advances the plot through Alain's soliloquy, without the aid of dialogue. Not only do we learn what has happened to Frantz, but we see Alain's inner struggle to cope with the horrible task of reporting the young soldier's death to his family:

> Now must I bring the dreadful word,
> They'll see him, no, never.
> Their hearts to crush, their world to end,
> Their hopes o'er forever.
> When the shot and shell came flying,
> Was it meant for him or me?
> Just a shot and he lay dying,
> And I heard his last breath sighing,
> Would I had died for thee.[22]

In perhaps the darkest moment in the show, Young reveals that Alain suffers from survivor guilt and actually foreshadows the events to follow: his impersonation of Frantz and denial of his own identity. In effect, he does die for Frantz. When he meets Frantz's family, he cannot bring himself to tell them the truth and willingly hides his feelings for Marlene, thinking that the truth will kill Frantz's mother. We can only imagine the effect this might have had on an audience waiting to find out if the United States would enter the war. As she had done so beautifully with "Mother Machree," Young knew that nothing would resonate with her audience more than tugging at the "mother" heartstrings.

"The Tired Business Man's Dream"

Critics and audiences embraced *Her Soldier Boy* as a welcome distraction from the terrible news coming from the war front in Europe. Critics praised Young and the cast for keeping the mood "lighthearted." The *New York Times* called it "one of the most enjoyable musical plays to pass this way in the last five seasons."[23] Charles Darnton remarked, "Rida Johnson Young has taken this simple story from Victor Leon and turned it, with lyrics of her own invention, to excellent account."[24] Arthur Hornblow in *The Theatre* praised Young's "real, honest-to-goodness plot" along with the attractive cast, calling it "The Tired Business Man's Dream."[25] The Baltimore *Evening Sun* gave it an ambiguous review:

> It is a little difficult to classify this particular offering because of the extremely serious note that is occasionally introduced in the dialogue, but the piece follows somewhat the general plan of the older and more dignified operettas

with their many romantic incidents and quiet charm. It gains little from being "adapted" for American audiences.[26]

And while the critics praised most of the songs, unfortunately for Young, the most popular song to come out of *Her Soldier Boy* was not one of hers. "Smile, Smile, Smile"—better known as "Pack Up Your Troubles in Your Old Kit Bag"—was an interpolation by George Asaf and Felix Powell.

While it does not possess the sophistication of *Naughty Marietta* or the rich dramatic depth of Young's next project, *Maytime*, *Her Soldier Boy* appealed to the wartime audience by wearing its sentimentality on its sleeve and giving a happy ending to a potentially tragic story. *Her Soldier Boy* does not entirely succeed as a piece of dramatic literature and relies heavily on its charm to entertain, but it serves as a prime example of Rida Johnson Young's ability to write musical shows with broad appeal. Young would strike gold twice because of this talent, first with *Her Soldier Boy* and immediately after with *Maytime*.

MAYTIME

Early in the spring of 1917, the Shuberts acquired the rights to the German operetta *Wie einst im Mai* (*As Once in May*) with libretto by Rudolf Schanzer and Rudolf Bernauer, and music by Walter Kollo and Willy Bredschneider. In the play, twelve-year-old Ottilie is the daughter of the wealthy Colonel von Henkeshoven and engaged to her seventeen-year-old cousin, Cicero. But her young heart belongs to Fritz Juterbog, a worker on the estate. When Cicero insults Fritz because of his lowly station, Fritz leaves, determined to build his wealth and make Ottilie his wife when she comes of age. Sadly, Ottilie's betrothal is binding, and the second act finds her married to an unfaithful husband who slowly gambles away their fortune. When the now-wealthy Fritz runs into the couple at a nightclub, Cicero reveals that he is suing Fritz for a small piece of property on the estate that belonged to Fritz's father. Fritz then schemes to expose Cicero's infidelity (along with that of all the other philandering husbands at the club), hoping that Ottilie will leave her husband. But she has become accustomed to the situation and chooses to stay. In the third act, an older Fritz celebrates his booming business with his adult son at their new home—Colonel von Henkeshoven's estate. At the same time, news arrives that Fritz has been knighted. Cicero has died, but the lawsuit over the Juterbog property is still carrying on. Ottilie arrives, now remarried and relatively poor. She has come to ask permission for her daughter, Vera, a secretary under Fritz's employ, to marry one of his clerks, which is against company policy. Even though Fritz's widowed son has designs on Vera, Fritz, still besotted with Ottilie, approves the marriage. In act 4, Ottilie and Fritz have died, but their grandchildren meet at Vera's dress shop. Fred and Tilla—played by the same actors who portrayed Fritz and Ottilie—fall in love, then find out that the property that supposedly belonged to Fritz was Ottilie's and Tilla now inherits it. Fritz and Ottilie's love story will now continue with their grandchildren.[27]

Box 6.1 Her Soldier Boy

Lyrics and libretto: Rida Johnson Young
Music: Sigmund Romberg (based on Emmerich Kálmán)
Additional music and Lyrics: George Asaf, Augustus Barratt, Clifton Crawford, Felix Powell
Astor Theatre, Lyric Theatre, and Shubert Theatre; opened December 6, 1916; closed May 25, 1917 (198 performances)
Producers: Lee and J. J. Shubert

Major Cast

Teddy McLane . . . Clifton Crawford
Marlene Delaunay . . . Beth Lydy
Frantz Delaunay . . . Frank Ridge
Amy Lee . . . Adele Rowland
Alain Teniers . . . John Charles Thomas
Monty Mainwaring . . . Cyril Chadwick
Alfred Appledorp . . . Ward DeWolfe
Vitus Appledorp . . . Harold Vizard

Songs

"Mother" . . . Frantz
"Song of Home" . . . Alain and Frantz
"Fairy Song" . . . Marlene
"All Alone in a City of Girls" . . . Teddy and Peasant Girls
"I Want to Go Home" . . . Amy and Chorus
"He's Coming Home" . . . Marlene
"Song of Home" (reprise) . . . Alain
"I'd Be Happy Anywhere with You" . . . Alfred and Desiree
"Smile, Smile, Smile" . . . Amy and Boys (music by F. Powell, lyrics by G. Asaf)
"Slavery" . . . Teddy (music and lyrics by C. Crawford)
"Golden Sunshine" . . . Marlene and Alain
"Amsterdam" . . . Elsje (music and lyrics by A. Barratt)
"Kiss Waltz" . . . Marlene and Alain
"History" . . . Teddy (music and lyrics by C. Crawford)
"Military Stamp" . . . Teddy, Amy, and Chorus (music and lyrics by C. Crawford)

The United States declared war on Germany on April 6, 1917. With the official declaration, the simmering animosity toward German cultural imports boiled over into outright contempt. Now the Shuberts found themselves in a bind: they had already enlisted Young and Romberg to adapt *Wie einst im Mai*, but it would have to be completely removed from its German origins. The producers insisted on a total overhaul: none of the original German songs would appear in the New York version, and the libretto and score would be updated with American characters and musical styles. Despite threatened legal action by the German authors' American management office, the Shuberts left all mention of Schanzer, Bernauer, Kollo, and Bredschneider out of publicity notices.[28] As far as American audiences were concerned, Young and Romberg wrote *Maytime* after an authorless German play. At least, until Channing Pollock of the *Green Book Magazine* revealed the secret to his readers: "'Maytime' . . . is set down as the work of Rida Johnson Young and Sigmund Romberg. As a matter of fact, this is a bit of camouflage. The present unpopularity of Germans serves as excuse for crediting our own countrymen with accomplishments not properly theirs. Thus does questionable honesty masquerade as patriotism." He then named the four German authors of *Wie einst in Mai*.[29] But another reviewer, impressed with Young's handling of the material, reassured audiences that "It has been so successfully naturalized that no one need fear he is jeopardizing his patriotism in going to see it."[30]

Young—whose librettos frequently received varied reviews from critics—scored a dramaturgical victory in her second collaboration with Romberg. The *New York Times* review of the original production praised the story at length, while only briefly mentioning Romberg's music.[31] *Maytime* charmed critics and audiences alike and became one of Young's greatest artistic and financial successes. Her treatment of this story of unfulfilled love stretching across seven decades shows off another of her skills as a playwright: an adeptness for writing in an episodic form. Many of her plays and librettos employ standard climactic structure, in which events in the play turn on a central conflict that is resolved in a compressed period of time (such as a few days or weeks), and the events play out in cause-and-effect fashion. The events of *Maytime* transpire over several decades and involve four complete sets of characters (only a few characters reappear throughout). Its epic scope demands a different dramaturgical approach from that required of something like *Naughty Marietta*. With *Maytime*, Young displays her range of ability: not only can she alternate between the genres of musical and non-musical theater, comic and serious, but she manages to cross dramatic structural forms with ease.

Once upon a Time in Washington Square

In uncertain times, the musical theater can transport audiences and provide comfort and reassurance in the form of songs, dances, and stories that reflect the values of a bygone era. Take, for instance, the overwhelming success of such shows as *Oklahoma!* in the middle of World War II, the 1971 revival of *No, No, Nanette* during the Vietnam War, and the rash of jukebox musicals like *Mamma Mia* and *Jersey Boys* following the September 11, 2001, terrorist attacks. Young filled *Maytime* with American—specifically New York—references, images, and people, infusing it all with a palpable nostalgia. Most of the action takes place at historic Washington Square in Greenwich Village, Manhattan. The opening stage directions call for a backdrop that "shows New York as it was in 1840."[32] The moment the curtain rose, the audience would have recognized the city as their parents and grandparents would have described it to them (or, if they were older than seventy, as they had known it themselves). Although long past, this world would have been familiar to them and given them an immediate point of reference. Young peppered the script with recognizable characters like Martin Van Buren, P. T. Barnum, Jenny Lind, Buster Brown, and Andrew Carnegie. Many of the songs provide a musical trip down memory lane, the most notable being the slightly naughty "It's a Windy Day on the Battery," which recalls the practice of promenading in pairs along the river, and a new take on the old minstrel song, "Jump, Jim Crow!" The waltz duet for the star-crossed lovers, "Will You Remember?" is classic romantic operetta.

The story of *Maytime* spans more than seventy years, beginning in 1840 and ending in the present day of 1917. Young retained some plot elements of *Wie einst im Mai* while converting it to an American location. Ottilie Van Zandt (sixteen years old in Young's version), the precocious daughter of a wealthy colonel and industrial supplier, falls in love with one of his workers, Richard Wayne ("Fritz" in the original). Colonel Van Zandt regards the love affair as "childish sweet-hearting" and, dismissing his daughter's pleas, insists that she marry one of her cousins to keep the money within the family. The lovers promise their enduring devotion to each other and seal their bond by placing mementos of their love under a young apple tree Richard has given Ottilie for her birthday. Included are a ring, a lock of Ottilie's hair, and the words to "their" song (the much-loved "Will You Remember?" also known as "Sweetheart") written on a sheet of blue paper that, unknown to the pair, also happens to be a promissory note from Richard's father, John Wayne, to Colonel Van Zandt for Wayne's farmhouse on 59th Street (later Columbus Circle). When Ottilie's cousin, Claude ("Cicero" in the original), catches the lovers together, the colonel orders Richard off the property. Richard leaves, vowing to return for Ottilie as soon as he has made an independent living.

The secondary plot and the comic-relief character are also introduced in the first act. Matthew, a lazy but good-hearted woman chaser, must marry the colonel's sister-in-law, Mathilde, who has recently come into an inheritance, or pay off all his debts to the colonel. This marriage will be the first of four for Matthew over the course of the show. In the original, he was "Methusalem," no doubt so named because he will live to be more than one hundred years old. He is a villain in *Wie einst im Mai*, but Young must have decided only one villain was necessary and that she could do more with a comic character.

Act 2 opens fifteen years later. Claude and Ottilie have been married for twelve years, and Claude spends his time wasting the family money gambling at Madame Delphine's nightclub. This particular night, Delphine announces that she has some very special guests coming: P. T. Barnum, with two of his leading entertainers, and none other than the millionaire Richard Wayne. Claude, furious at this news, grills Matthew about the lost promissory note that would transfer the Wayne property to his wife and, by extension, to him. In the meantime, Ottilie sneaks into the parlor with her friend Alice, intending to spy on Claude. Richard arrives to find Ottilie a changed woman. They sadly remember the old days, realizing that they can never be together as they had once dreamed. When Claude catches them together and threatens to drag Ottilie's name through the

Figure 6.3 Peggy Wood as young Ottilie in Maytime. *Photo by White Studio. © Billy Rose Theatre Division, The New York Public Library for the Performing Arts.*

mud, Matthew tells him that Richard is actually there to propose to Alice—which he does, to Ottilie's relief and heartbreak.

Act 3 takes place twenty-five years later, back in the Washington Square home, which Ottilie, faced with her late husband's gambling debts, must sell in order to live. Richard arrives to see Ottilie one last time, bringing along his young grandson, Dicky, to whom he has taught the love song Richard and Ottilie sang in the first act. He secretly purchases the house and all its contents and delivers the property deed through his personal assistant, sneaking away before Ottilie can refuse his gift. This brief act transitions into act 4 and the present day. Ottilie's granddaughter, also named Ottilie (and played by the same actress as the older Ottilie) now runs a dressmaker's shop in the Washington Square house. Dicky Wayne (the now-grown grandson of Richard, also played by the same actor) has been buying gowns for the "Follies" girls as an excuse for visiting the shop and wooing Ottilie. She views his extravagance as wasteful and disapproves of his attitude toward his own inheritance. She reveals that business has not been as good as she has led him to believe and expresses the fear that she may have to close. Meanwhile, the old apple tree has died, and Ottilie is having it removed. Dicky protests, reminding her that the tree belongs to both of them and represents the love that their grandparents had for each other. In an effort to win her over, he sings Richard and Ottilie's love song, causing Ottilie to change her mind about removing the tree, but it is too late: the tree has fallen. A worker enters with the old jewel case. Matthew, now ninety years old, recognizes the blue paper as the lost promissory note. They all realize that because the property has dramatically increased in value, Ottilie is now a rich woman. She and Dicky turn to each other and sing "Will You Remember?" fulfilling the promise of their grandparents' love.

Money Changes Everything

Like *Naughty Marietta*, class structure plays a large part in the lives of the characters. While the characters in *Naughty Marietta* attempt to escape their class distinctions, their views on class do not affect the action or the show's central plot of Marietta's search for her true love. In *Maytime*, class conflicts have a direct bearing on the actions of the characters and create the situation that keeps the primary couple apart. Young uses the gap between the wealthy and the working class to heighten the dramatic tension and drive the plot.

Throughout the first act, the Van Zandts take care to remind Richard that his working-class status makes him unworthy of a place in their family. Although Colonel Van Zandt thinks very highly of Richard, his admiration does not extend to regarding him as an equal. He does not mind Richard's attention toward Ottilie as long as they are children, but when Richard insists that he will marry Ottilie, the colonel flatly refuses to even consider it:

> COLONEL. Silence! There must be an end of this nonsense. You must remember your station, young man.
> RICHARD. I'll better my station, sir. You'll see. I'll work to be worthy of her.
> COLONEL. Ottilie, come to me at once—
> OTTILIE. I love him father, I'll never give him up!
> COLONEL. You will do as I say. Understand Richard, my daughter is not for you.[33]

Young uses language to highlight class differences, distinguishing them by speech patterns, as in this exchange between Claude and Richard:

> CLAUDE. Same rude specimen of health as ever, I see.
> RICHARD. You haven't changed much, either. I think I could whale the tar out of you just as I used to.

OTTILIE. I hope you two aren't going to quarrel again.
CLAUDE. I never quarrel with my social inferiors.[34]

It seems that class distinction is stronger than moral character, and not just for the older members of the family. Despite having played with him when they were children, Claude Van Zandt displays an overt disgust for Richard. The difference in tone between Claude's use of "specimen" and "inferiors" and Richard's use of "whale the tar out of you" illustrates the social gap separating them. Even the somewhat dotty Mathilde calls Richard one of the "proletariat" and looks down her nose at him.[35]

The missing promissory note also provides a vehicle for the class conflict evident in *Maytime*. Claude's relentless pursuit of the 59th Street property stems from both his greed and his dislike for Richard because of his status, not because he feels any jealousy about Ottilie's feelings for him. Securing the property would solidify his own status and keep Richard down, as well as bring an additional source of income. Even when Richard returns as a millionaire, Claude cannot see Richard as his equal. The note serves a somewhat symbolic purpose as well; how they value money defines many of the characters in *Maytime*. Wayne gives Colonel Van Zandt the promissory note because he has borrowed money from the colonel and puts up the property as collateral. Van Zandt, although he is a successful businessman who appreciates the value of hard work and marries Ottilie to Claude specifically to protect the family fortune, is surprisingly cavalier about the money he lent to Wayne. He clearly does not grasp how seriously Wayne regards this money, calling it a "trifle." To the colonel, the loan is merely pocket change, but Wayne stakes the money against his integrity and his good name. When Van Zandt loses the note, he gives up the search quickly, again calling the debt a trifle. Matthew, present at this moment, also displays indifference to the debt. Matthew's lack of concern for the promissory note reflects his own attitude toward money. He simply feels entitled to financial freedom: he should not have to lift a finger to get it. He marries four times, to very wealthy women, and anytime the idea of working for a living comes up, he dismisses it. Claude also feels entitled, but his sense of entitlement leads to his bankruptcy. At the other end of the spectrum, Richard, like his father, sees earning money as a way to better himself, not because he is greedy but because making an honest living gives him pride. Unlike the younger Van Zandt men, he does not waste his money on frivolities but spends it carefully and unselfishly.

The financial situation of the Waynes and the Van Zandts is reversed in acts 3 and 4. Both Ottilies (grandmother and granddaughter) have seen reversals in their fortunes. The first Ottilie must sell everything her father has left to her, while Richard has attained great wealth. The second Ottilie resembles the young Richard, running her own shop and struggling to make ends meet. She is disgusted and dumbfounded by Dicky's apparent disregard for his fortune, telling him, "You're a waster—I'm a worker."[36] She has somehow developed the working-class ethic her family rejected at the beginning of the show, and Dicky, rather than following in his grandfather's footsteps, squanders the money Richard worked all his life to earn. They are, in effect, mirror images of the first Richard and Ottilie: one works hard to make an honest living, while the other takes money for granted with ignorant bliss.

Because *Maytime* attempts to depict a realistic love story, Young creates credible characters in their speech, behavior, and development. Even the more comic characters, like Matthew and his wives, resist outright caricature. The episodic structure of the piece aids in the realistic character portrayal as the characters grow and change over time. Ottilie undergoes the most drastic changes, particularly if we consider her granddaughter as an extension of herself. In the first act, sixteen-year-old Ottilie is on the brink of moving from childhood to adulthood. Her love for Richard blinds her to the reality of his social class, and her idealism gives her confidence that love will overcome her family's objections. She does not understand the power her family's money wields and cannot foresee that it will eventually destroy her life. Not only is she optimistic, but she also displays an adolescent penchant for melodrama:

> OTTILIE. Dick, I'll just wither up and fade away in the bloom of my youth and they'll bury me beneath the lilies in the vale, just like Lily Dale, and then perhaps you'll be sorry.
> RICHARD. Oh, don't, Ottilie!
> OTTILIE. Well, I won't then, because I know you wouldn't be mean enough to go back on all our plans. How we're going to defy the stern parent and live in our little cottage way out in the country with a big garden full of tulips and lilacs and love-lives-bleeding and heartsease . . .[37]

The young Ottilie is headstrong, ready to stand up to her father fearlessly when he forbids her to marry Richard. She has an unwavering belief in the power of love. But in act 2, we meet a very different Ottilie, whose forced marriage to a man she does not love has failed miserably. The loving spirit that had emanated from her seems to have disappeared, replaced by unhappiness and even bitterness: "I'm a frivolous woman now, Dick, living on the surface. Getting what I can from the froth of life."[38] When Claude enters and sees them together, it is easy to see why this marriage has left her devoid of any joy. Claude has forced her into a life of shallow decadence. The contrast in settings between act 1 and act 2—gentility versus debauchery—symbolizes the turn Ottilie's life has taken. By act 3, Ottilie has recovered some of the grace, strength, and gentility her marriage took from her. She admits to Richard that "I used to be bitter and resentful . . . but now I know better. I live in the sweet memories of the past."[39] The act 4 Ottilie embodies the headstrong spirit of her grandmother, as well as her sentimentality. She is determined to be self-sufficient and retain the house her grandmother left her, and she flatly refuses Dicky when he does not live up to the same standard as his grandfather. But the apple tree and the old love song attached to it force her to relent to her deep love for him.

Although Richard is one half of the main couple, he spends less time onstage than Ottilie or even Matthew, and his character does not change as drastically as Ottilie. His devotion to her remains strong throughout the play, even when he is forced to leave her three times. He is kind, chivalrous, dependable, and

Figure 6.4 Peggy Wood as an older Ottilie in Maytime. *Photo by White Studio. © Billy Rose Theatre Division, The New York Public Library for the Performing Arts.*

loving from beginning to end. His biggest change is not that he goes from rags to riches but that the determination to do so gives him the courage to stand up to Ottilie's father. When Richard and Van Zandt first appear together, Richard is respectfully meek toward the colonel, compelling Ottilie to call him a coward. The combination of the colonel's harping on the young lovers and Claude's brutal treatment of Richard seems to push him over the edge. He retains his dignity, but he will no longer stand for being called an inferior. This change comes to fruition by act 3 in a telling exchange with his assistant, Rutherford. When Rutherford hesitates to carry out his boss's wishes, Richard tersely responds, "I am accustomed, Rutherford, to having my instructions obeyed, no matter how difficult or expensive."[40] Not only has Richard attained his goal of financial independence, but he has gone beyond it to a position of power. However, the only trait he passes on to Dicky is his love for Ottilie. Dicky is willing to change his ways for her, but the money means little to him.

Because of its epic scope, Young gives *Maytime*'s secondary and tertiary characters ample attention, fleshing them out into fully realized characters whose actions relate strongly to the main plot. Although ostensibly the comic character in *Maytime*, Matthew Van Zandt provides more than comic relief. True, he spends most of the show wooing women and singing the uptempo dance numbers; rarely does a profound thought cross his mind. But unlike Silas Slick, for example, whose only function in *Naughty Marietta* is to play the clown, Matthew also advances two vital plot points, and in both instances he proves himself to be a sympathetic ally to Richard and Ottilie. In act 2, when Claude accuses Richard and Ottilie of trying to renew their love affair, the quick-thinking Matthew, remembering that the gypsy at Ottilie's birthday party predicted that Richard would marry Alice, comes up with a plan:

> MATTHEW. You'll see, my dear cousin, that you are sadly mistaken. You say that you found your wife here with Wayne and in tears. Well, I happen to know they were tears of happiness for her friend, Miss Tremaine. You'll forgive me, Wayne, for thus making your little romance public, but I think we owe it to Ottilie.
> RICHARD. Go on.
> MATTHEW. Our very good friend, Richard Wayne, has come back to America with the avowed purpose of asking Miss Tremaine to be his wife! . . . Am I right, Wayne?[41]

Matthew has no personal stake in what transpires between Claude and Richard, but his love for Ottilie and her daughter compels him to intervene. After Richard proposes to Alice, Matthew rushes to Ottilie's side to steady her, and when she faints, he holds her in his arms. He continues to play a role in Ottilie's life, returning in the third and fourth acts to revisit their old home. Also, Matthew is present in act 1 when Colonel Van Zandt loses the promissory note from Wayne. By the last act, he is the only surviving family member who knows anything about the note and therefore recognizes the significance of the faded blue paper found in the jewel casket. Most important, he serves as a symbolic foil for Richard and Ottilie. While they struggle to find a way to be together, Matthew finds marital bliss four times. He ostensibly marries these women for their money, but each of the marriages lasts until the respective wife dies, and Matthew speaks of each of them lovingly.

Under the Apple Tree

Through the apple tree that Ottilie and Richard plant, Young employs a strong central image symbolizing the show's theme of true love surviving insurmountable odds and living on after death. The tree's three stages—as a seedling, in full bloom, and at death—mirror the stages of Richard and Ottilie's love, though not as obviously as we might expect. Richard inadvertently foreshadows their affair's demise when he brings out the tree and tells Ottilie, "I had a time persuading Father to let me transplant it. He said it was too young."[42] Just as the tree may not survive an early upheaval, so Richard and Ottilie are too young and naive to defy their families' objections, and therefore, their love will not be allowed to thrive. When they try to assert themselves, the colonel cuts them off, choking the relationship before it can grow any further. The tree's absence in the second act leaves the audience to assume that the tree has died, as Richard implied it might. Hope is renewed when, in act 3, the apple tree has come into full bloom. Perhaps the lovers will unite after all? But this time, the tree's blossoms deceive: though Richard and Ottilie still love each other deeply, they can never fully realize that love and must part again. They regretfully let go of the dream of their children playing under the tree. At the same time, young Dicky runs around it, possibly foreshadowing another love blossoming under the tree. But the tree's death in act 4 seems to put an end to that possibility. The second Ottilie is removing the dead tree, essentially ending the love affair that began more than seventy years earlier. However, the death of the tree finally comes to symbolize the birth of a new love, the seeds of which have been passed down through the generations. Rather than ending Richard and Ottilie's love, the tree's demise renews it in their grandchildren.

The tree even inspired a publicity stunt. With her love for gardening well known, Young planted an apple tree on her estate in Stamford with the help of the show's stars, Peggy Wood and Charles Purcell. And a photographer from *Theatre Magazine* just happened to be there to capture it (see figure 6.5).[43]

Young's flair for nostalgic images resonates beautifully in the three major duets for Richard and Ottilie, "In Our Little Home, Sweet Home," "Will You Remember?" and "The Road to Paradise." They dream of a quiet life together, uncomplicated by money or concerns about social status. "In Our Little Home, Sweet Home" and "The Road to Paradise" are really two halves of the same song. The first contains traditional domestic images, like a "little kettle on the fire" and a "little home," which reflect the values of the early Victorian era. However, the prevailing imagery rings with the surreal and unattainable dreams of two people who have yet to experience the real world:

> There's a home in the land, the fair land of my dreams,
> That's waiting for you and me,
> And love to that haven will show us the way,
> And give us the golden key.
> We'll enter therein and shall know all the joy,
> In the Kingdom of Heart's desire.[44]

The lyrics are heartbreakingly idealistic, even childish. The audience must guess that they will at least run into a few snags trying to find that "golden key." However, the poetic nature of the song also reflects the sentiment of the 1840s. The twentieth century brought with it a change in the old values. Women

Figure 6.5 Rida Johnson Young (center), Peggy Wood, and Charles Purcell planting a tree on Young's estate in a publicity photo for Maytime. *Theatre Magazine, July 1918. Billy Rose Theatre Division, The New York Public Library.*

began to enter the workforce, some out of necessity, but many because they felt they finally had a choice; it was no longer enough to strive for the "hearth and home." More and more people lived in urban areas, so the image of that hearth and home had also changed dramatically. The original audiences at *Maytime* may have appreciated revisiting the simpler era in which Richard and Ottilie live. As in *Naughty Marietta*, Young uses a slightly archaic language to place the characters in their world. As the show moves forward in time, the language changes. When Richard and Ottilie meet fifteen years later, their song is now an expression of the dream they have lost:

> To Paradise, ah dear, I've lost the way,
> So far I've gone astray.
> No hand to clasp in mine,
> No guiding star!
> Ah, Love! Lead me where you are,
> In your loving eyes,
> There my Paradise lies.[45]

The song becomes even more poignant when sandwiched between the two scenes featuring P. T. Barnum and his performers. In the first scene, Barnum lectures his stars about the importance of "selling" themselves: the operatic tenor must "try to look as if [he] had lived and suffered," and the Spanish dancer must not let on that she has a family to support. When the dancer protests that she is a respectable woman, Barnum cries, "For the love of heaven, Amorita, forget your husband and your respectability! . . . Wouldn't you rather be popular than respectable?"[46] These scenes serve two key purposes: one is to set act 2 firmly in 1855 and give the audience a chance to revisit one of America's greatest impresarios; the other is to juxtapose the life Richard and Ottilie wanted for themselves, a life of quiet gentility, with the looser morals of the life into which Claude forces Ottilie. When Richard and Ottilie recall the "Paradise" they had hoped to find together, the preceding scene renders that paradise pathetic. Ottilie would love nothing more than to settle down with the safe and loving Richard, but she must keep up appearances as Claude's wife. She must "sell" herself just as Barnum's performers do.

To give the act a nostalgic flavor, Young includes diegetic songs modeled after some popular tunes of 1855, most notably her own version of the minstrel song "Jump Jim Crow." The original debuted around 1828, written and performed by Thomas D. Rice in his blackface minstrelsy act in London. His version is extremely problematic today, filled with racist diction and images:

> Come listen all you galls and boys, I's jist from Tuckyhoe,
> I'm going to sing a little song, my name's Jim Crow,
> Weel about and turn about and do jis so,
> Eb'ry time I weel about and jump Jim Crow.[47]

Young's version does away with most of the racial overtones and focuses on the social-dance aspect:

> It's a dance that's rather shocking
> To a spinster or a frump,
> For it's apt to show your stocking
> When you make the little jump.
> They tell me that Victoria,
> Who's very strict you know,
> Bars everybody from the court
> Who jumps Jim Crow.
> Jump, jump, oh, jump, Jim Crow!

> Take a little twirl and around you go!
> Slide, slide and point your toe,
> You're as naughty as a devil
> When you jump Jim Crow![48]

While minstrelsy was reaching the height of its pre–Civil War popularity in 1855, it is unclear why Young chose that particular song to rewrite. Perhaps she thought it would be the most recognizable title, or that adapting a Stephen Foster tune would not go over well, as his songs were still extremely popular at the beginning of the twentieth century. While Young's version does not entirely divorce itself from its source—the dance portion is similar and the implication that the dance makes one "naughty as a devil" could be interpreted as racist—she thankfully stays away from the problematic plantation caricature that Rice and later minstrel performers normalized.

"Will You Remember?"

Young and Romberg borrowed a technique from *Wie einst im Mai* with multiple reprises of a love song for Ottilie and Richard that would ultimately transfer to their grandchildren. The German Fritz and Ottilie sing:

> SHE: That was in Schonberg in the month of May
> HE: There was a little maid so bright and gay
> SHE: She kissed the little boy right merrily
> HE: For that's in Schonberg the thing to do.[49]

Ottilie and Fritz sing this twice: at the end of act 1, when Fritz leaves to pursue his fortune, and at the end of act 3, when they regretfully part for the last time. Tilla and Fred (their respective grandchildren) declare that they will "make up for all that Grandmama missed" and refrain it one last time with the new words: "And now the play is done / As fades the day / 'Twas once in Schonberg / In the month of May."[50]

Young and Romberg came up with a decidedly more romantic sentiment for their version. If the apple tree visually represents Richard and Ottilie's love, "Will You Remember?" is its musical equivalent. In much the same way that "Ah! Sweet Mystery of Life" operated as a plot device, "Will You Remember?" uses nostalgia as a dramatic tool. The lyrics anticipate the song's reprisal:

> I'll love you in life's gray December,
> The same as I love you today,
> My heart, ever young, will remember
> The thrill it knew that day in May.
> Sweetheart, sweetheart, sweetheart,
> Will you love me ever?
> Will you remember this day,
> When we were happy in May,
> My dearest one?

> Sweetheart, sweetheart, sweetheart,
> Though our paths may sever,
> To life's last faint ember
> Will you remember
> Springtime, love time, May?[51]

The first time Richard and Ottilie sing this, they are looking to the future and assuming that they will be sitting under the tree with their children when they reminisce about this day. As with "In Our Little Home, Sweet Home," the dream seems too good to be true. We wonder if they will remember, or if time and circumstance will pull them apart. Note Young's use of the long "a" vowel in "gray," "same," "day," and "May." Of the three duets for the lovers, this one uses the simplest rhyme scheme, illustrating their youth and idealism. The rhymes come easily because their love is pure and true. Young uses a similar rhyme scheme in "The Road to Paradise," but this time the sound voices a lament:

> To Paradise, the land so far away,
> The land of endless day!
> To Paradise, ah dear, I've lost the way,
> So far I've gone astray.[52]

With this song, the realization that they will never see their dream come true hits them fully, only to be brutally reminded of what they have lost when Barnum's tenor enters and sings "Will You Remember?" For the other characters in the show, the song is merely beautiful and a little sad, but it taunts Richard and Ottilie. The song they were supposed to have treasured has become painful to hear. However, just as the tree blossoms in act 3, "Will You Remember?" finally acquires its long-awaited nostalgic tone. When Dicky and Ottilie sing it in act 4, it is a new love song for them, but it has become nostalgic for the audience. This moment solidifies Young's genius for reaching a wartime audience: by having the characters of two generations later reprise the song, it reassures the audience that the world they know will live on through their children. In a review—or, perhaps more accurate, an emotional response—to the show, *New York Times* writer John Corbin waxed philosophical about its more profound themes: "In the world of today, as it seems, the hope of personal immortality is fading—of a heaven that will give us all that earth denied; but many in whom hope still springs unquenchable look forward to immortality of a sort in their children, and their children's children."[53]

Maytime went on to a hugely successful run of 492 performances, two national tours, and a Canadian production in 1921. Though reviews were lukewarm—*Theatre Magazine* opined that "it has so slight a plot, and is so filled with episode and obvious theatrical expedients to piece out with, that it is astonishing what charm it has"—the public loved it.[54] Corbin, having obviously enjoyed the show, took Young to task, saying that she "has done some violence to our local color and atmosphere, [but] the essentials of the story are retained."[55] Apparently, his vision of old New York differed from hers.

Maytime *on Film*

With the success of the stage version, the Shuberts wanted to shop around the film rights to *Maytime*. As always, Young was adamant about her compensation:

> I am not willing to sell the motion picture rights to my adaptation of "Wie Einst Im Mai" which you produced under my title of "Maytime" for less than five thousand dollars as my share. We sold the picture rights to "Captain Kidd, Jr." for ten thousand dollars and I am sure that "Maytime" has a far better commercial value than that play.[56]

Louis J. Gasiner directed a silent version in 1923, with Ethel Shannon and Harrison Ford in the leading roles. Clara Bow—the original "It Girl"—appeared as Alice Tremaine. Segments of the original film have since been lost, but the movie stayed faithful to the stage version. MGM made another version in 1937, the third vehicle for Jeanette MacDonald and Nelson Eddy. The film of *Naughty Marietta* had been a breakout hit for the new pair, followed by *Rose-Marie* in 1936. Director Robert Z. Leonard and writer Noel Langley scrapped Young's libretto and Romberg's score, keeping only "Will You Remember?"[57] The film's plot bears no resemblance to the stage version and contains not a single line of Young's libretto. Instead, MacDonald plays an opera singer who gives up love (in the form of another opera singer, played by Eddy) for her career. Perhaps the original plot was considered quaint and dated twenty years later, or maybe the filmmakers thought that making MacDonald and Eddy into opera singers would create more opportunities for them to sing onscreen. In any case, Young's work—as well as Romberg's—is virtually absent from the film version of *Maytime*.

Box 6.2 Maytime

Lyrics and libretto: Rida Johnson Young
Music: Sigmund Romberg
Additional lyrics: Cyrus Wood
Shubert Theatre, 44th Street Theatre, Broadhurst Theatre, and Lyric Theatre; opened August 16, 1917; closed October 19, 1918 (492 performances)
Producers: Lee and J. J. Shubert

Major Cast

Ottilie Van Zandt / Ottilie (act 4) . . . Peggy Wood
Richard Wayne / Dicky Wayne (act 4) . . . Charles Purcell
Claude Van Zandt . . . Douglas J. Wood
Alice Tremaine . . . Laura Arnold
Matthew Van Zandt . . . William Norris
John Wayne . . . Richard Morgan
Colonel Van Zandt . . . Carl Stall

> **Songs**
>
> "In Our Little Home, Sweet Home" . . . Ottilie and Richard
> "It's a Windy Day on the Battery" . . . Matthew, Alice, and Girls
> "Gypsy Song" . . . Rudolfo
> "Will You Remember (Sweetheart)?" . . . Ottilie and Richard
> "Jump Jim Crow" . . . Matthew and Chorus
> "The Road to Paradise" . . . Ottilie and Matthew
> "Will You Remember?" (reprise) . . . Signor Vivalla
> "Odd Lots, Job Lots" . . . Ensemble
> "Reminiscence" . . . Little Dicky
> "Selling Gowns" (lyrics by C. Wood) . . . Ottilie and Girls
> "Dancing Will Keep You Young" (lyrics by C. Wood) . . . Matthew and Ermintrude
> "Only One Girl for Me" . . . Dicky and Girls
> "Will You Remember?" (reprise) . . . Ottilie and Dicky

LITTLE SIMPLICITY

With music by Augustus Barratt, *Little Simplicity* premiered days before the armistice ending World War I. As the war had been winding down for several weeks, perhaps the time was right for a more comic look at soldiers in the midst of war. As she had done with *Her Soldier Boy* and *Maytime*, Young kept the war at arm's length, only referencing it in the third act and in a lighthearted tone. Once again, she populated the script with a handful of American characters who begin the play as expatriates and wind up as soldiers in the end, much like the American characters in *Her Soldier Boy* who join the Red Cross to aid their brothers in the cause. Young also ended *Little Simplicity* on a somewhat somber note: the lovers are last seen going to the front lines together. The violence and bloodshed wrought by new military technology in this "war to end all wars" had stunned the world and brought a sobering new perspective to the concept of war, which Young captures somewhat in the final moments of *Little Simplicity*.[58]

Originally titled *Miss I-Don't-Know*, *Little Simplicity* went through several title changes and at least one full draft before being submitted for rehearsals. In a letter to the Shuberts on January 3, 1918, Young explains that she wants to add six new songs and asks, "Will you kindly have Romberg or whomever you wish to do this music call me up and make an appointment to see me about the numbers." A few weeks later, she wrote again to make some casting suggestions, even proposing a specialty dance number for Fred and Adele Astaire.[59] (Sadly, she did not get her request.)

Unfortunately, the skillful epic writing Young demonstrated in *Maytime* merely a year earlier is strangely absent in *Little Simplicity*. Despite all of Young's experience writing musicals up to this point, *Little Simplicity* suffers from an uneven script that takes place over five years and three locations. This may be partly due to the fact that *Little Simplicity* incorporates a great deal of comedy, both verbal and physical, with stage directions for "business" scattered throughout the script. It mirrors the unevenness of Her Soldier Boy, which suggests Young's own difficulty finding an appropriate balance between comedy and sentiment in a wartime show. *Little Simplicity* does not traffic in sentimentality, but neither does it reach for high comedy; it seems stuck somewhere in between and struggles to achieve the right tone. As with *Sometime*, this appears to be a musical comedy with operetta-like characters in the lovers Alan and Veronique, who are separated because of a misunderstanding and only come back together as Alan heads to certain death on the front lines. Meanwhile, the other characters engage in a farce in which the nervous egghead Professor Erasmus Duckworth (Ducky) tries to escape from the dangerous feminine clutches of the worldly Lulu, Veronique's self-appointed guardian. The juxtaposition of the main plot (Alan and Veronique) and the subplot (Ducky and Lulu) is fundamentally the same as in *Her Soldier Boy* and *Sometime*. *Little Simplicity* works somewhat better than *Her Soldier Boy* because the primary characters interact more with the secondary characters, but *Sometime* balances the plots more easily: the lines between the comic and the sentimental blur, giving both plots a similar tone. *Little Simplicity* cannot decide whether it is a comedy or a drama, so the audience gets pulled in two directions throughout.

Little Simplicity represents Young's most ambitious foray into exotic operetta. The first act takes place in Tunisia in 1912, where a French expatriate and his daughter, Clavelin and Lulu, run a cafe and supply the local nobles with harem girls. The favorite is the beautiful Veronique, nicknamed "Little Simplicity" for her purity and innocence. As the show opens, a cry calling the people to prayer interrupts a harem girl's performance:

> *At end of dance, people without any shouts or other applause knock with knuckles on floor to signify approval. . . . One hears outside a voice intoning.*
> MAN. Allah! Allah! Mohammed Resul Allah! Allah il Allah, Mohammed Resul Allah! [sic]
> *After this, there is a beat of tom-toms from outside and girl . . . runs to door where the Sheik suddenly appears. She shrinks back, throwing herself on ground before him. Everyone salaams.*
> SHEIK. Bishmallah. [sic]
> *People rise and stand, evidently in awe of Sheik.*[60]

Young supplies specific details about Islamic behavior and language and employs the expressions "La ilah illa Allah, Mohammed Rasul Allah" ("No god but Allah, Mohammed is the messenger of Allah") and "Bismillah" ("In the name of God.").[61] She also makes it clear that this will not be a Montgomery and Stone comedy about Americans getting into mischief in Africa; she calls for the tom-toms to be heard again "to give a sort of mystery and menace to the scene."[62] Act 2 takes place in Paris's Latin Quarter. Here, Young depicts the bohemian life, indicating artistic graffiti on the walls and an old tree growing out of the concrete courtyard. References to the evening's masked ball, for which all the young men have planned to dress as Pierrot, the "sad clown" of commedia dell'arte, enhance the romantic mood. Setting the third act in an American army camp near the front lines provides the audience with a glimpse into army life without the imminent battle encroaching on the scene, as it does in the prologue of *Her Soldier Boy*. All the play's locations lend exoticism to the story, enhanced by the operetta plot and tempered by the familiarity of American characters.

Yet again, Young uses class conflict as a major plot element. The main issue occurs in the relationship between Alan and Veronique. Veronique has worried all along that Alan would dismiss her because he is from a higher class, and she confides to Lulu that she feels Alan is above her. In what may be Young's most revealing piece of dialogue, Lulu answers, "No man is above any woman."[63] Their story borders on the tragic, particularly when Alan's father arrives to separate the two because his son is highborn and Veronique is an orphan of questionable values. Lulu aptly comments that the elder Van Cleeve's arrival smacks of the "Camille" story and snaps, "Don't expect me to supply the weeps."[64] We have seen similar plot lines in *Maytime* and *Naughty Marietta*. However, Ottilie and Marietta stand up to those who try to keep them with members of their own class; even the quadroon Adah eventually seizes an opportunity to break out of her oppressive position. Veronique does not stand up for herself; rather, she allows herself to be intimidated by those of the higher classes. She only rises to fame in the end because of Lulu. Young also hints at a class tension between Lulu and Ducky. Ducky is slightly afraid of Lulu because of her status as a streetwise entertainer, and it is Ducky who sends for Alan's father to break up the relationship. Ducky's academic standing puts him in a higher class than Lulu; ironically, by the third act, he has abandoned the academic life and become a nightclub owner. Class roles are reversed by the end of the show: Veronique is famous thanks to Lulu's guidance, Ducky is now part of the "lowbrow" class, and Alan is a soldier.

Little Simplicity premiered exactly one month after *Sometime*, which may explain some of the script's weaknesses. Young's libretto seems thrown together, save for the attention to detail in the first act. Many of the scenes are so overwritten they become tedious. Young's usual talent for dramatic economy fails her in scenes such as one in which the following events take place: Jack tries to convince Lulu to choose him over Ducky; Ducky enters and confronts Lulu about her reputation for dating several men at once; Jack tricks Ducky into thinking Lulu only wants him for his money; then, when Lulu gets angry and leaves, Jack gives Ducky a pistol with which to threaten to kill himself so that Lulu will forgive him. The scene lasts for twelve pages (and contains two songs), during which time no other character enters the stage. Young completely abandons the Alan/Veronique plot for a scene that might have worked better had it been cut in half. Because it is so long, the various tricks Jack contrives to break up Lulu and Ducky never pay off. Other scenes are simply too short to be effective. Much of Young's dialogue is flat, as in this excerpt from act 2:

> DUCKY. I know you are going to lose your temper. Time and time again you have been taken home from a cabaret by a man.
> LULU. It has happened.

DUCKY. Now I know you are going to lose your temper. You unlock the door—
LULU. Naturally.
DUCKY. Now I know you are going to lose your temper.
LULU. Then—
DUCKY. Oh gee—oh gosh—and he—oh, Lulu, he goes in with you.
LULU. No, that man has never been born. . . . I have had my eyes open to the world since I was that high, I saw that men liked to spend their money on the kind they think I am, but I am not the kind they think I am, I'm the kind they think I'm not—and if they think I am—
DUCKY. Just a minute, I think I am losing the connection.[65]

So is the audience. *Little Simplicity*'s characters talk in circles, rarely make coherent points, and repeat themselves. This is not the quick, sparkling dialogue we have come to expect from Young.

She also seems to have transplanted the main characters from *Sometime* to *Little Simplicity*. Veronique starts out as a lowly flower girl, then rises to celebrity status as Victorine Del Mar, world-famous opera singer, much as Enid Vaughn goes from invisible chorus girl to leading lady. The cynical Lulu might be an older version of Mayme, and the half-nerdy, half-slick Ducky a younger Loney. Although operettas and musical comedies of the early twentieth century often featured similar character types, these feel too similar to be mere coincidence. Since Young had to have been working on both shows at the same time, it stands to reason that the characters would blend together. All of these issues are symptomatic of the pressure lyricists, librettists, and composers were under to produce as many works as they could whenever a powerful producer like J. J. Shubert called.

Box 6.3 Little Simplicity

Lyrics and libretto: Rida Johnson Young
Music: Augustus Barratt
Astor Theatre and 44th Street Theatre; opened November 4, 1918; closed February 8, 1919 (112 performances)
Producers: Lee and J. J. Shubert

Major Cast

Lulu Clavelin . . . Marjorie Gateson
Alan Van Cleeve . . . Carl Gantvoort
Veronique . . . Carolyn Thomson
Clavelin . . . Eugene Redding
Erasmus "Ducky" Duckworth . . . Charles Brown
The Sheik of Kudah . . . Ben Hendricks
Morgan Van Cleeve . . . Robert Lee Allen
Jezirah and Zillah . . . The Cameron Sisters

Songs

"Women" . . . Joseph
"Days of Youth" . . . Lulu, Alan, Jack, Pierre, Philip, and Joseph
"National Airs" . . . Lulu, Alan, Jack, Pierre, Philip, Joseph, and Ducky
"My Caravan" . . . Jack and Chorus
"Flower Song" . . . Veronique
"My Lulu" . . . Lulu, Ducky, and Jack
"You Don't Know" . . . Alan and Veronique
"First Love" . . . Pierre, Jack, and Philip
"Just a Little Sunshine" . . . Veronique
"Hush! Hush!" . . . Veronique, Alan, Pierre, Philip, Jack, and Grisettes
"Maybe You'll Look Good to Me" . . . Lulu, Ducky, and Girls
"Learning to Love" . . . Veronique, Alan, and Ducky
"Boomerang" . . . Veronique and Pierre
"I Cannot Leave You Now" . . . Veronique and Alan
"Voice Calling Me" . . . Alan
"Fox Trot Military Tune" . . . Maude, Jezirah, Zillah, and Girls
"Same Old Way" . . . Jack
"March" . . . Lulu, Ducky, and Girls

Even the Shuberts' publicity department had trouble selling the idea of *Little Simplicity*. A marketing pamphlet had this dubious tagline: "Girls—Fun and Music—Mostly Girls."[66] Reviews for *Little Simplicity* were very mixed. Most critics agreed that the music was pleasant and many of the performances enjoyable. They had particularly high praise for the sister dance act the Cameron Sisters (Madeline and Dorothy), graduates of the *Ziegfeld Follies*, as exotic sisters Jezirah and Zillah. But the general consensus was that, while entertaining, *Little Simplicity* was just another formulaic musical romance. "'Little Simplicity' achieves no distinction in either [music or libretto]; yet there are many men who enjoy calling on a bread-and-butter miss, and there are thousands of theatregoers who enjoy seeing a bread-and-butter musical comedy," declared the *Globe*.[67] The *American* called it "another of those delightful musical comedies with a real story, full of heart interest, like 'Maytime,' in which the lovers are separated through two acts and through no fault of their own and then reunited at the final curtain to the satisfaction of all concerned and the delight of the audience." That reviewer praised "Rida Johnson Young, than whom there is no more prolific or entertaining writer."[68] However, the *New York Star* tersely reported, "The book is by Rida Johnson Young. She has turned out much better ones."[69] Charles Darnton of the *Evening World* did not mince words: "The book and lyrics by Rida Johnson Young are dull beyond words, and the music by Augustus Barratt, except for a pleasing waltz song, is lacking in spirit and melody. Most of the tunes were evidently ground out by hard labor."[70] Only the *New York Dramatic Mirror* found "a measure of novelty in this musical play—a fact which calls for a fair amount of praise. Any piece which starts its line of action in Algeria in 1912, journeys on to the Latin Quartier of Paris and depends for its finale upon the war, should furnish quite a bit of surprise. And so 'Little Simplicity' is meritorious from such a standpoint."[71]

Despite any flaws, *Little Simplicity* proved good enough for a healthy run of 112 performances. But it does not adequately represent Young's breadth of talent as a librettist. The flat dialogue, two-dimensional characters, and uneven script point to a hastiness in production or perhaps a personal disinterest in the material. Whatever the reasons for its lackluster book, Young would quickly find her stride again by returning to the past.

7

DREAM GIRL
• • •
END OF A CAREER

> If I had my own way, I would not write at all. I should devote myself to my home and the entertainment of my friends. If I had a dozen children I should have been happier, but fate has made me a playwright and I must be content.
>
> Rida Johnson Young[1]

By her prodigious output, one might assume that Rida Johnson Young worked constantly. And she did—to a point. She spent every morning at her typewriter, working a minimum of four hours whether or not inspiration struck. But afterward, her gardens beckoned. Many articles and publicity photos situated Young outdoors—planting trees, playing with her dogs, filling flowerpots in her shed—but this was more than the magazines asserting her feminine domesticity. Young thrived in the outdoors. Perhaps to counterbalance the hours spent in darkened theaters, all of her homes had ample room for gardens. She wrote in the morning so as to have the better part of the day free for the pleasures of her home and social life. And even though she could never spend as much time there as she wanted to, the garden seemed to be always on her mind:

> "And this summer!" She drew in a deep breath. "This summer I'm going to get a vacation if it's my last act. I've bought a new country place at Southfield Point, near Stamford. And I'm going to dig and hoe and scratch in the ground to my heart's content. . . . I'd rather be outdoors working in a garden than doing anything else. I'm going to plant anything I get my hands on, flowers and trees and vegetables. And I'm going to earn a niche in the Hall of Fame by giving away the potatoes I raise. Just now it is taking all the royalties I can earn to buy fertilizer. It's worth its weight in gold."[2]

She pledged to raise spinach for the Stage Women's War Relief in 1917, along with Billie Burke, Elsie Janis, Marie Dressler, and Louise Drew, among other notable women in theater.[3] She remarked once that the act of writing was like tending a garden. "You learn a lot about plays by writing in a garden," she mused, "for the

Figure 7.1 Rida Johnson Young in her garden. New York American, December 1920. Billy Rose Theatre Division, The New York Public Library.

gentle art of pruning is an essential part of a dramatist's work, and you learn to develop situations, to weed out extraneous dialogue, to carefully tend and water the growing idea that is at once the seed and fruit of your work—all these things you learn in a garden."[4] As happened so often, Young betrayed a dichotomous attitude about her profession: in one interview, she might call writing a thankless chore that she only did for the money and, in the next, divulge the quiet passion that fueled her work ethic.

After *Little Simplicity*, Young returned to her original chosen dramatic form, the straight play. *Little Old New York* opened at the Plymouth Theatre in September 1920, partly inspired by the world she had created with *Maytime*. Set in 1810 and featuring such historical luminaries as Washington Irving, John Jacob Astor, and Cornelius Vanderbilt, the play delighted audiences and critics with its depiction of "the New York that heard laughing parties go blackberrying in Maiden Lane and shook with derision at the thought of that mad Mr. Astor buying lots way up in the swamp land where Gramercy Park stands now."[5] The subject matter served her well, because *Little Old New York* and *Maytime* were her longest-running shows, at 308 performances and 492 performances, respectively. (Incidentally, Douglas J. Wood starred in both: first as Claude, Ottilie's philandering husband, then as another member of the upper class, Cornelius Vanderbilt.) A film of *Little Old New York* starring Marion Davies and Young's novelization of the film followed in 1923.

But after *Little Old New York* opened, Young had only the second lengthy Broadway hiatus of her career. Although she was working on several plays, no new Rida Johnson Young production would open on Broadway for three years. But her work was heard and seen elsewhere. In 1921, "Mother Machree" was featured in the Shuberts' revue *The Midnight Rounders of 1921*. That same year, Arthur Hammerstein produced *The Front Seat* at Poli's Theatre in Washington, D.C. Hammerstein planned to bring it to New York, but negative reviews halted its progress. Coming on the heels of this failure was a vehicle for Vivienne Segal called *A Wise Child*, this time produced by Charles Dillingham. Segal, who was best known for musicals, took on her first dramatic role as a vaudeville performer hired to impersonate a wealthy man's long-lost daughter. Despite very strong reviews for its Boston tryout, Dillingham opted not to take *A Wise Child* to Broadway.

THE DREAM GIRL

Despite their roaring success with *Naughty Marietta*, Young and Victor Herbert did not collaborate on another musical until *The Dream Girl* in 1924, the year of Herbert's death (although Herbert's daughter found parts of a score for an unproduced musical with lyrics by Young called *Three Little Widows* among his papers after he died).[6] *The Dream Girl* was based on the 1906 fantasy play *The Road to Yesterday* by Beulah Marie Dix and Evelyn Greenleaf Sutherland. Correspondence from Young and Herbert indicates that they began work on it as early as 1921, so it is unclear what delayed its production. Herbert biographer Neil Gould cites a 1923 letter from Herbert saying that he "wrote the piece two years ago."[7] And a couple of letters from Young to the Shuberts in 1922 and 1923 compare it to some of her other shows in an effort to get the producers on board: "Mr. Herbert's score for this play is on the style of the music he wrote for 'Naughty Marietta' and has several surefire hits in it."[8] By April 1923, they were evidently in negotiations and just waiting to get approval from the agents for Dix and Sutherland:

> I hope everything is going along satisfactorily about making arrangements for the production of "The Dream Girl." I know in this play I'll give you something that will make a bigger sensation than "Maytime." There are a lot of old English, very quaint dances and songs in the dream part of the play, and up to date jazzy stuff in the first and last acts, so we'll be sure to please all sorts of tastes with the variety we have.[9]

Young must have been very confident in the piece to invoke *Naughty Marietta* and *Maytime*. It certainly had all the right ingredients: Dix and Sutherland's original play had run for more than two hundred performances, Herbert was one of America's best-loved composers, and Young was at the height of her career.

The Dream Girl represents a bit of a departure for Young in that it is a fantasy. An American girl named Elspeth visits London for the first time and is so enchanted with its romantic history that she dreams her way into an earlier century. While Young had written shows that took place in the distant past, she had not had to mix past and present so radically within one show. The first act takes place in the London studio of a painter named Will. Other artists use the studio, including Bobby Thompson, who is searching for the right male model for his painting of "The Knight of the Road, Fifteenth Century Adventurer." Also visiting the studio are a group of young women from America, traveling with their chaperone, Aunt Harriet. When the handsome American athlete Jack Warner comes in to see his friends, the girls gather around him and convince Bobby that Jack should be his model. Jack refuses until he finds out that Elspeth—whom he has never met but whose picture he has fallen in love with—will be there. He thinks he knew her at one time but cannot remember where or when. One of the other girls, Malena, believes she was a gypsy in a past life, so she is especially intrigued by Jack's confusion. A superstitious servant, Nora, reminds them all that it is Midsummer's Eve and whatever wish they make that night will come true. Malena wishes to go back in time. Elspeth and Dolly enter breathlessly, having had the most wonderful day in London seeing the historical sights. When Elspeth exclaims that she wishes she had lived in another century, Malena brings up her theory again about them all having had past lives. Jack puts on his costume for the painting, and Malena is shocked, certain that she has seen him that way before. He returns to Elspeth's picture—she has left the room before he entered, and they will continue to miss meeting each other for the rest of the act—and wonders if she is his "Dream Girl" from another life. Later, Elspeth has a vision of Jack. Convinced that she is just overtired, she goes to bed.

Elspeth wakes in act 2 to find herself in the London of three hundred years ago. All of the characters from act 1 are there, but they seem to actually live in this world, while Elspeth is aware that she is in another time. She is now a "serving wench" to Aunt Harriet; Jack is an adventurer, the same one in the painting; Malena is indeed a gypsy. Nora appears to tell Elspeth that she is Lady Elizabeth and that the evil Lord Strangevon wants her for his wife, even though he is already married. Elspeth disguises herself as a boy to avoid him, but Jack recognizes her. He offers to marry her, but Strangevon enters and kidnaps her—and Jack runs away. Elspeth is equally afraid of Strangevon and annoyed with Jack for abandoning her. In Strangevon's castle, Elspeth meets Dolly, a dancer, and Elinor, Strangevon's wife. They dress her for her upcoming wedding to Strangevon. But Jack reappears to rescue her.

Elspeth wakes in act 3 to find Jack standing over her, but she doesn't realize that she is back in the London studio in the present day. Jack is still in his knight costume, so Elspeth thinks she has conjured him from her dream. Malena enters and explains who he is. Elspeth realizes she is talking to a stranger, but Jack is convinced that they are meant to be together. He explains that when he first saw her picture, he thought he knew her. They realize that they really were in love in a past life, and now they will get married in this one.

There are two extant scripts of *The Dream Girl*, one at the New York Public Library and one at the Shubert Archive. Neither is clearly dated, but the NYPL one does not contain the character of Jimmie Van Dyke, played by vaudeville and burlesque actor Billy B. Van. According to some of the reviewers, Van was brought in late to the production to provide "humor":

> In rehearsals and trials, seemingly, it was discovered that the piece lacked comic interest. Accordingly, Mr. Billy B. Van was summoned to deck it with a personage that is merely his wiry self variously costumed and with quips in his best vaudevillian vein, barely pinned to Mrs. Rida Johnson Young's play and for the most part quite at odds with it.[10]

And this review lays the blame for his performance on another writer: "The play was . . . harnessed somewhat unwillingly to jokes by Mr. Harold Atteridge and clowning by Mr. Billy B. Van. Neither artist, one fears, was at his best."[11] Harold Atteridge was one of the Shuberts' staff writers and had written lyrics and librettos for most editions of their annual revue, *The Passing Show* (various productions from 1912 to 1924). He often bragged about his speed and agility when adding new material during short rehearsal periods. Because the revues were topical, Atteridge had to keep up with the audience: "They are looking for catchy words, something that can shock them into laughter, and dancing, but most of all they want sensationalism and scenic effects and they want speed," he said.[12] This explains the major stylistic differences between the scripts at the NYPL and the Shubert Archive and helps to clarify the authorship of *The Dream Girl*. It appears that Atteridge only wrote Billy B. Van's dialogue, as none of Van's material exists in the earlier script. When Van is not in a scene, the script is nearly identical to the first version. Unlike Young's previous collaborations, her style and Atteridge's do not mix, and the critics picked that up. If Atteridge was indeed brought onto the production late, while Young had already worked on the script for at least two years, they would not have had time to shape a coherent piece with a new character. Young's original is romantic and charming; Van's dialogue lumbers through it like a chatty bull in a china shop, not unlike Ed Wynn's additions to *Sometime*.

For comparison, let us examine two versions of a scene from act 1. Elspeth returns from her day in London and sings about all the wonderful sights. In the original script, a painter named Tubby (renamed Bobby in the later version) has been searching for just the right model for his modern "Venus," and he thinks Elspeth may be the one:

> ELSPETH. I haven't told half. Wait till I get my second wind.
> TUBBY. Stop! Stop! *(Points dramatically to her arm)* I've found my elbow!
> ELSPETH. I beg pardon. That's *my* elbow. At least, I think it is. I can't seem to feel that anything belongs to me!
> TUBBY. My Venus is complete. I've found my elbow. *(Kisses her arm)*

ELSPETH. Take him away. He's going to bite.

MALENA. Don't be silly, Tubby.

TUBBY. You'll pose for my elbow. Oh, say you'll pose for my elbow. *(Kneels before her)*

MALENA. You must put on a negligee and lie down and rest.

NORA. And I'll brew ye a nice cup of tea.

ELSPETH. Oh, that sounds good. Lend a hand, somebody. I'm dizzy from flying back so many centuries. Please hold that threshold until I get through.[13]

The same scene in the second version of the script has Jimmie (Van) tinkering with a radio. It begins the same way, Elspeth having just finished singing about the sights of London:

ELSPETH. Wait till I get my second wind.

JIMMIE. I beg your pardon. Who's making all this noise? You are interrupting my work. I was just painting a miniature. Oh, it's you. You're going to get yourself all tired out. Where have you been all day?

ELSPETH. Everywhere!

JIMMIE. That's a broad assertion. Well, I suppose you've been looking at all the old ruins. Have you seen them all?

ELSPETH. Yes!

JIMMIE. You didn't happen to see my wife anywhere? You had better watch out, you will get yourself all tired out. I tell you what, come on over and listen to my radio. I'll radio you to sleep with a Chicago Stock Market quotation and wake you up with the Medford Hillside Police Reports.

ELSPETH. Oh, you funny radio man. I don't want to think of radios or anything modern. I'm still living in past centuries.

JIMMIE. Well, ain't you the old-fashioned thing. Living in past centuries. I'll bet that you still believe that all the trouble in the Garden of Eden was caused by an apple. Don't believe it. It was caused by a green pear. Don't you want to have Uncle Wiggley tell you about Puss in Boots and Peter Rabbit—

ELSPETH. Oh, you're so silly.

JIMMIE. You think so? Well, I can see that you're not interested in me. But I don't care. A woman scorned Napoleon once. Goodbye, I'm signing off until 8:15.

MALENA. Come, Elspeth, you must put on a negligee and lie down and rest.

ELSPETH. Oh, no.

NORA. And I'll brew you a nice cup of tea.

ELSPETH. Oh, that sounds good. Lend a hand, somebody. I'm dizzy from flying back so many centuries. Please hold that threshold until I get through.[14]

In the first example, Young established Tubby's search for the Venus model in an earlier scene, so when he briefly interrupts Elspeth's excited report about her day, the audience is in on the joke. Tubby also plays on Elspeth's fascination with the past by gallantly kneeling in front of her, so that even this pause in the action stays thematically within the story. In contrast, Jimmie rambles in non sequiturs and basically hijacks the scene. Not one of his lines makes sense or connects to something he said earlier. And even though this is an early scene, it is Jimmie's second long appearance. He tries to "woo" Aunt Harriett in a previous section—that scene, too, is filled with repetitions, bad jokes, and non sequiturs and goes on for about four pages. Frankly, every time Jimmie opens his mouth, he forces all the air out of the play. And the effect is not only on the page—many critics questioned Van's contribution to the show, such as this one: "His jokes and mannerisms brought forth a large amount of tolerant first-night laughter, but it cannot be said that there was any substantial basis for this tolerance."[15] There was nothing unusual about producers bringing in a specialty performer or additional writers to boost ticket sales or fix a troubled script. But the Shuberts' decision to add Van and Atteridge truly baffles. Rida Johnson Young was an established, celebrated playwright whom the Shuberts had employed many times for nearly twenty years, and *The Dream Girl*'s source material was a known property. Neither Young nor Herbert—a wildly successful and beloved composer—would have needed extra help to make the show work. In this instance, the seasoned producers made an egregious misstep.

Dream Songs

Young wrote the majority of the lyrics, with the exception of one song solely attributed to Atteridge, "I Want to Go Home" (with music by Sigmund Romberg, brought in after Herbert's sudden death in May 1924). However, Gould suggests that Herbert himself made lyric changes when Young's did not fit his music. Gould points to notes in Herbert's papers that show the development of a song called "Bubbles" that have Young's lyrics scratched out and replacement ones in his handwriting. They are minor changes—Herbert suggests "Hush! Hush!" instead of the harder-to-sing "Shh! Shh!"—but informative nonetheless.[16] It is likely that Young would have welcomed Herbert's suggestions, as he had composed music for operatic voices for most of his career.

Many of the songs printed in the NYPL typescript were changed for the later version and are considerably shorter. I am fascinated by one of the cut songs because it is the only example of a "list" song that I have come across by Young. Elspeth sings "Sights of London" in her first scene:

> There's such a lot of things to see,
> The very thought bewilders me.
> There's churches and their patron saints,
> So many that my memory faints.
> St. Paul's, St. Pride's, St. Gabriel,
> St. John's, St. Peter's, Clerkenwell,
> St. Mary's scattered by the dozens,
> St. George and all his saintly cousins.
> St. Pancras old, St. Pancras new,

> St. Ann and St. Bartholomew,
> St. Bololph, old and very quaint,
> St. Giles in Fields, where no fields ain't![17]

She goes on for three more verses: one about taverns, one about city gates, and one about dungeons. In the rewrite of *The Dream Girl*, "Sights of London" was replaced with the much shorter—and less interesting—"Dancing Round":

> I've had such a wonderful, wonderful day,
> Just like a seventeenth century play,
> I've been to the Abbey, I've been to the Tower,
> I've seen Windsor Castle and sweet Ellen's bower.
> I've been so excited that really I've found,
> That I could not keep my feet down on the ground.[18]

There is only the one verse and a simple refrain. It's perfectly fine but lacks the charm and breathlessness of the list song. Was the better song sacrificed to make room for Billy Van? If so, the play suffered for it. Many critics argued that the show was overly long, but it would not have been if not for Van's scenes.

The title song, "My Dream Girl," demonstrates once again Young's ability to match her style to her composer's. Victor Herbert was the undisputed master of the romantic operetta ballad, and Young knew that her words not only must match his music but must allow it to dominate. He would write a soaring melody, and her words would ride on the wave. Her lyrics for "My Dream Girl" do just that:

> VERSE.
> O silent lips if you could only answer,
> O lovely eyes if you could only tell,
> Why every single fiber of my being
> Responds to you as to some magic spell.
> Why do I feel as though I'd always known you,
> What is this thrill of mingled joy and pain,
> Oh, have we met before through all the ages,
> And will we meet and love once more again?
> REFRAIN.
> My dream girl, my one only dream girl,
> I'm waiting, for I'll meet you I know.
> Oh, tell me that you'll know me and love me,
> For I've loved you,
> Loved you long ago.[19]

These lyrics share some characteristics of those she wrote for *Naughty Marietta*, especially "I'm Falling in Love with Some One." She begins with a complex verse for the character to work through his confusion and longing, then gives him a free-flowing verse to let the emotion take flight. It fits beautifully with Herbert's melody.

Directed by Laura Hope Crews and J. C. Huffman, *The Dream Girl* opened at the Ambassador Theatre on August 20, 1924, and lasted for 117 performances. For all of Young's predictions that *The Dream Girl* would rival the Shuberts' other operetta hits, it failed to live up to its predecessors. It garnered positive reviews for its stars, Fay Bainter and Walter Woolf, and was a fitting legacy for Victor Herbert, who died of heart failure a few months before the show opened. But critics found the play long and lacking in the charm and romance of its source material. Young turned back to writing and shifted away from musical theater. She could not have known that she would not return to it.

Box 7.1 The Dream Girl

Lyrics and libretto: Rida Johnson Young and Harold Atteridge
Music: Victor Herbert
Additional music: Sigmund Romberg
Ambassador Theatre; opened August 20, 1924; closed November 29, 1924 (117 performances)
Producers: Lee and J. J. Shubert

Major Cast

Elspeth . . . Fay Bainter
Jack Warren . . . Walter Woolf
Malena . . . Vivara
Dolly Follis . . . Wyn Richmond
Wilson Addison . . . George Lemaire
Jimmie Van Dyke . . . Billy B. Van
Aunt Harriet . . . Maude Odell
Elinor Levison . . . Alice Moffat
Nora . . . Clara Palmer
Will Levison . . . John Clarke
Bobby Thompkins . . . Frank Masters

Songs

"Making a Venus" . . . Bobby, Malena, Models, and Boys
"All Year Round" . . . Jack and Chorus
"Dancing Round" . . . Elspeth and Chorus
"My Dream Girl (I Loved You Long Ago)" . . . Jack
"Old Songs" . . . Maidens
"Maiden, Let Me In" . . . Will and Boys
"Gypsy Life" . . . Malena and Chorus
"Stop, Look and Listen" . . . Elspeth, Jimmie, and Bobby
"The Broad Highway" . . . Jack and Chorus
"My Hero" . . . Elspeth and Jack
"I Want to Go Home" . . . Elspeth (lyrics by H. Atteridge)
"Bubbles" . . . Dolly and Chorus
"Make Love in the Morning" . . . Jimmie and Specialty Dancers
"Saxophone Man" . . . Bobby, Dolly, and Chorus
"Dream Girl" . . . Elspeth, Jack, and Company

A CAREER CUT SHORT

Soon after *The Dream Girl,* Young premiered what was to be her final play. *Cock o' the Roost* (originally titled *The Rabbit's Foot*) was the second production of a fledgling group called the Dramatists Theatre. The feel-good tale of a man who wins over his true love through the power of positive thinking got pleasant reviews—"Miss Young has a trick or two of stagecraft and a flair for dialogue that carry her a long way"[20]—but lasted only twenty-four performances. Young had more than enough to keep her busy. She wrote four novellas in four years: *Little Old New York* (1923), based on her play; *The Story of Mother Machree* (1924), based on the immensely popular song she had written fifteen years before; and two new works, *Out of the Night* (1925) and *The Red Owl* (published after her death, in 1927).

But her health was also failing: Rida had breast cancer. By Christmas of 1925, she had deteriorated to the point where medical specialists were called to her home. The papers reported that she was "dangerously ill," with the implication that she would probably not live to see the new year.[21] The papers also reported that she was a Christian Scientist, meaning that she might not have sought medical treatment but would likely have relied on prayer for physical healing. I have not found any interviews with her that confirm that she identified as a Christian Scientist, but she had been a strong proponent of "New Thought," an offshoot of Christian Science. She explained her spiritual leanings in a 1917 interview:

> Did you ever try a course in New Thought reading? It's better than a spring tonic. And Theosophy, too! I'm not a dyed in the wool Theosophist, but I'm a sort of a kind of a one. . . . I had an idea for [a play]. It dealt with occultism, and as I was decidedly shy of any real knowledge of the subject I went to the library and began to read up on it. My reading had the totally unexpected result of converting me to Theosophy. Maybe I have a weak nature, but I can't seem to get along without some belief to tie to. I had somehow grown away from those I had been brought up on, and Theosophy furnished me a new and reasonably satisfactory explanation of the scheme of things.[22]

Perhaps her family or friends had finally convinced her to consult the doctors. Or perhaps, desperate for a cure, they had insisted on bringing doctors in. She did rally that winter and held on a few months longer.

"AN ALERT AND AMBITIOUS MIND"

Rida succumbed to her cancer on May 8, 1926. She left behind her mother and one brother and an estate of $90,411—a little more than $1.3 million in today's dollars.[23] Young bequeathed $15,000 to her mother, $5,000 to her brother, $2,000 to friends Constance Bellamy and Lyle Kerr, and the remainder of the estate to her nephew and executor, William A. Schroeder. The tributes that flowed from the pens of other writers spoke volumes about the respect with which her peers regarded her. The woman who had merely written "trifles" had accomplished more than she realized. The *Baltimore Sun* spoke lovingly of that city's favorite daughter:

> Mrs. Young's successes as a playwright were more than the product of an alert and ambitious mind. This she had, but she understood even in Baltimore at the beginning of her career the need of careful training for the work which she expected to perform. Her early appearances on the stage were definitely for the purpose of gaining a knowledge of stage technique and the limitations within which a writer of plays must make his points. This serious approach to the profession which she planned to pursue presaged competent workmanship. She served an apprenticeship in performance as a preliminary to designing, as an architect learns something of framing and stone cutting before he designs structures. This is the traditional and effective course which complacent youngsters like to omit. And the fact that Mrs. Young followed it adds to the sorrow with which the Baltimore public learns of her death. She had laid the foundation for work even better than what she had achieved, and the close of her career has come grievously soon.[24]

The New York newspaper columnist O. O. McIntyre lamented:

> In the passing of Rida Johnson Young, America lost one of its foremost playwrights. She wrote a half a hundred plays and at least a dozen were conspicuous successes. She was a beautiful, queenly looking lady and one of the kindliest I ever met. Somehow she didn't seem at home in the theater yet she understood it and its tricks perhaps more than anyone of her generation.[25]

Young never saw herself as an important playwright and probably did not expect her eulogies to say much more than "She wrote plays and tended her garden." Would she be surprised to hear some of her own songs in popular culture more than a hundred years after she wrote them? Could she ever have predicted that she would be named to the Songwriters Hall of Fame, alongside George Gershwin, George M. Cohan, and her old collaborator Chauncey Olcott? Would the woman who wrote "Will You Remember?" expect anyone to remember her name?

CONCLUSION

I chose the title of *Sweet Mystery* for this book not just because of Rida Johnson Young's most famous song. From the day I first heard her name, I could not understand why this incredibly prolific writer was virtually lost in the annals of theater history. How could someone so well known in her lifetime, whose works are still occasionally produced and whose career was so lucrative, be relegated to the footnotes? There are so many possible explanations: lots of her contemporary writers who also had rich careers seldom make a dent in the books beyond biographical information; early musical theater history studies have disproportionately favored male writers over females; perhaps the brief runs of many of her plays deemed her not "popular" enough for further study. Add to all of these that few historians have shown much interest in pre–Golden Age musical theater beyond a handful of seminal artists, shows, and forms. Except for some significant studies of vaudeville, burlesque, and operetta, few books have taken a deeper dive into the era. I am thrilled to read newer works like Jonas Westover's *The Shuberts and Their Passing Shows: The Untold Tale of Ziegfeld's Rivals* (2016), Anne Ommen van der Merwe's *The Ziegfeld Follies: A History in Song* (2009), and Kathleen Riley's *The Astaires: Fred and Adele* (2012) for their meticulous archival research into this under-studied period. Their work uncovers a wealth of songs, scripts, scores, productions, business practices, and anecdotes that have lain dormant for too long and bring clarity to a complex and seemingly messy era. And, happily, these efforts open new doors for historians interested in similar research avenues.

Rida Johnson Young's work informs and enhances what we know about the theater at the beginning of the twentieth century. She forged a career by adhering to the conventions of the time while subtly pushing against the limits of tradition. She was versatile, productive, collaborative, and business-minded. She approached her work with little ego and held no delusions that she would be any more successful or important than her contemporaries. She understood that her words only constituted one part of a play, inviting input from her fellow writers, directors, and performers, so long as that input served the play. As a lyricist and librettist, she understood the relationship between words and music, between composer and wordsmith, between performer and material. She took immense pride in her profession, her work ethic, and her ability to collaborate with her fellow theater makers. She listened to audiences, responded to them, catered to them, and affected them.

It is also important to acknowledge that, as a lyricist *and* a librettist, Young was one of the last of a generation of writers to take on both roles in musical theater writing. With the notable exceptions of Oscar Hammerstein II and Alan Jay Lerner, later writers increasingly specialized in creating lyrics or librettos but not both. This resulted in the typical triumvirate musical writing team of composer, lyricist, and book writer (no longer called a librettist), a practice still in place today. There have been several *composer*-lyricists, such as Cole Porter, Irving Berlin, Frank Loesser, Stephen Sondheim, and Jason Robert Brown, but the lyricist-librettist remains comparatively rare.

Rida was also very much a feminist. She championed her fellow women playwrights, fought for her own equal pay, and defined her place in the boys' club that was professional theater. Her shows are largely female-centric, and she wrote herself into all of her female characters; Marietta, Sophie, Ottilie, Eloise, and Elspeth all symbolized parts of her. Independent, daring, hopeful,

Figure 7.2 Rida Johnson Young with one of her dogs. Green Book, May 1912. Billy Rose Theatre Division, The New York Public Library.

they walked a tightrope between the old and the new. Young looked forward, and so did they.

Ultimately, Rida Johnson Young had an impressive career in the theater, one that should be recognized as having made a major contribution in its era and beyond. She wrote more than thirty plays, hundreds of songs, and four novels. Many of her plays were turned into movies, and an entire generation experienced her songs through Jeanette MacDonald and Nelson Eddy. A new cohort of musical theater fans know them because of *Thoroughly Modern Millie*. And I think she would have a hearty laugh at Madeline Kahn's version of "Ah! Sweet Mystery of Life" in *Young Frankenstein*. As with everything in her life, Rida Johnson Young took both success and failure in her stride: "One must make it a business. That is the real reason I have succeeded. I have never undertaken anything really big; I have contented myself with writing plays that are popular and within my ability."[26]

I would say she was being modest.

APPENDIX LIST OF WORKS BY RIDA JOHNSON YOUNG

SOURCES: Gerald Bordman and Richard Norton, *American Musical Theatre: A Chronicle*, 4th ed.; Brenda Coven, *American Women Dramatists of the Twentieth Century: A Bibliography*; Kurt Gänzl, *The Encyclopedia of the Musical Theatre*, 2nd ed.; Virginia L. Grattan, *American Women Songwriters: A Biographical Dictionary*; Alice M. Robinson, Vera Mowry Roberts, and Milly S. Barranger, eds., *Notable Women in the American Theatre: A Biographical Dictionary*; Internet Broadway Database (www.ibdb.com).

FULL PRODUCTIONS

Plays and Plays with Music

Lord Byron, 1900
Brown of Harvard, 1906 (incidental songs with Melville Ellis)
The Boys of Company "B," 1907
The Lancers, 1907 (co-written with J. Hartley Manners)
Glorious Betsy, 1908
The Lottery Man, 1909
Ragged Robin, 1910 (co-written with Rita Olcott)
Barry of Ballymore, 1911 (featuring "Mother Machree," with music by Ernest Ball and Chauncey Olcott)
Next! 1911
Macushla, 1912
The Isle o' Dreams, 1913 (incidental songs with Ernest Ball and Chauncey Olcott)
The Girl and the Pennant, 1913 (co-written with Christy Mathewson)
Shameen Dhu, 1914
Captain Kidd, Jr., 1916
Little Old New York, 1920
Cock o' the Roost, 1924

Musicals

Just One of the Boys, 1910 (music by William Schroeder)
Naughty Marietta, 1910 (music by Victor Herbert)
The Red Petticoat, 1912 (book and lyrics co-written with Paul West, music by Jerome Kern)
When Love Is Young, 1913 (co-written with William Cary Duncan, music by William Schroeder)
Lady Luxury, 1914 (music by William Schroeder)
Her Soldier Boy, 1916 (music by Emmerich Kálmán and Sigmund Romberg)

His Little Widows, 1917 (co-written with William Cary Duncan, music by William Schroeder)
Maytime, 1917 (music by Sigmund Romberg)
Sometime, 1918 (music by Rudolf Friml)
Little Simplicity, 1918 (music by Augustus Barratt)
The Dream Girl, 1924 (co-written with Harold Atteridge, music by Victor Herbert and Sigmund Romberg)

One-Acts and Unproduced Plays

Barbara's Dilemma, a Monolog Sketch, 1906
Chatterton, a Dramatic Monolog, 1906
Last of the Cargills, 1906
What's Bred in the Bone, ca. 1909
Old Town Folks, ca. 1909
Wanted—A Sister, 1910
The Candidate, ca. 1910
The Yellow Streak, ca. 1910
John Clayton, Actor, 1915
Lot 79, 1918
The Front Seat, 1921
A Wise Child, 1921

Novels

Little Old New York, 1923
The Story of Mother Machree, 1924
Out of the Night, 1925
The Red Owl, 1927 (published posthumously)

NOTES

* * *

PREFACE

1. The Tony Award category includes lyrics as part of the score for a musical.
2. Recalling the offers that came pouring in after *Naughty Marietta*'s success, she ruefully admitted that "not being made of the stern stuff that enables one to look an advance royalty in the face and cut it, I fell for another contract for a musical play." Rida Johnson Young, "Lo! The Poor Librettist," *New York Tribune*, June 3, 1917.
3. Philip Furia and Michael Lasser, *America's Songs: The Stories behind the Songs of Broadway, Hollywood, and Tin Pan Alley* (New York: Routledge, 2006), 6.
4. David Ewen, *The Life and Death of Tin Pan Alley: The Golden Age of American Popular Music* (New York: Funk and Wagnalls, 1964), 335–342.
5. For an excellent biography of Dorothy Fields, please read Charlotte Greenspan's *Pick Yourself Up: Dorothy Fields and the American Musical* (Oxford: Oxford University Press, 2010), also part of Oxford University Press's Broadway Legacies series.
6. Ewen, *The Life and Death of Tin Pan Alley*, 159.
7. George Jessel, "And Then They Wrote . . ." *Variety*, January 9, 1946, 268.
8. See Sherry Engle, *New Women Dramatists in America* (New York: Palgrave Macmillan, 2007); Bud Coleman and Judith A. Sebesta, eds., *Women in American Musical Theatre* (Jefferson, NC: McFarland, 2008); Thomas S. Hischak, *Boy Loses Girl: Broadway's Librettists* (Lanham, MD: Scarecrow Press, 2002).
9. *The Theatre* originated in May 1901, published by Meyer Bros and Co. and edited by Arthur Hornblow, Jr. The title changed to *Theatre Magazine* in August 1917 and ran under that name until 1931. I have made every effort to ensure that the correct title is used in each reference to the magazine.

CHAPTER 1 The Women Who Wrote

1. Helen Ten Broeck, "Rida Young—Dramatist and Garden Expert," *The Theatre*, April 1917, 250.
2. Ada Patterson, "Wealth Not a Bar to Playwriting," *Theatre Magazine*, May 1918, 296.
3. Ada Patterson, "The Only Woman Librettist in America," *The Theatre*, June 1915, 305–306.
4. Mary B. Mullett, "She Holds the Season's Record for Stage Successes," *New York Sun*, May 6, 1917, 16.
5. Ten Broeck, "Rida Young—Dramatist and Garden Expert," 250.
6. Virginia Frame, "Women Who Have Written Successful Plays," *The Theatre*, October 1906, 265.
7. Helen Christine Bennett, "The Woman Who Wrote 'Mother Machree,'" *American Magazine* 90 (1920), 187.

8. Ten Broeck, "Rida Young—Dramatist and Garden Expert," 202.
9. Bennett, "The Woman Who Wrote 'Mother Machree,'" 187.
10. New York Public Library (hereafter NYPL) clippings file.
11. Isidore Witmark and Isaac Goldberg, *The Story of the House of Witmark: From Ragtime to Swingtime* (New York: Lee Furman, 1939), 348.
12. Mullett, "She Holds the Season's Record."
13. "Dramatists—No. 3," *Baltimore Sun*, February 21, 1909.
14. "Jas. Young, Jr., Weds: Actor's Bride, Miss Rida Louise Johnson, of This City," *Baltimore Sun*, September 19, 1901.
15. "Woman Playwright's Secret of Success," *Syracuse Herald*, November 18, 1917.
16. "Women Writers Now Occupy Important Place on American Stage," *Brooklyn Times*, January 27, 1911.
17. Cady Whaley, "The Woman Playwright of the Current Season," *The Billboard*, December 15, 1906, 16.
18. Thomas S. Hischak, *Word Crazy: Broadway Lyricists from Cohan to Sondheim* (New York: Praeger, 1991), 189.
19. *The Fortune Teller*, comic opera in three acts as presented by the Alice Nielson Opera Company, libretto by Harry B. Smith, music by Victor Herbert (New York: M. Witmark, 1898), 19–20.
20. Henry Blossom, "Thine Alone," music by Victor Herbert (New York: M. Witmark & Sons, 1917).
21. Rida Johnson Young, "Kiss Waltz," music by Sigmund Romberg (New York: G. Schirmer, 1916).
22. *Brooklyn Daily Eagle*, November 14, 1912.
23. *Dramatic News*, April 10, 1909. Robinson Locke Collection, New York Public Library.
24. George Jean Nathan, *The Theatre, the Drama, the Girls*, (New York: Alfred A. Knopf, 1921), 56–57.
25. Otto Harbach, "The Writing of a Musical Comedy," *Theatre Magazine*, November 1925, 10.
26. Arthur Hornblow, "Mr. Hornblow Goes to the Play," *The Theatre*, January 1917, 64.
27. "Vote of Thanks to Rida Johnson Young," *New York Dramatic Mirror*, July 21, 1917.
28. *The Billboard*, July 20, 1907, 29.
29. Rida Johnson Young, "Lo! The Poor Librettist," *New York Tribune*, June 3, 1917.
30. Mullett, "She Holds the Season's Record."
31. Young, letter to J. J. Shubert, July 26, 1918, Shubert Archive (hereafter SA).
32. J. J. Shubert, letter to Young, July 30, 1918, SA.
33. Young, letter to Shuberts, March 7, 1910, SA.
34. Young, letter to Shuberts, June 22, 1911, SA.
35. Young, letter to Shuberts, January 5, 1910, SA.
36. J. J. Shubert, letter to Young, November 17, 1919, SA.
37. Young, letter to J. J. Shubert, November 19, 1919, SA.
38. Ibid.

39. Young, letter to Shuberts, January 24, 1918, SA. The show became *Little Simplicity*, and, it should be noted, Young did not get any of her initial casting choices.
40. Young, letter to Shuberts, September 19, 1917, SA.
41. Young, letter to Shuberts, January 25, 1919, SA.
42. John Franceschina, *Harry B. Smith: Dean of American Librettists* (New York: Routledge, 2003), 3.
43. Frame, "Women Who Have Written Successful Plays."
44. Ibid., 178.
45. Harbach, "The Writing of a Musical Comedy," 10.
46. R. B. Sheridan, "Some Secrets of the Dramatists' Workshop," *The Theatre*, May 1910, 144.

CHAPTER 2 An Old Story in a New Dress: The Emerging Playwright

1. Helen Christine Bennett, "The Woman Who Wrote 'Mother Machree,'" *American Magazine* 90 (1920), 182.
2. The *Baltimore Sun* notice of her divorce from James Young gave her name as "Marie Louise Johnson." I have not been able to ascertain whether this was a misprint or whether "Rida" was a nickname. Kurt Ganzl's *Encyclopedia of the Musical Theatre*, 2nd ed. (New York: Schirmer, 2001), lists her birth name as "Ida Louise Johnson," but I have not found this information in any other source. Her year of birth is given variously as 1869 and 1875. The 1875 date is based on a census record from that year, which only indicates that a child exists, not her actual birthdate. The *ASCAP Biographical Dictionary of Composers, Authors and Publishers* (New York: Bowker, 1980) lists her birth year as 1869. *Women in Particular: An Index to American Women*, Kali Herman, ed. (Phoenix: Oryx Press, 1984), lists the date as "1869/75."
3. Sherry D. Engle, *New Women Dramatists in America* (New York: Palgrave Macmillan, 2007), 224.
4. "Jas. Young, Jr., Weds," *Baltimore Sun*, September 19, 1901.
5. Rida Johnson Young Alumnae File, C. Elizabeth Boyd '33 Archives, Wilson College.
6. Bennett, "The Woman Who Wrote 'Mother Machree,'" 184.
7. Ibid., 185.
8. Isidore Witmark and Isaac Goldberg, *The Story of the House of Witmark: From Ragtime to Swingtime* (New York: Lee Furman, 1939), 348–349.
9. Bennett, "The Woman Who Wrote 'Mother Machree,'" 185.
10. "Theatres Last Night," *Baltimore Sun*, May 15, 1900.
11. "New Novel by Miss Johnson," *Baltimore Sun*, February 15, 1901.
12. "Jas. Young, Jr., Weds."
13. *Baltimore Sun*, January 3, 1904.
14. Rida Johnson Young, *Brown of Harvard: A Play in Four Acts* (New York: Samuel French, 1909). That colorful description of the college students is given in the *dramatis personae*.
15. "A College Play at the Princess," *Baltimore Sun*, February 25, 1906.

16. Young, *Brown of Harvard*, 36.
17. New York Public Library (hereafter NYPL) clippings file dated June 11, 1906.
18. "A Woman Dramatist," *Augusta Herald*, undated clipping, NYPL.
19. Correspondence with Anna Hocker, Schlesinger Library Research Services, Harvard University.
20. Promotional pamphlet for *Brown of Harvard*, NYPL clippings file.
21. Acton Davies, "Some Dramas of the Day," *Theatre Magazine*, undated clipping, NYPL.
22. *Life*, March 8, 1906, 313.
23. Rida Johnson Young and Melville Ellis, "When Love Is Young," (New York: M. Witmark & Sons, 1906).
24. *Brown of Harvard* (short), directed by Colin Campbell, Selig Polyscope Company (1911); *Brown of Harvard*, directed by Harry Beaumont, Perfection Pictures (1918); *Brown of Harvard*, directed by Jack Conway, Metro-Goldwyn-Mayer (1926).
25. Bennett, "The Woman Who Wrote 'Mother Machree,'" 186.
26. *Brooklyn Eagle*, October 9, 1907.
27. "A Betsy Patterson Play," *Baltimore Sun*, November 14, 1906.
28. "Glorious Betsy," NYPL clippings file.
29. Ibid.
30. "Mrs. Young Writes Again," *Baltimore Sun*, November 15, 1908.
31. "A Bright Comedy Enlivens an Otherwise Uneventful Seven Days," *New York Dramatic Mirror*, January 11, 1910, 6.
32. "The Lottery Man," NYPL clippings file.
33. Ibid.
34. Ibid.
35. George Jean Nathan, "What the Theater Got in Its Stocking," *Smart Set*, February 1910, 145.
36. "At the Playhouses," *The Theatre*, January 1910, 5.
37. Bennett, "The Woman Who Wrote 'Mother Machree,'" 180.
38. "The Lottery Man," NYPL clippings file.
39. "Mrs. Young Tells What," *Evening Sun*, November 1, 1912.
40. "No Theft in Play Steals, Says Brady," *New York Times*, November 1, 1912; "Writer Sues Shuberts," *New York Times*, October 29, 1912.
41. Shirley Burns, "Women Dramatists," *Green Book Album* (September 1910): 634.
42. W. A. Phelon, "Olcott Captures House as Usual," NYPL clippings file.
43. Ernest R. Ball, Chauncey Olcott, and Rida Johnson Young, "Mother Machree," (New York: M. Witmark & Sons, 1910). The word *machree* is a bastardization of a Gaelic term meaning "my dear" or "my heart."
44. Bennett, "The Woman Who Wrote 'Mother Machree,'" 34.
45. "Chauncey Olcott," NYPL clippings file.
46. Philip Furia and Michael Lasser, *America's Songs: The Stories behind the Songs of Broadway, Hollywood, and Tin Pan Alley* (New York: Routledge, 2006), 6–7.
47. Bennett, "The Woman Who Wrote 'Mother Machree,'" 34.
48. Ibid., 180.
49. For a comprehensive analysis of *The Girl and the Pennant*, see Travis W. Stern, "From the Ball Fields to Broadway: Performative Identities of Professional

Baseball Players on the Nineteenth and Twentieth Century American Stage," PhD diss., University of Illinois, 2011.
50. Ibid., 112.
51. Ibid., 122.
52. "'Matty' Does a Play," NYPL clippings file.
53. Stern, "From the Ball Fields to Broadway," 115.
54. "Women's Year in the Drama," *Chicago Daily Tribune*, February 17, 1907.
55. David Belasco, "The Grand Opportunity of the Woman Dramatist," *Good Housekeeping Magazine*, November 1911, 627–628.
56. Ibid.
57. Shubert Archive correspondence file.
58. "The Great American Playwright Belt," *San Francisco Call*, September 4, 1910.
59. Eve Sullivan, "Gilded Age Shines On," *Stamford Advocate*, May 4, 2014.
60. "Local Interest in Young Divorce," *Baltimore Sun*, July 30, 1909.
61. Quoted in "Miss Young's Success as Playwright," unmarked clipping, NYPL clippings file.
62. Ibid.
63. "James Young Divorced," *Baltimore Sun*, July 29, 1909.
64. "James Young Has Done It Again," *New York Telegraph*, September 4, 1911.
65. NYPL clippings file.
66. Bennett, "The Woman Who Wrote 'Mother Machree,'" 186.
67. "'Mother' Song Aids College Fund," Rida Johnson Young Alumnae File, C. Elizabeth Boyd '33 Archives, Wilson College.
68. Bennett, "The Woman Who Wrote 'Mother Machree,'" 179.
69. Burns, "Women Dramatists," 634.
70. Ibid.
71. "Cheer from a Tragic Life," *Hartford Courant*, May 16, 1926.
72. "Dramatists—No. 3," *Baltimore Sun*, February 21, 1909.

CHAPTER 3 Ah! Sweet Mystery of Life: *Naughty Marietta*

1. Mary B. Mullett, "She Holds the Season's Record for Stage Successes," *New York Sun*, May 6, 1917, 16.
2. Schroeder is referred to as her nephew in some sources, a family friend in others. Whatever the relationship, Young named him executor of her estate after her death.
3. *Washington Post*, March 8, 1910.
4. Mullett, "She Holds the Record."
5. Dominic Symonds, *We'll Have Manhattan: The Early Work of Rodgers and Hart* (New York: Oxford University Press, 2015), 13.
6. The location held some irony for Hammerstein; the Olympia proved a disastrous venture, and he was forced to auction it off. In 2016, the remains of the orchestra pit were discovered underneath the Toys "R" Us store in Times Square.
7. Unidentified newspaper clipping, New York Public Library (hereafter NYPL).
8. Neil Gould, *Victor Herbert: A Theatrical Life* (New York: Fordham University Press, 2008), 402.

9. Raymond Knapp, *The American Musical and the Performance of Personal Identity* (Princeton: Princeton University Press, 2006), 35–36.
10. Richard Traubner, *Operetta: A Theatrical History*, rev. ed. (New York: Routledge, 2003), 372. Since its premiere, the script has undergone at least two major revisions, first for the 1935 film and then in 1959 for amateur performance (revision by Phil Park), neither of which involved Young herself, as she died in 1926.
11. Henry Blossom, quoted in Louis Cline, "The Tribulations of a Librettist," *The Theatre*, June 1917, 334.
12. Frederick S. Roffman, "Ah, It's Sweet Mystery Time," *New York Times*, May 11, 1975.
13. Edward N. Waters, *Victor Herbert: A Life in Music* (New York: Macmillan, 1955), 356.
14. Rida Johnson Young, "Lo! The Poor Librettist," *New York Tribune*, June 3, 1917.
15. Waters, *Victor Herbert*, 360.
16. Originally, this character was a Jewish-Irish immigrant and a broad stereotype. His name was changed to Silas Slick, a comic character with an unidentified ethnicity, in the show's second year (Gould, *Victor Herbert*, 402).
17. Rida Johnson Young, *Naughty Marietta*, typescript, Shubert Archive, New York, 1.1.29. Pagination for the typescripts I consulted were wildly inconsistent, sometimes changing styles between acts. I have tried to make page numbers as clear as possible for this book. Where there are three numbers given, the first number indicates the act, the second number indicates the scene, and the third number indicates the page. If only two numbers are given, they indicate act and page. In this instance, 1.1.29 refers to act 1, scene 1, page 29..
18. French scenes divide the action into smaller units than printed scene divisions, usually when any character enters or leaves the stage.
19. William A. Everett, *Sigmund Romberg* (New Haven: Yale University Press, 2007), 16.
20. The 1928 operetta *The New Moon* essentially used the same version of New Orleans, also in the wrong decade. The lyrics and libretto were by Oscar Hammerstein II, and music was by Sigmund Romberg.
21. Shannon Lee Dawdy, *Building the Devil's Empire: French Colonial New Orleans* (Chicago: University of Chicago Press, 2008), 3.
22. Herbert Asbury, *The French Quarter: An Informal History of the New Orleans Underworld* (New York: Garden City, 1938), 12.
23. Grace King, *New Orleans: The Place and the People* (New York: Macmillan, 1895), 54.
24. Roffman, "Ah, It's Sweet Mystery Time."
25. "Naughty Marietta and Trentini a Hit," *New York Times,* November 8, 1910.
26. Waters, *Victor Herbert*, 361.
27. Young, *Naughty Marietta*, 1.6.
28. Two excellent resources in this vein are John Bush Jones, *Our Musicals, Ourselves: A Social History of the American Theatre* (Waltham, MA: Brandeis University Press, 2003);and Raymond Knapp, *The American Musical and the Formation of National Identity* (Princeton: Princeton University Press, 2005).

29. French-Canadian fur traders.
30. Young, *Naughty Marietta*, 1.5.
31. Rida Johnson Young, *The Boys of Company "B,"* typescript, NYPL, 7.
32. Young, *Naughty Marietta*, 1.11.
33. Ibid., 2.1.5.
34. Ibid., 2.1.1.
35. Rida Johnson Young and Victor Herbert, *Naughty Marietta*, vocal score (New York: M. Witmark & Sons, 1910), 61–62.
36. Historically, quadroon women were free but were often the kept mistresses of wealthy Creole men. By law, they could not marry white men. Young stretched historical fact to heighten the precariousness of Adah's position.
37. There is some debate about whether the Quadroon Ball and its accompanying common-law arrangement, *plaçage*, actually existed in historical New Orleans. For more information, see Kenneth Aslakson, "The 'Quadroon-Plaçage' Myth of Antebellum New Orleans: Anglo-American (Mis)interpretations of a French-Caribbean Phenomenon," *Journal of Social History* 45.3 (Spring 2012): 709–734.
38. Young, *Naughty Marietta*, 2.1.5.
39. Candice Marie Coleman, "Gender Issues as Reflected in the Lives and Plays of Three Women Playwrights: 1900–1930," PhD diss. Kent State University, 1993, 153–157.
40. Young, *Naughty Marietta*, 1.1.14.
41. Ibid., 1.1.19.
42. Ibid., 2.2.13.
43. Young and Herbert, *Naughty Marietta*, 49–51. The final lines are paraphrased from Longfellow's poem "There Was a Little Girl."
44. "Emma Trentini—The 'Little Devil' of the Opera House," *The Theatre*, March 1911, 86.
45. Young, *Naughty Marietta*, 2.1.3.
46. Young and Herbert, *Naughty Marietta*, 118–119.
47. The expected spelling is "Someone," but as Young separates "some" and "one" in both the printed script and the score, Dick is specifying Marietta as the "one" he loves. Because of this, he is able to say "Some one girl" in the second line of the refrain.
48. Young and Herbert, *Naughty Marietta*, 175–177.
49. The most famous is "My Ship" from Kurt Weill and Ira Gershwin's *Lady in the Dark* (1941), but this was more recently (and less successfully) used in John Kander and Fred Ebb's *Curtains* (2006), with "In the Same Boat."
50. Young and Herbert, *Naughty Marietta*, 185–186.
51. *The Theatre*, December 1910, 166.
52. Charles Darnton, "'Naughty Marietta' Makes Broadway Open Its Ears," NYPL clippings file.
53. "'Naughty Marietta' Falls Flat in New York Theatre," NYPL clippings file.
54. NYPL clippings file.
55. "Film Reviews," *Variety*, March 27, 1935, 15. Joseph Breen served as the head of the Production Code Administration, which censored Hollywood film scripts from 1930 to 1967.
56. Gould, *Victor Herbert*, 235.

CHAPTER 4 The Old-Fashioned Things Must Go: Musical Comedies

1. Mary B. Mullett, "She Holds the Season's Record for Stage Successes," *New York Sun*, May 6, 1917, 16.
2. "Miss Young's Success as Playwright," New York Public Library (hereafter NYPL) clippings file.
3. Young, letter to J. J. Shubert, Shubert Archive (hereafter SA).
4. Young, letter to J. J. Shubert, SA.
5. Young, telegram to Lee Shubert, September 23, 1914, SA. Because the telegram contains no punctuation, I had to guess at sentence breaks.
6. Lee Shubert, letter to Young, September 24, 1914, SA.
7. Young, telegrams to Lee Shubert, SA.
8. John James Hickey, "The Lure of 'Lady Luxury': A Musical Gem That Was Lost and Found," *The Passing Show: Newsletter of the Shubert Archive* 30 (2013–2014): 31.
9. Rida Johnson Young, *Lady Luxury*. The extant script is from Mills Music Library, University of Wisconsin–Madison. A notation inside says, "This Manuscript has been corrected and brought up to date by Leo Stark, and is the piece as played by the Charles H. Wuerz company of Lady Luxury. April 7, 1915."
10. Correspondence file, SA.
11. Hickey, "The Lure of 'Lady Luxury,'" 35.
12. Young, *Lady Luxury*, 1.25.
13. Ibid., 1.23.
14. Ibid., 1.12.
15. Ibid., 1.34.
16. "'Lady Luxury' Is Quite Pleasing," *New York Times*, December 26, 1914.
17. Young, *Lady Luxury*, 1.2.
18. Ibid., 1.3.
19. Later examples include "It's a Windy Day on the Battery" from Young's *Maytime*, the title song from *Lady, Be Good!* (Gershwin), and "When the Sea Is Calling" from *No, No, Nanette* (Caesar/Harbach/Youmans).
20. Rida Johnson Young, "I'll Take You All," *Lady Luxury*, vocal score (New York: M. Witmark & Sons, 1914), 5–6.
21. Young, *Lady Luxury*, typescript, 1.41.
22. Young, "Dream On, My Princess," *Lady Luxury*, vocal score, 2–3.
23. Young, *Lady Luxury*, typescript, 2.6.
24. Ibid., 2.18.
25. Ibid., 2.20.
26. Ibid., 2.38.
27. Ibid., 2.24-25.
28. Ibid., 1.37.
29. Ibid., 2.9-10.
30. Ibid.
31. "'Lady Luxury' Is Quite Pleasing."
32. "'Lady Luxury' Here to Cheer You Up," Robinson Locke Collection, NYPL.
33. "'Lady Luxury' at Casino," *New York Sun*, December 26, 1914.

34. "'Lady Luxury' a Sad Dame on Casino Stage," *New York World,* December 26, 1914.
35. "The New Plays," *The Theatre,* February 1915, 60.
36. Robinson Locke Collection, NYPL.
37. "Sweet and Mild Is 'Lady Luxury,'" Robinson Locke Collection, NYPL.
38. Robinson Locke Collection, NYPL.
39. Hickey, "The Lure of 'Lady Luxury,'" 43.
40. Gerald Bordman, *American Musical Comedy: From* Adonis *to* Dreamgirls (New York: Oxford University Press, 1982), 7.
41. "'Sometime' Comes, with Ed Wynn," *New York Times,* October 5, 1918.
42. Gerald Bordman and Richard Norton, *American Musical Theatre: A Chronicle,* 4th ed. (New York: Oxford University Press, 2011), 385; and William A. Everett, *Rudolf Friml* (Urbana: University of Illinois Press, 2008), 27.
43. Bordman cites this as "one of the earliest uses of flashback" (Bordman and Norton, *American Musical Theatre,* 382).
44. Rida Johnson Young, *Sometime,* typescript, SA, 1.4. The word *flivver* was slang for an old, battered car.
45. Ibid., 1.5.
46. This character is listed alternatively as "Carter" and "Dick."
47. Young, *Sometime,* 1.34.
48. Ibid., 1.14.
49. Ibid., 1.38.
50. Rida Johnson Young and Rudolf Friml, *Sometime,* vocal score (New York: G. Schirmer, 1919), 15–16.
51. Young, *Sometime,* 2.9
52. Everett, *Rudolf Friml,* 28.
53. Sherry D. Engle, *New Women Dramatists in America, 1890–1920* (New York: Palgrave Macmillan, 2007), 182.
54. Young and Friml, *Sometime* , 39–40.
55. Ibid., 27–28.
56. Young, *Sometime* , 1.27.
57. Ibid., 1.42.
58. Ibid., 1.2.
59. Ibid., 1.6.
60. John H. Raftery, "'Sometime' at the Shubert Theatre," *New York Telegraph,* October 6, 1915.
61. "'Sometime' Comes, with Ed Wynn."

CHAPTER 5 Just One of the Boys: Young as Co-Writer

1. Mary B. Mullett, "She Holds the Season's Record for Stage Successes," *New York Sun,* May 6, 1917.
2. Duncan's middle name is variably written as "Cary" and "Carey." As it is "Cary" on published sheet music, I have opted for that spelling.
3. Young, letter to Shuberts, dated October 19, 1910, Shubert Archive (hereafter SA).

4. Young, letter to Shuberts, dated February 21, 1911, SA.
5. Young, letter to Shuberts, dated April 11, 1911, SA.
6. Young, letter to Shuberts, dated August 3, 1911, SA.
7. Rida Johnson Young, *Next!* typescript, 2.1–2 Houghton Library, Harvard University.
8. For an in-depth analysis of Jerome Kern's score for *The Red Petticoat*, please see J James Kenneth Randall, "Becoming Jerome Kern: The Early Songs and Shows, 1903–1915," PhD diss., University of Illinois, 2004.
9. Ibid., 186.
10. Johnson Briscoe, *The Actors' Birthday Book, [First]–Third Series: An Authoritative Insight into the Lives of the Men and Women of the Stage Born between January First and December Thirty-First* (New York: Moffat, Yard1907–1909), 37.
11. "Paul West Missing, Is Believed Dead," *New York Sun*, October 26, 1918.
12. Gerald Bordman, *Jerome Kern: His Life and Music* (New York: Oxford University Press, 1980), 75.
13. Young, letter to Shuberts dated May 16, 1912, SA.
14. Young, letter to Shuberts, dated September 17, 1912, SA.
15. Bordman, *Jerome Kern*, 76.
16. Rida Johnson Young and Paul West, *The Red Petticoat*, typescript, SA.
17. Program found in New York Public Library (hereafter NYPL) clippings file and attached to file box in SA.
18. NYPL clippings file.
19. Lee Shubert, letter to Young, dated April 16, 1912, SA.
20. Young, letter to Lee Shubert, dated April 26, 1912, SA.
21. Young, *Next!* 19.
22. "'The Red Petticoat,'" *New York Tribune*, November 14, 1912.
23. Young and West, *The Red Petticoat*, 1.1.
24. Bordman, *Jerome Kern*, 75.
25. Young and West, *The Red Petticoat*, 1.14.
26. A job for which we now use the term "manicurist."
27. Young and West, *The Red Petticoat*, 1.16–17.
28. Ad in *Buffalo Evening News*, November 4, 1912.
29. *Los Angeles Times*, June 9, 1912.
30. Young and West, *The Red Petticoat*, 1.5.
31. Ibid., 1.17.
32. Ibid., 1.23.
33. Ibid., 2.8.
34. Ibid., 1.24.
35. Young, *Next!* 1.37.
36. "'Red Petticoat' Bright with Fun," *Boston Globe*, February 11, 1913.
37. "An Actress in the Making," *New York Sun*, November 17, 1912.
38. "'The Red Petticoat,' and Some Others," *New York Times*, November 14, 1912.
39. Young, letter to Shuberts, dated December 4, 1912, SA.
40. Young, letter to a Mr. Morris—possibly William Morris of the William Morris Agency—dated June 11, 1921, SA.
41. Sigmund Spaeth, "Music for Everybody," *Oakland Tribune*, June 13, 1954.

42. Rida Johnson Young, *The Boys of Company "B,"* typescript, NYPL, 1.24.
43. Rida Johnson Young and William Cary Duncan, *When Love Is Young*, typescript, SA, 1.30–31.
44. Young, *The Boys of Company "B,"* 3.26.
45. Young and Duncan, *When Love Is Young*, 3.52–53.
46. Ibid., 1.51.
47. William Cary Duncan, "The Girl That Dreams of Me" (New York: M. Witmark & Sons, 1913).
48. Rida Johnson Young, and William Schroeder, "The Tango Glide," (New York: M. Witmark & Sons, 1913).
49. Unmarked clippings, NYPL clippings file.
50. Mullett, "She Holds the Season's Record."
51. Unmarked clipping, NYPL clippings file.
52. Rida Johnson Young and William Cary Duncan, *His Little Widows*, typescript, Tams-Witmark Collection, University of Wisconsin–Madison, 18.
53. Ibid., 6.
54. Ibid., 53.
55. Lewis Sherwin, "'His Little Widows' Presented at the Astor," *Globe*, May 1, 1917, NYPL clippings file.
56. Rida Johnson Young and William Schroeder, "My Love Is a Secret" (New York: Jos. W. Stern & Co., 1917).
57. Rida Johnson Young and William Schroeder, "That Creepy Weepy Feeling" (New York: Jos. W. Stern & Co., 1917).
58. William Cary Duncan and William Schroeder, "Oh, You Girls!" (New York: Jos. W. Stern & Co., 1917).
59. *The Theatre*, June 1917, 343.
60. *New York Evening Mail*, May 1, 1917, NYPL clippings file.
61. *Globe*, May 1, 1917, NYPL clippings file.
62. Charles Collins, "Mormon Widows in Musical Show," *Chicago Post*, March 26, 1918, NYPL clippings file.

CHAPTER 6 Will You Remember? Operetta in Wartime

1. Helen Christine Bennett, "The Woman Who Wrote 'Mother Machree,'" *American Magazine* 90 (1920), 180.
2. Mary B. Mullett, "She Holds the Season's Record for Stage Successes," *New York Sun*, May 6, 1917.
3. *Brooklyn Life*, November 25, 1916, 28.
4. Foster Hirsch, *The Boys from Syracuse: The Shuberts' Theatrical Empire* (Carbondale: Southern Illinois University Press, 1998), 160.
5. William A. Everett, *Sigmund Romberg* (New Haven: Yale University Press, 2007), 83.
6. Gerald Bordman and Richard Norton, *American Musical Theatre: A Chronicle*, 4th ed. (New York: Oxford University Press, 2011), 365.
7. Mullett, "She Holds the Season's Record."
8. Obituary, *Theatre Magazine*, July–August 1920, 69–70.

9. Clifton Crawford, telegram to Lee Shubert, October 24, 1916, Shubert Archive (hereafter SA).
10. Lee Shubert, letter to Clifton Crawford, October 24, 1916, SA.
11. Clifton Crawford, telegram to J. J. Shubert, October 26, 1916, SA.
12. J. J. Shubert, letter to Clifton Crawford, February 17, 1917, SA.
13. Rida Johnson Young, *Her Soldier Boy*, Typescript, SA, New York, P.1. The script is divided into a prologue and two acts. "P" refers to the prologue.
14. Ibid., P-4.
15. Several of the songs were interpolations by Crawford, who played Teddy. Augustus Barratt also contributed "Amsterdam." For the purposes of this study, I only discuss songs written by Young.
16. Rida Johnson Young, "I'd Be Happy Anywhere with You" (New York: G. Schirmer, 1918).
17. Young, *Her Soldier Boy*, 2.12.
18. Everett, *Sigmund Romberg*, 89.
19. Young, *Her Soldier Boy*, 1.16.
20. Ibid., P.9.
21. Rida Johnson Young, "Song of Home" (New York: G. Schirmer, 1916).
22. Ibid.
23. "Mirth and Melody in 'Her Soldier Boy,'" *New York Times*, December 7, 1916.
24. Charles Darnton, "'Her Soldier Boy' Hits the Bull's-Eye," *Evening World*, December 7, 1916.
25. Hornblow, "Her Soldier Boy," *The Theatre*, January 1917, 24.
26. "Lilting Tunes in Musical Piece," *Evening Sun*, November 28, 1916.
27. *Wie einst im Mai*, English translation by Grace Isabel Colbron, International Play Agency, 1917.
28. Letter to J. J. and Lee Shubert from International Play Agency, August 9, 1917, SA.
29. Channing Pollock, "Squaring Washington Square," *Green Book Magazine* (August 1918): 207.
30. "'Maytime' Is Delightful," *Times Union*, August 17, 1917.
31. "'Maytime' Scores at the Shubert," *New York Times*, August 7, 1917.
32. Rida Johnson Young, *Maytime*, typescript, SA, 1.1.
33. Ibid., 1.30.
34. Ibid., 1.20.
35. Ibid., 1.7.
36. Ibid., 4.14.
37. Ibid., 1.6.
38. Ibid., 2.14.
39. Ibid., 3.13.
40. Ibid., 3.12.
41. Ibid., 2.19.
42. Ibid., 1.29.
43. *Theatre Magazine*, July 1918, 13.
44. Rida Johnson Young and Sigmund Romberg, *Maytime*, vocal score (New York: G. Schirmer, 1917), 11–12.

45. Ibid., 39–40.
46. Young, *Maytime*, 2.9, 2.10.
47. W. T. Lhamon, Jr, *Jump Jim Crow: Lost Plays, Lyrics, and Street Prose of the First Atlantic Popular Culture* (Cambridge, MA: Harvard University Press, 2003) 95–96.
48. Rida Johnson Young, "Jump Jim Crow" (New York: G. Schirmer, 1917).
49. *Wie einst im Mai,* trans. Colbron, act 1.
50. Ibid., act 4.
51. Young and Romberg, *Maytime*, 23–24.
52. Ibid., 39–40.
53. John Corbin, "'Maytime,' and after That, 'The Deluge,'" *New York Times*, August 26, 1917.
54. *Theatre Magazine* (October 1917): 205.
55. Corbin, "'Maytime' and After That, 'The Deluge,'" 75.
56. Young, letter to J. J. Shubert, July 12, 1918, SA.
57. Even though some sources list other songs from the stage musical as being in the film version, they are not. It is possible that they are used as underscoring, but none is sung, and therefore, Young's lyrics are absent.
58. As I have been unable to locate a score or sheet music for individual songs, and the lyrics do not appear in the script, I can only analyze Young's libretto.
59. Young, letter to J. J. Shubert, SA.
60. Rida Johnson Young, *Little Simplicity*, typescript, SA, 1.1.
61. The difference in spelling in Young's script may be due to a typist's error, a change in the accepted English spelling, or Young's own interpretation of what she heard someone chanting.
62. Young, *Little Simplicity*, 1.2.
63. Ibid., 2.2.
64. Ibid., 2.24.
65. Ibid., 2.13.
66. New York Public Library (hereafter NYPL) clippings file.
67. "Little Simplicity," *Globe,* November 5, 1918, NYPL clippings file.
68. "Little Simplicity," *American,* November 6, 1918, NYPL clippings file.
69. "'Little Simplicity' at the Astor," *New York Star*, November 13, 1918, NYPL clippings file.
70. Charles Darnton, "'Little Simplicity' Conventional Musical," *Evening World*, November 7, 1918, NYPL clippings file.
71. "'Little Simplicity' New Musical Sounds Novel Patriotic Note," *New York Dramatic Mirror*, November 6, 1918, NYPL clippings file.

CHAPTER 7 Dream Girl: End of a Career

1. "Woman Playwright's Secret of Success," *Syracuse Herald*, November 18, 1917.
2. Mary B. Mullett, "She Holds the Season's Record for Stage Successes," *New York Sun*, May 6, 1917.
3. "Actresses to Grow War Relief Crops," *New York Times*, May 6, 1917.
4. Helen Ten Broeck, "Rida Young—Dramatist and Garden Expert," *The Theatre*, April 1917, 202.

5. Alexander Woollcott, "The Play," *New York Times*, September 9, 1920.
6. Neil Gould, *Victor Herbert: A Theatrical Life* (New York: Fordham University Press, 2008), 532.
7. Ibid., 502.
8. Young, letter to Shuberts, December 10, 1922, Shubert Archive (hereafter SA).
9. Young, letter to Shuberts, April 14, 1923, SA.
10. Unmarked clipping, New York Public Library (hereafter NYPL) clippings file.
11. Percy Hammond, "The Theatres," NYPL clippings file.
12. Foster Hirsch, *The Boys from Syracuse: The Shuberts' Theatrical Empire* (Carbondale: Southern Illinois University Press, 1998), 137.
13. Rida Johnson Young and Harold Atteridge, *The Dream Girl*, typescript, NYPL, 19–20.
14. Young and Atteridge, *The Dream Girl*, SA, 21–22.
15. "Herbert Melodies in 'The Dream Girl,'" NYPL clippings file.
16. Gould, *Victor Herbert*, 503.
17. Young and Atteridge, *The Dream Girl*, NYPL, 17.
18. Young and Atteridge, *The Dream Girl*, SA, 19.
19. Ibid., 21.
20. NYPL clippings file.
21. "Rida Johnson Is Ill," *Billboard*, December 26, 1925.
22. Mullett, "She Holds the Season's Record."
23. "Rida Johnson Young Left $90,411 Estate," *Billboard*, August 27, 1927.
24. "Rida Johnson Young," *Baltimore Sun*, May 10, 1926.
25. O. O. McIntyre, "Gossip and a Few Prejudices!" *Miami News*, July 4, 1926.
26. Helen Christine Bennett, "The Woman Who Wrote 'Mother Machree,'" *American Magazine* 90 (1920), 185.

SELECTED BIBLIOGRAPHY
• • •

Books and Essays

Auster, Albert. *Actresses and Suffragists: Women in the American Theater, 1890–1920.* New York: Praeger, 1984.

Banfield, Stephen. *Jerome Kern.* New Haven: Yale University Press, 2006.

Bordman, Gerald. *American Musical Comedy: From* Adonis *to* Dreamgirls. New York: Oxford University Press,1982.

Bordman, Gerald. *American Operetta: From* H.M.S. Pinafore *to* Sweeney Todd. New York: Oxford University Press, 1981.

Bordman, Gerald. *Jerome Kern: His Life and Music.* New York: Oxford University Press, 1980.

Bordman, Gerald, and Richard Norton. *American Musical Theatre: A Chronicle*, 4th ed. New York: Oxford University Press, 2011.

Brown, Dorothy M. *Setting a Course: American Women in the 1920s.* Boston: Twayne, 1987.

Chafe, William H. *The American Woman: Her Changing Social, Economic, and Political Roles, 1920–1970.* London: Oxford University Press, 1972.

Chafe, William H. *The Paradox of Change: American Women in the 20th Century.* New York: Oxford University Press, 1991.

Chinoy, Helen Krich, and Linda Walsh Jenkins, eds. *Women in American Theatre.* New York: Theatre Communications Group, 1987.

Citron, Stephen. *The Wordsmiths: Oscar Hammerstein 2nd and Alan Jay Lerner.* New York: Oxford University Press, 1995.

Coleman, Bud, and Judith A. Sebesta, eds. *Women in American Musical Theatre.* Jefferson, NC: McFarland, 2008.

Commire, Anne, and Deborah Klezmer, eds. *Women in World History: A Biographical Encyclopedia.* Waterford, CT: Yorkin, 2002.

Coven, Brenda. *American Women Dramatists of the Twentieth Century: A Bibliography.* Metuchen, NJ: Scarecrow Press, 1982.

Davis, Lee. *Bolton and Wodehouse and Kern: The Men Who Made Musical Comedy.* New York: James H. Heineman, 1993.

Davis, Ronald L. *A History of Music in American Life*, Vol. 2: *The Gilded Years, 1865–1920.* Huntington, NY: Robert Krieger, 1980.

Dumenil, Lynn. *The Modern Temper: American Culture and Society in the 1920s.* New York: Hill and Wang, 1995.

Engel, Lehman. *Words with Music.* New York: Macmillan, 1972.

Engle, Ron, and Tice L. Miller, eds. *The American Stage: Social and Economic Issues from the Colonial Period to the Present.* Cambridge: Cambridge University Press, 1993.

Engle, Sherry D. *New Women Dramatists in America.* New York: Palgrave Macmillan, 2007.

Erenberg, Lewis A. *Steppin' Out: New York Nightlife and the Transformation of American Culture, 1890–1930*. Chicago: University of Chicago Press, 1981.
Everett, William A. *Rudolf Friml*. Urbana: University of Illinois Press, 2008.
Everett, William A. *Sigmund Romberg*. New Haven: Yale University Press, 2007.
Everett, William A., and Paul R. Laird, eds. *The Cambridge Companion to the Musical*, 2nd ed. Cambridge: Cambridge University Press, 2008.
Ewen, David. *Complete Book of the American Musical Theater*. New York: Henry Holt, 1958.
Ewen, David. *The Life and Death of Tin Pan Alley: The Golden Age of American Popular Music*. New York: Funk and Wagnalls, 1964.
Franceschina, John. *Harry B. Smith: Dean of American Librettists*. New York: Routledge, 2003.
Furia, Philip, ed. *Dictionary of Literary Biography*, Vol. 265: *American Song Lyricists, 1920–1960*. Detroit: Thomson Gale, 2002.
Furia, Philip. *Ira Gershwin: The Art of the Lyricist*. New York: Oxford University Press, 1996.
Furia, Philip. *The Poets of Tin Pan Alley: A History of America's Great Lyricists*. New York: Oxford University Press, 1990.
Furia, Philip, and Michael Lasser. *America's Songs: The Stories behind the Songs of Broadway, Hollywood, and Tin Pan Alley*. New York: Routledge, 2006.
Gänzl, Kurt. *The Encyclopedia of the Musical Theatre*, 2nd ed. New York: Schirmer Books, 2001.
Gilbert, James, et al. *The Mythmaking Frame of Mind: Social Imagination and American Culture*. Belmont, CA: Wadsworth, 1993.
Gilbert, Sandra M., and Susan Gubar. *No Man's Land: The Place of the Woman Writer in the Twentieth Century*. New Haven: Yale University Press, 1988.
Glenn, Susan A. *Female Spectacle: The Theatrical Roots of Modern Feminism*. Cambridge, MA: Harvard University Press, 2000.
Gould, Neil. *Victor Herbert: A Theatrical Life*. New York: Fordham University Press, 2008.
Grattan, Virginia L. *American Women Songwriters: A Biographical Dictionary*. Westport, CT: Greenwood Press, 1993.
Heilbrun, Carolyn G. *Writing a Woman's Life*. New York: Ballantine, 1989.
Heller, Adele, and Lois Rudnick, eds. *1915, the Cultural Moment: The New Politics, the New Woman, the New Psychology, the New Art and the New Theatre in America*. New Brunswick, NJ: Rutgers University Press, 1991.
Hirsch, Foster. *The Boys from Syracuse: The Shuberts' Theatrical Empire*. Carbondale: Southern Illinois University Press, 1998.
Hischak, Thomas S. *Boy Loses Girl: Broadway's Librettists*. Lanham, MD: Scarecrow Press, 2002.
Hischak, Thomas S. *The Oxford Companion to the American Musical: Theatre, Film, and Television*. Oxford: Oxford University Press, 2008.
Hischak, Thomas S. *Word Crazy: Broadway Lyricists from Cohan to Sondheim*. New York: Praeger, 1991.
Hyland, William G. *The Song Is Ended: Songwriters and American Music, 1900–1950*. New York: Oxford University Press, 1995.

Iger, Arthur L. *Music of the Golden Age, 1900–1950 and Beyond: A Guide to Popular Composers and Lyricists*. Westport, CT: Greenwood Press, 1998.

Jones, John Bush. *Our Musicals, Ourselves: A Social History of the American Musical Theatre*. Waltham, MA: Brandeis University Press, 2003.

Kerber, Linda K., and Jane De Hart-Mathews, eds. *Women's America: Refocusing the Past*, 2nd ed. New York: Oxford University Press, 1987.

Knapp, Raymond. *The American Musical and the Formation of National Identity*. Princeton: Princeton University Press, 2005.

Knapp, Raymond. *The American Musical and the Performance of Personal Identity*. Princeton: Princeton University Press, 2006.

Knapp, Raymond, Mitchell Morris, and Stacy Wolf, eds. *The Oxford Handbook of the American Musical*. New York: Oxford University Press, 2011.

Lamb, Andrew. *150 Years of Popular Musical Theatre*. New Haven: Yale University Press, 2000.

Logan, Mary S. *The Part Taken by Women in American History*. Wilmington, DE: Perry-Neale, 1912.

Mates, Julian. *America's Musical Stage: Two Hundred Years of Musical Theatre*. Westport, CT: Greenwood Press, 1985.

McLean, Lorraine Arnal. *Dorothy Donnelly: A Life in the Theatre*. London: McFarland, 1999.

McMillin, Scott. *The Musical as Drama: A Study of the Principles and Conventions behind Musical Shows from Kern to Sondheim*. Princeton: Princeton University Press, 2006.

McNamara, Brooks. *The Shuberts of Broadway*. New York: Oxford University Press, 1990.

Miller, Nathan. *New World Coming: The 1920s and the Making of Modern America*. New York: Scribner, 2003.

Mordden, Ethan. *Better Foot Forward: The History of the American Musical Theatre*. New York: Grossman, 1976.

Mordden, Ethan. *Broadway Babies: The People Who Made the American Musical*. New York: Oxford University Press, 1983.

Mordden, Ethan. *Make Believe: The Broadway Musical in the 1920s*. New York: Oxford University Press, 1997.

Mordden, Ethan. *That Jazz! An Idiosyncratic Social History of the American Twenties*. New York: G. P. Putnam's Sons, 1978.

Norton, Richard C. *A Chronology of American Musical Theatre*. Oxford: Oxford University Press, 2002.

Robinson, Alice M., Vera Mowry Roberts, and Milly S. Barranger, eds. *Notable Women in the American Theatre: A Biographical Dictionary*. New York: Greenwood Press, 1989.

Smith, Cecil. *Musical Comedy in America*. New York: Theatre Arts Books, 1950.

Snyder, Robert W. *The Voice of the City: Vaudeville and Popular Culture in New York*. New York: Oxford University Press, 1989.

Stagg, Jerry. *The Brothers Shubert*. New York: Random House, 1968.

Steyn, Mark. *Broadway Babies Say Goodnight: Musicals Then and Now*. London: Faber and Faber, 1997.

Thomas, James. *Script Analysis for Actors, Directors, and Designers*, 3rd ed. Burlington, MA: Focal Press, 2005.

Traubner, Richard. *Operetta: A Theatrical History*, rev. ed. New York: Routledge, 2003.

Turk, Edward Baron. *Hollywood Diva: A Biography of Jeanette MacDonald*. Berkeley and Los Angeles: University of California Press, 1998.

Walsh, David, and Len Platt. *Musical Theatre and American Culture*. Westport, CT: Praeger, 2003.

Waters, Edward N. *Victor Herbert: A Life in Music*. New York: Macmillan,1955.

Westover, Jonas. *The Shuberts and Their Passing Shows: The Untold Tale of Ziegfeld's Rivals*. New York: Oxford University Press, 2016.

Wilson, Margaret Gibbons. *The American Woman in Transition: The Urban Influence, 1870–1920*. Westport: Greenwood Press, 1979.

Witmark, Isidore, and Isaac Goldberg. *The Story of the House of Witmark: From Ragtime to Swingtime*. New York: Lee Furman, 1939.

Wolf, Stacy. *A Problem Like Maria: Gender and Sexuality in the American Musical*. Ann Arbor: University of Michigan Press, 2002.

Zeitz, Joshua. *Flapper: A Madcap Story of Sex, Style, Celebrity, and the Women Who Made America Modern*. New York: Three Rivers Press, 2006.

Zinsser, William. *Easy to Remember: The Great American Songwriters and Their Songs*. Jaffrey, NH: David R. Godine, 2000.

Journal Articles

Block, Geoffrey. "Revisiting the Glorious and Problematic Legacy of the Jazz Age and Depression Musical." *Studies in Musical Theatre* 2.2 (2008): 127–146.

Hickey, John James. "The Lure of 'Lady Luxury': A Musical Gem That Was Lost and Found." *The Passing Show: Newsletter of the Shubert Archive* 30 (2013–2014): 23–46.

Knapp, Margaret M. "Integration of Elements as a Viable Standard for Judging Musical Theatre." *Journal of American Culture* 1.1 (1978): 112–119.

Mates, Julian. "Experiments on the American Musical Stage in the Twenties." *Journal of American Drama and Theatre* 8 (Spring 1996): 12–25.

McNicholl, B. T. "There Is Nothin' Like a Dame: Women Writers in the Musical Theatre." *The Dramatist* 1 (1998): 20–28.

Peck, Ellen Marie. "'Ah, Sweet Mystery': Rediscovering Three Female Lyricists of the Early Twentieth-Century American Musical Theater." *Contemporary Theatre Review* 19.1 (2009): 48–60.

Magazines and Newspaper Articles

Andrews, Charleton. "Wanted—A Librettist." *Theatre Magazine* (October 1918): 204.

Bennett, Helen Christine. "The Woman Who Wrote 'Mother Machree.'" *American Magazine* 90 (1920): 34–187.

Burns, Shirley. "Women Dramatists." *Green Book Album* (September 1910): 632–639.

Frame, Virginia. "Women Who Have Written Successful Plays." *The Theatre* (October 1906): 265.

Harbach, Otto. "The Writing of a Musical Comedy." *Theatre Magazine* (November 1925): 10.

Mullett, Mary B. "She Holds the Season's Record for Stage Successes." *New York Sun*, May 6, 1917, 16.

Patterson, Ada. "The Only Woman Librettist in America." *The Theatre* (June 1915): 305–306.

Patterson, Ada. "Wealth Not a Bar to Playwriting." *Theatre Magazine* (May 1918): 296–297.

Ten Broeck, Helen. "Rida Young—Dramatist and Garden Expert." *The Theatre* (April 1917): 202–250.

"Vote of Thanks to Rida Johnson Young." *New York Dramatic Mirror*, July 21, 1917, 6.

Wilmore, Carl. "American Operetta and Its Possibilities." *New York Dramatic Mirror* 10 (March 1917): n. p.

Young, Rida Johnson. "Lo! The Poor Librettist." *New York Tribune*, June 3, 1917.

Scripts and Scores

Young, Rida Johnson. *The Boys of Company "B."* Typescript. New York Public Library, New York.

Young, Rida Johnson. *Brown of Harvard: A Play in Four Acts.* New York: Samuel French, 1909.

Young, Rida Johnson. *Her Soldier Boy.* Typescript. Shubert Archive, New York.

Young, Rida Johnson. *Lady Luxury.* Typescript. Tams-Witmark Collection, University of Wisconsin–Madison.

Young, Rida Johnson. *Little Simplicity.* Typescript. Shubert Archive, New York.

Young, Rida Johnson. *Maytime.* Typescript. Shubert Archive, New York.

Young, Rida Johnson. *Naughty Marietta.* Typescript. Shubert Archive, New York.

Young, Rida Johnson. *Next!* Typescript. Houghton Library, Harvard University.

Young, Rida Johnson. *Sometime.* Typescript. Shubert Archive, New York.

Young, Rida Johnson, and Harold Atteridge. *The Dream Girl.* Typescripts. New York Public Library and Shubert Archive, New York.

Young, Rida Johnson, and William Cary Duncan. *His Little Widows.* Typescript. Tams-Witmark Collection, University of Wisconsin–Madison.

Young, Rida Johnson, and William Cary Duncan. *When Love Is Young.* Typescript. Shubert Archive, New York.

Young, Rida Johnson, and Rudolf Friml. *Sometime.* Vocal score. New York: G. Schirmer, 1919.

Young, Rida Johnson, and Victor Herbert. *Naughty Marietta.* Vocal score. New York: M. Witmark & Sons, 1910.

Young, Rida Johnson, and Sigmund Romberg. *Maytime.* Vocal score. New York: G. Schirmer, 1917.

Young, Rida Johnson, and William Schroeder. *Lady Luxury.* Vocal score. New York: M. Witmark & Sons, 1914.

Young, Rida Johnson, and Paul West. *The Red Petticoat.* Typescript. Shubert Archive.

Dissertations and Theses

Coleman, Candice Marie. "Gender Issues as Reflected in the Lives and Plays of Three Women Playwrights: 1900–1930." PhD diss., Kent State University, 1993.

Peck, Ellen Marie. "Blossom Time: Three Lyricist-Librettists and the Early Twentieth-Century American Musical Theatre." PhD diss., University of Illinois, 2009.

Peck, Ellen Marie. "Forgotten Words: Lyricists and the American Musical Theatre, 1890–1930." MA thesis, University of Illinois, 2006.

Randall, James Kenneth. "Becoming Jerome Kern: The Early Songs and Shows, 1903–1915." PhD diss., University of Illinois, 2004.

Stern, Travis W. "From the Ball Fields to Broadway: Performative Identities of Professional Baseball Players on the Nineteenth and Twentieth Century American Stage." PhD diss. , University of Illinois, 2011.

Archives

Billy Rose Theatre Division, New York Public Library.
Shubert Archive, New York.
Rida Johnson Young Alumnae File. C. Elizabeth Boyd '33 Archives, Wilson College.

INDEX

• • •

Figures and boxes are indicated by *f* and *b* following the page number

For the benefit of digital users, indexed terms that span two pages (e.g., 52–53) may, on occasion, appear on only one of those pages.

"Ah! Sweet Mystery of Life (Dream Melody)" xviii–xix, xx, 35, 36–37, 48–50, 51*b*, 121, 143–44
"Any Kind of Man," 70–71, 75*b*
Atteridge, Harold, 135–37, 139*b*, 146

Bainter, Fay, 138–39, 139*b*
Ball, Ernest, 24–25, 145
Barratt, Augustus, 109*b*, 124, 127*b*, 128–29, 146
Barry of Ballymore, 24–25, 145
Belasco, David, 28, 78–79
Blossom, Henry, 5–6, 7, 34, 35–36
Boys of Company "B", The, 20–21, 41, 86–88, 89, 145
Brown of Harvard, xviii, 18–21, 26–27, 30, 82, 99, 145

Caldwell, Anne, xvii–xviii, 2
Captain Kidd, Jr., 91, 99, 123, 145
Cock o' the Roost, 140, 145
"Correspondence School, The," 83, 87*b*
Crawford, Clifton, 100–1, 104*f*, 109*b*
Crews, Laura Hope, 18, 138–39

"Dancing Round," 138, 139*b*
Donnelly, Dorothy, xvii–xviii, 11–12, 41–42
"Don't You Really Think I'd Do?" 59–60, 66*b*
Dream Girl, The, xviii, 18, 49, 80, 133–40, 139*b*, 146
"Dream On, My Princess," 60–61, 66*b*
Duncan, William Cary, 66*b*, 77, 86–88, 90, 91, 92*b*, 95–96, 97*b*, 98, 145, 146

Eddy, Nelson, xx, 35, 49–50, 123, 142–43
Ellis, Melville, 20, 145

Fields, Dorothy, xvii
Friml, Rudolf, xix, 8, 53, 66–67, 71, 72, 74*b*, 146
Frohman, Charles, xix, 16, 20–21
Frohman, Daniel, xix, 16–17, 20–21, 31–32
Furness, Edith Ellis, 5, 23

Gershwin, George, xviii–xix, 70, 141
Gershwin, Ira, xviii–xix, 70, 71, 83
Girl and the Pennant, The, 26–28, 27*f*, 80, 145
Glaser, Lulu, 33–34, 86–88
Glorious Betsy, 9–10, 20–21, 80, 145
"Golden Sunshine," 102–3, 105, 109*b*

Hammerstein, Arthur, 67, 74*b*, 133
Hammerstein, Oscar, xix, 34–35, 40, 44–45, 51*b*
Hammerstein II, Oscar, xviii–xix, 8, 41–42, 47, 61, 142
Harbach, Otto, xviii–xix, 8, 12, 58
Harrold, Orville, 35, 51*b*
Herbert, Victor, xviii–xix, xx–xxi, 5–6, 34–38, 40, 45–46, 48–50, 51*b*, 67, 86–88, 133–34, 136–37, 138–39, 139*b*, 145, 146
Her Soldier Boy, xviii, 6, 8, 12, 25–26, 66–67, 72, 91, 99–108, 109*b*, 124–26, 145
His Little Widows, xviii, 53–54, 77, 86–88, 91–98, 97*b*, 146

"If I Were Anybody Else But Me," 42–43, 51*b*
"I'd Be Happy Anywhere with You," 105, 109*b*
"I'll Take You All," 58–59, 66*b*

"I'm Falling in Love with Some One,"
    xviii–xix, xx, 20, 35, 47–48, 51*b*,
    83, 138
"I Want to Go Home," 103–6, 109*b*
"In Our Little Home Sweet Home," 118,
    122, 124*b*
"Italian Street Song," 42, 51*b*
"It's Written in the Book of Destiny,"
    61–62, 66*b*

"Jump Jim Crow," 110–11,
    120–21, 124*b*
Just One of the Boys, 10, 33–34,
    86–88, 145

"Keep On Smiling," 72–73, 75*b*
Kern, Jerome, xviii–xix, 7, 77, 79,
    87*b*, 145
"Kiss Waltz," 6–7, 102–3, 109*b*

Lady Luxury, xviii, 53–65, 65*b*, 72, 80,
    86–88, 145
Little Old New York, 132–33, 140, 145
Little Simplicity, xviii, 99–100, 124–29,
    127*b*, 132–33, 146
"Longing Just for You," 60, 66*b*
Lottery Man, The, 5, 10, 22–23, 29–30,
    77–78, 145
Lowell, Helen, 77–79, 80, 85, 86, 87*b*

MacDonald, Jeanette, xx, 35, 49–50,
    86–88, 123, 143–44
Mannering, Mary, 20–21, 22
Mathewson, Christy, xix, 26–28,
    27*f*, 145
Maytime, xviii, 10, 12, 62, 68, 72,
    80, 99–100, 105, 108–22,
    123*b*, 124–25, 126, 128–29,
    132–34, 146
Maytime (film), 49–50, 123
Miller, Henry, 18, 30
"Mother Machree," xviii–xix, 24–26,
    107, 133, 145
"My Dream Girl," 138, 139*b*
"My Love Is a Secret," 96, 97*b*

Nathan, George Jean, 7, 22
Naughty Marietta, xviii–xix, xx, 12–13,
    20, 34–50, 51*b*, 62, 67, 68, 72,
    82, 83, 89, 105, 106, 108, 110,
    113, 117, 118–19, 126, 133–34,
    138, 145
"Naughty Marietta," 46, 51*b*
Naughty Marietta (film), xx, 49–50, 123
"Neath the Southern Moon," 43, 51*b*
New York Public Library, xvii–xviii, xxi,
    67, 135, 137
Next!, 77–79, 80, 84–86, 145

Olcott, Chauncey, xix, 23–26, 24*f*, 77,
    141, 145
"Old Fashioned Things, The," 58–59, 66*b*
"Oh, You Girls!" 96, 97*b*

"Pick, Pick, Pickaninny," 62, 66*b*
Purcell, Charles, 118, 119*f*, 123*b*

Ragged Robin, 23–24, 145
Red Petticoat, The, xviii, 7, 77–86,
    87*b*, 145
"Road to Paradise, The," 118–20,
    122, 124*b*
Romberg, Sigmund, xix, 8, 11, 12, 41–
    42, 66–67, 99–100, 105–6, 109–10,
    109*b*, 121, 123, 123*b*, 124, 137,
    139*b*, 145, 146

Schroeder, William, 20–21, 33–34,
    53–54, 55, 58, 65*b*, 77, 86–88, 92*b*,
    97*b*, 98, 140–41, 145, 146
Shubert Archive, xvii–xviii, xix, 28, 55–
    56, 67, 79–80, 135
Shubert Brothers, xix–xx, 8, 9–12, 16–
    17, 20–21, 22–23, 28, 31–32, 33–
    34, 44, 53–55, 69, 77–80, 86, 87*b*,
    91–92, 99–101, 108–10, 109*b*, 123,
    123*b*, 124, 127*b*, 128–29, 133, 135,
    136–37, 138–39, 139*b*
Shubert, J. J., 9–10, 22, 86, 99–100, 127
Shubert, Lee, 29–30, 54–55, 79–80
"Sights of London," 137–38

"Sing, Sing, You Tetrazzini," 83, 84, 87*b*
Smith, Harry B., 5–6, 7, 12, 34
Sometime, xviii, 53, 66–74, 74*b*, 80, 124–25, 126, 127, 135, 146
"Sometime," 71, 75*b*
"So Near, So Far Away," 72
"Song of Home," 106–7, 109*b*
Sothern, E. H., xix, 16–17
"Sweet By and By," 45, 51*b*

"That Creepy Weepy Feeling," 96, 97*b*, 98
"Those Awful Tattle Tales," 57–58, 66*b*
"Tramp! Tramp! Tramp!" 41, 51*b*
Trentini, Emma, 35, 36, 40, 46, 49, 51*b*, 67
"Tune You Can't Forget, The," 71, 75*b*

Van, Billy B., 135–37, 138, 139*b*

West, Mae, 67–68, 70–71, 74, 74*b*
West, Paul, 77, 78–80, 83–85, 87*b*, 145
"What Do You Have to Do?" 70, 75*b*
When Love Is Young, xviii, 20–21, 77, 86–91, 92*b*, 145
"When Love Is Young in Springtime," 20, 48
Whitney, Fred C., 54, 65*b*
"Will You Remember? (Sweetheart)" 110–11, 112–13, 118, 121–22, 123, 124*b*, 141
Witmark & Sons, 4–5, 12–13, 16–17, 20
Wood, Peggy, 112*f*, 116*f*, 118, 119*f*, 123*b*
Woodruff, Henry, 18, 19, 22
Wynn, Ed, 67–68, 73–74, 74*b*

"You Marry a Marionette," 46–47, 51*b*
Young, James, xviii, 16–17, 18, 22, 30

www.ingramcontent.com/pod-product-compliance
Ingram Content Group UK Ltd.
Pitfield, Milton Keynes, MK11 3LW, UK
UKHW022153230426
12049UKWH00003BA/84